Robert J. Spitzer

The Presidency and Public Policy:

The Four Arenas of Presidential Power

The Presidency
and Public Policy:

The Four Arenas of

Presidential Power

Robert J. Spitzer

With best regards,

Robert Spitzer

The University of Alabama Press

Copyright © 1983 by
The University of Alabama Press
University, Alabama 35486
Manufactured in the United States of America

Library of Congress Cataloging in Publications Data

Spitzer, Robert J., 1953–
    The presidency and public policy.

    Revision of the author's thesis (Ph.D.)—Cornell
University.
    Bibliography: p.
    Includes index.
    1. Presidents—United States. 2. Executive
power—United States. 3. United States. Congress.
I. Title.
JK585.S65   1982   353.03'1   81-19802
ISBN 0-8173-0109-7   AACR2

to Bill and Jinny Spitzer

Contents

Tables and Figures

Tables

Figures

Acknowledgments

In many ways the most pleasurable task connected with the production of this work is reflected on this page. The book's writing (and rewriting, and rewriting, and rewriting...) was a satisfying and rewarding experience, but many of its pleasures stemmed directly from exchanges with many good people, whose help I gratefully acknowledge here.

My former advisors at Cornell University provided the initial guidance necessary to keep the project on track when it was a dissertation. My thanks go to E. W. Kelley, Peter Katzenstein, and Benjamin Ginsberg, and especially to Theodore Lowi for his intellectual and personal guidance throughout the writing and rewriting process.

Two individuals read the entire manuscript and provided detailed, careful comments and suggestions. I extend heartfelt thanks to Werner Dannhauser and Richard Bensel for their efforts.

A number of other good friends and acquaintances have provided less systematic, but incisive (and, fortunately, irreverent) comments and suggestions. My thanks to Michael Brown, Gary Bryner, Bruce Detwiler, Arch Dotson, Peter Galderisi, Edward Harpham, John Green, Patricia Leeds, John Mearsheimer, Jack Moran, Peggy Murphy, Steve Newman, G. Olivia O'Donnell, Martin Shefter, Henry Steck, and Jeff Tarbox.

I would also like to gratefully acknowledge the impartial efforts of the director of The University of Alabama Press, Malcolm MacDonald, and the comments of one of the Press's readers, Bert A. Rockman of the University of Pittsburgh.

Finally, I would like to thank Gertrude Fitzpatrick for her fine efforts in typing and editing the initial manuscript, and Jean Fowler for her patience and efficiency in typing revisions and alterations.

Preface

Students of history and politics have long been enamored of the great leaders of history and their impact on their political times.[1] Indeed, analysis of political history often centers on the biographies of famous men associated with important events. In the United States, the political figure most often associated with the compelling moments of history has been the president. While military men fulfill this role in most nations (through military means), America's lack of a military tradition has encouraged its military leaders to seek greater influence through civilian political office, leaving aside the military rank and trappings (though not the initial popularity associated with successful military ventures). The military men we are most likely to remember in the United States are those who assume the highest civilian office.

Quite clearly, Americans reserve a special place for the chief executive. What heart has not been stirred by the genius of Thomas Jefferson, the dynamism of Andrew Jackson, the foresight of Abraham Lincoln, the determination and strength of Franklin Roosevelt, or the youthful vigor of John Kennedy? Even mediocre men are assessed in the light of their "great moments," and bad presidents are censured because they do not measure up to the standards of "greatness," leaving aside for the moment the question of what those standards might be.[2]

If this form of hero worship were simply a part of American political mythology, it would be innocent enough. But it does not stop there. It permeates much of what we refer to as the "scholarly literature" on the presidency. It manifests itself in various contexts, from historical biographies to contemporary analyses of power (see Chapter 1 for examples and a more detailed discussion of this).

The academic version of this normative bias, to label it thus, has yielded a very particular perspective on the presidency. Simply stated, the fates and fortunes of presidents have been ascribed heavily, indeed too heavily, to each president's own personal political acumen, skills, resources, desires, and dispositions. As much as any other student of the presidency, Richard Neustadt has perpetuated this image of presidential "rugged individualism." To wit: success as a president (meaning the successful exercise of presidential power) accrues to those presidents who master the persuasive arts—that persuasion being successfully employed by bargaining. Presidents who have mastered the bargaining skills are thus likely to be the ones written about by adoring presidential antiquarians. This perspective has cultivated at least two dubious assumptions: that the more power a president exercises, the more good he can do, and therefore the better off both he and the country will be; and that presidential success or failure, however defined, rests fundamentally with the president himself.

The first assumption has been subject to a fair amount of revision since Vietnam and Watergate. It took a forced resignation by a less-than-revered president to make us realize that Watergate was not an anomaly, but the logical extension of the presidential activism extolled by most students of the presidency. In spite of this rethinking, most of us still secretly hope for the man on the white horse to lead us from our present travails. Though it is comforting to conjure up such daydreams, we know that to try to bring them to life would be to court political tyrannies and excesses antithetical to our constitutional traditions.

If we are indeed a government of laws and not of men, then are we not fools to pin our hopes solely on "good men" (as if voters thought they were electing a crook when they voted for Nixon)?[3] To be more specific, if we do not have the kind of presidents or presidency that we want, and if we are confused by the behavior of both, ought we simply to look at the men in the office, and the effects they have upon it? The point is that leadership, while important, is by its character highly situational. But its variable nature from one administration to another is seldom taken into account. More than that, to focus solely on leadership in the presidential context is to limit one's view of the office by ignoring other, fundamental consistencies.

It may be evident to the reader that I am suggesting another avenue that, by contrast, is regular and indeed inescapable. That avenue, stemming from the very apparatus of the state, employs the concrete products of presidents and the presidency—policy. When we refer to presidential accomplishments and achievements, we are usually referring to the policies enacted and implemented by presidents. Policies are definable, measurable, and comparable, insofar as we can rely upon what is written into policy proposals and law. If we view policies as the expressed intentions of government, then we can consider them in the context of presidential policy making to be the best (or worst) efforts of presidents, that is, the tangible products of an administration.

Beyond the focus on presidential policies and policy making, there is another component to the argument, set in contradistinction to the second assumption mentioned above—an assumption that, by and large, has not been questioned. The second element of my argument is that there are some very particular factors associated with policies and policy types that have specific, verifiable effects on the behavior of presidents, the nature of the political process they must deal with, and by extension the ultimate outcome. The political forces that result from policies to be identified

herein, emanating from basic policy characteristics, are not easily manipulated by presidents or other actors in the short term, though this does not
constitute a denial of the importance of basic political skills. Again, my view
rests not on some vague attribution of presidential outcomes to the currents of history or macroeconomic and political forces; rather, it identifies
specific characteristics of policies proposed by presidents that shape
what the president can do and how well he can do it. In other words,
policies structure the interests involved and help to determine the political
arenas in which decisions are contested or made. Policy attributes can be
identified, observed, and compared across administrations, and they incorporate the full range of presidential policy-making activities, not simply
a few great moments and critical decisions. For all the attention that has
been focused on a few compelling decisions and policies—the Cuban
missile crisis, the seizure of the steel mills, and integration at Little Rock,
Arkansas, for example—one would think that presidents act as leaders
only in times of crisis. Obviously, this is not so. And there are significant
limits to what we can learn about the presidency from a few critical, atypical
cases.

Here, then, is the indictment: against the "great-man" view of the presidency, against presidential "rugged individualism," against looking at
power without seriously examining the question, Power to do what? Here
also is the alternative to be explored: to examine the presidency as an
ongoing institution, focusing on the products of presidential efforts (policies), but arguing that the nature of those products, as seen in the political
process associated with their formation, actually shapes what presidents
can do and how the political environment responds.

Specifically, this study will examine the president's annual domestic
legislative program (his policy proposals to Congress) over a twenty-year
period, in order to see how and in what ways the characteristics of those
proposals affect his success in dealing with Congress (success being
defined as Congress's passing the president's legislative proposals in the
forms offered). The effects of policy characteristics will be observed
throughout the legislative process. Presidential skills matter, but I will show
that the successful application of those skills is relatively easy for some
policies and next to impossible for others. In the end it will be clear that
certain consistent patterns predominate regardless of who sits in the Oval
Office, and that to a great extent those patterns prescribe presidential
behavior.

In addition, advance knowledge of policies and policy characteristics
should allow us to predict, at least in broad outline, the quality of the
political obstacles presidents may face in their dealings with Congress.
This has certain prescriptive implications, which will be discussed in the
final chapter.

The Presidency and Public Policy:

The Four Arenas of Presidential Power

1: Studying the Presidency

We know almost everything about
Presidents...but far too little
about the Presidency.
                    —James MacGregor Burns

The presidency of the United States has sometimes been described as the most powerful office in the free world, if not on earth, and at other times the president has been likened to the wretched Sisyphus, who was condemned forever to roll a stone up a hill in Hades, only to watch it roll down again as soon as he neared the top. What is odd about these two characterizations is that they exist simultaneously, even in harmony, as descriptions of the American presidency. This peculiar conjunction of power and impotence reflects both the complex reality and the general lack of understanding of the presidency. If the best wisdom that can be offered of a political institution is that it both possesses and lacks the same set of characteristics, then we are sorely lacking in wisdom. Such an acknowledgment assumes even more startling dimensions when the presidency is described as "the most important political institution in American life."[1] Students of the presidency are just now coming to grips with the conceptual, methodological, and substantive gaps in our understanding. While the literature on the presidency is voluminous (a recently published annotated bibliography of works on the presidency cites over twenty-five hundred entries published since the New Deal era),it is notably deficient in "basic empirical research"[2] and "systematic scholarly study."[3] Anthony King has delivered this severe indictment:

> To read most general studies of the United States presidency...is to feel that one is reading not a number of different books but essentially the same book over and over again. The same sources are cited; the same points are made; even the same quotations ("bully pulpit," etc.) appear again and again. In addition, the existing literature is mainly descriptive and atheoretical: general hypotheses are almost never tested. Largely for this reason, a subject that might be thought to bristle with difficulties has so far aroused remarkably

little scholarly—as distinct from purely political—controversy, about either methodology or substantive research findings.[4]

There are several reasons or, perhaps more properly, excuses that attempt to explain this lacuna in the study of the presidency. First, access to information about presidents is sometimes limited for reasons of national security. Much presidential activity involves matters of defense and international affairs. The military and political sensitivity of some material allows the use of the national-security justification for maintaining secrecy. Beyond that, many other presidential dealings are conducted in secret and are revealed only at the discretion of the president himself.[5] Such disclosures are seldom made voluntarily, unless disclosure works to the president's advantage.[6] While the published accounts of former presidential aides and confidants abound, such works have a reputation for being selective and self-serving. The same has been said of presidential memoirs as well. As a former presidential aide dryly observed, "The inaccuracy of most Washington diaries is surpassed only by the immodesty of their authors."[7]

Second, few numerical indicators can be readily utilized. There are no roll calls, judicial votes, or survey research available. Indeed, the existence of masses of readily available data from the Institute for Social Research, the National Opinion Research Center, the Gallup, Harris, and Roper organizations, and the like indicate how the existence of readily available data can spawn research, as these data have for the study of voting, attitudes, and mass behavior. In the case of studying the president, it is not clear what the level or unit of analysis should be, nor how hypotheses might be operationalized and tested.[8]

Third, the structure and evolution of the institution of the presidency itself is viewed as largely idiosyncratic and accidental. Many have noted, for example, how the assassinations of William McKinley, Lincoln, and Kennedy dramatize, especially to those who engage in "what if…"history, the important role of unanticipated events in shaping the presidency.[9] Clinton Rossiter emphasizes the role of chance in the formation of the presidential institution. The ambiguous nature of article two of the Constitution and the uncertainty surrounding it at the Constitutional Convention, as compared with article one, left open to interpretation many of the prerogatives and initiatives that were later to become accepted norms.[10]

A fourth factor contributing to the absence of systematic research is the simple fact that the institution of the presidency is tied to the man occupying the Oval Office. On that basis, obvious difficulties attend any attempt to generalize from thirty-nine cases over a two-hundred-year period. While there is clearly a great deal of continuity in terms of both internal and external forces and structures, the standard way of "cutting up" the presidency analytically is by the successive administrations of each president. One assumes that each man leaves his own unique mark on the office. Each president's style, temperament, personality, skill, and "charisma" all contribute to the perceptions of individuality by which each administration is viewed, despite continuities in institutional and environmental forces.[11]

Another factor that surely inhibits the application of social-scientific rigor is the fact that many, if not most, of the important scholarly writers on the presidency have themselves been intimately bound up not just in a presidential administration, but with the chief executive himself. Such authors as James MacGregor Burns, Stephen Hess, Emmet J. Hughes, Richard Neustadt, Arthur Schlesinger, Jr., and Rexford Tugwell have all had personal ties to one or more presidents. Personal experience is certainly important in obtaining a fuller understanding of how the presidency operates, but such experiences surely have had an effect on how presidents and their administrations are evaluated and compared. Few would not be awed by the majesty of the office and the presence of the chief executive. It is a recurrent problem among journalists covering the White House.[12] To be personally tied to a president is undoubtedly useful for obtaining certain kinds of detailed information about presidents, but it also creates a situation of observer-as-participant, which strikes directly at the ideals of dispassionate third-person analysis that lie at the heart of social-science research. Perhaps this factor more than any other is responsible for what has been identified by political scientists as "the Presidential worship that has pervaded our professional literature."[13]

Finally, there is often more than a little ambiguity over exactly what is being studied. Does a reference made to "the presidency" point only to the man in the Oval Office, or does it include the White House Office as well? What about the Executive Office, the cabinet, and the departments under each cabinet head? What about the rest of the bureaucracy? These are primarily organizational and definitional questions, which should pose no great obstacle. But terms such as *the president, the presidency* and *the executive branch* have been used interchangeably.

Taken together, these difficulties do present an obstacle; but obstacles exist to be overcome.[14] One should not lose sight of the fact that the presidency is a political institution founded in a long constitutional, legal, and political tradition. Consequently, the president and his minions behave in certain systematic, even predictable ways in the context of that institution. In this investigation, similarities and parallelisms existing across administrations will be sought out and analyzed by turning traditional frameworks on their heads. The argument I will advance is that policy determines presidential behavior.

The Policy Approach

The president sits at the center of government. From that vantage he surveys the entire governmental apparatus. More than that, however, he is actively involved in formulating and implementing the product of that apparatus—policies. Thus it is that presidents are defined and perceived in terms of the policies they choose to identify themselves with. Given the intimate relation between a president and his policies, the fundamental argument being made here is that *the type of policy with which the president deals determines the nature and effects of his political response and therefore his ultimate success.* The precise policy types and their differing effects will be discussed in the next chapter. While the logic of this argument can apply to all phases of presidential policy making, the analysis here will be confined to domestic-policy proposals made by the president to the Congress. The importance of this policy interaction for the president, the Congress, and the country is dramatized almost daily in news headlines emanating from Washington.

The analysis of policies with respect to the presidency is not new. Many important case studies have focused on presidential policy making and its effects. However, policy has generally been thought of as a dependent variable, that is, the product of political forces. Further, most studies have focused on a few critical cases. The analysis here will incorporate an examination of the full range of legislative policy proposals emanating from the White House. More important, the use of a policy typology will allow for more than simple description. The relationship between what has been done and what will be done here will be examined more fully in the next section.

The focus on presidential policy making is based on the assumption that the president operates and can be understood as a policy maker with conscious and relatively consistent policy interests and goals. Stated another way, the presumption is that the president pursues policy making as a purposive activity,[15] and that it is important to examine and understand his policy proposals and enactments because of what they reveal about the behavior of the president and his success in dealing with the political environment and because the nature of policies themselves has an independent effect on political processes and outcomes. The goal of the president's purposive activity is to realize the enactment of his policy program.

The analysis that composes the body of this project incorporates the domestic legislative program of presidents from 1954 to 1974. The focus is on that subset of legislative activity with which the president is most centrally concerned—his annual legislative program.[16] With this subuniverse of bills the president probably maximizes his efforts and expenditures of resources. I will argue that the president's political response to

Congress, and therefore the fate of these bills, varies with the nature of the policies themselves. And in his pursuit of policy making via the legislative route, the president goes a long way toward prescribing the outcome by committing himself to certain types of policies over others.

The President's Policy Proposals

An examination of the universe of legislative proposals that compose the annual congressional agenda reveals that there are four sources from which legislation is offered. Two of them, the chief executive (in conjunction with the White House Office) and the bureaucracy, are executive. A third source is congressmen themselves, and a fourth is interest groups. In an earlier age, political parties might have constituted a fifth source. But in today's political setting, the president and individual congressmen are themselves the important party leaders.

Within the executive, all proposed legislation passes through the Office of Management and Budget in order that it may be subjected to central clearance. The purpose of clearance is to insure that "the hundreds of legislative proposals generated by federal departments, bureaus, and independent agencies are coordinated and reviewed to assess their acceptability as component parts of the presidential program."[17] According to a recent estimate, the OMB handles approximately sixteen thousand proposals annually. About 80 to 90 percent of those proposals are generated by the bureaucracy. But much of the other 10 to 20 percent constitutes legislation adopted by the president and his aides in the White House Office as "The President's Program."[18] This distinctive function performed by the president was formally and permanently established by Dwight Eisenhower in 1954 and was first identified as such by Richard Neustadt. His description of the process, as valid today as then, bears repeating:

> Throughout [the administration's proposals], one theme was emphasized: here was a comprehensive and coordinated inventory of the nation's current legislative needs, reflecting the President's own judgements, choices, and priorities in every major area of Federal action; in short, his "legislative program," an entity distinctive and defined, its coverage and its omissions, both, delimiting his stand across the board. And—quite possibly—this stand was being taken, this program volunteered in order to give Congress an agenda, Republicans a platform, and voters a yardstick in 1954.
>
> Thus, one year after his inaugural, Eisenhower espoused a sweeping concept of the President's initiative in legislation and an elaborate mechanism for its public expression.[19]

In practical terms, the president's legislative program sets forth the main issues for each congressional session and in doing so, establishes general parameters for what will and will not be acceptable to the president—specifically, where the veto might be employed. Presidential identification with major bills is the important boost a piece of legislation can receive,[20] as the Area Redevelopment Act illustrates. Throughout the 1950s Senator Paul Douglas repeatedly proposed a redevelopment act, only to be thwarted at various points in the legislative process. During the 1960 presidential campaign, John Kennedy promised a redevelopment act during a speech in West Virginia. In 1961 he engineered the bill's passage with the cooperation of Douglas. While it is clear that Douglas sired the initial concept, introducing the bill as a part of the president's program led to its passage.[21] So it is that a "bill that originally emerges in the Congress may have absolutely no chance of passing until adopted or sometimes changed by the President."[22]

However, in considering the president's program as submitted to Congress, it is important to clarify the question of whether in fact his program can be interpreted as consistent with his policy preferences (as his purposive behavior would indicate). Three objections to this view present themselves at once; I will label them expedience, prior influence, and end product.

Expedience. It could be argued that the president's program, as submitted to Congress, primarily if not entirely reflects the president's perception of what Congress is likely to pass. While the validity of this assertion is not entirely denied, there are several points that militate against this argument. First, as a practical matter the legislative process affords a great deal of leeway. A bill introduced in a form that is perceived as unacceptable to a majority can be manipulated without seriously altering the basic content of the bill. The ultimate form of a bill, especially a controversial one, will often not be known until the final vote.[23] Yet manipulation of the form of the bill, while satisfying some congressmen, may not alter the basic bill. The debate over the Panama Canal Treaty provides a good example. If the amount of initial congressional outcry over the treaty was any indication, the treaty would have stood no chance of passage; yet it was ultimately ratified by the necessary two-thirds vote in the Senate, with several votes held in reserve (a few senators would have voted with Carter if he had needed the extra votes for ratification).[24] The final form of the treaty was manipulated by the introduction of a series of amendments and reservations; those changes served primarily to placate constituents as well as generalized opposition, which was considered to be widespread.

Second, it is argued (in contrast to the first objection) that the president is at least as concerned with what he proposes, for electoral and policy reasons, as he is with whether the proposal passes. Naturally, the passage of a proposed piece of legislation is important to the president's interests as he perceives them, and he is surely prepared to compromise in order to obtain passage. However, it is just as true that a president often finds it desirable to rail against a "do-nothing" Congress rather than passively to accept whatever proposals are laid before him by Congress.

Finally, it is clear that there are times when the president looks for a legislative "win" strictly for its own sake. News reports in the late summer of 1978 indicated that President Carter was searching for some sort of legislative victory to bolster his sagging image. But as the Carter example illustrates, the president's selection of an issue is invariably made among the proposals composing his own established legislative agenda. In the case of Carter, two frequently mentioned issues were the test of strength on his veto of a $38 billion defense appropriation that included $2 billion for a Nimitz-class nuclear carrier he did not want (the House sustained the veto), and the passage of part or all of the administration's energy program.

Another example comes from an interview with Bill Moyers in which Carter discussed the compromises he had made over a tax bill. In the light of Carter's hackneyed campaign slogan that the tax system was "a disgrace to the human race," Moyers inquired why Carter had not vetoed the bill rather than settle for a compromise. Carter's response was revealing: "When I met a few days before the Congress adjourned with the leaders of the House and Senate—Al Ullman in the House, Russell Long in the Senate—and said, 'This is what I will and will not accept,' they complied with my request substantially. And although it was short of what I would have preferred, my vetoing of that bill would have been a very serious mistake."[25]

This example illustrates the limits within which Carter was willing and able to compromise while still maintaining the integrity of his proposals. Presidents do bargain and compromise with Congress, and they have a variety of resources at their disposal with which to enforce or punish, from threatening vetos and holding bills hostage to patronage and appeals to public opinion.[26]

Prior influence. It could be argued that the president's program is primarily the product of prior influence. That is, its composition may in fact be greatly affected by the ideas of congressmen, bureaucrats, and private groups, or by public clamor. The implication is that unless proposals spring from the president and his aides, they cannot legitimately be labeled the president's. Quite the reverse is true. Indeed, I do not dispute the observation that most bills incorporated into the president's program were not conceived in the White House Office. But the point of origin of a policy proposal matters little, even assuming it can be ascertained. As with the case of the Area Redevelopment Act, I am primarily concerned with the way ideas fare once they become part of the president's program. It might be fairly said that in politics, as in political science, a completely original idea is a truly rare thing. In the case of the president's program, "the ideas germinating in Congress are like a shopping list to presidential assistants from which they select those ideas most appropriate for presidential coop-tation."[27] When a bill is incorporated into the president's program and advanced in his state of the union message, economic message, or other public pronouncement, it must be taken seriously by both houses. While passage is far from assured, the bill automatically becomes more impor-tant and is accorded due consideration. Presidential advocacy of a bill can attract for it new enemies as well as new friends, but that very fact indicates the importance at.ached to the identification of a bill with the president."[28]

End product. Finally, a bill may pass through Congress and reach the president's desk so altered that it bears no resemblance to his original proposal and thus does not represent a real achievement for the president. It is quite clear, however, that presidents remain informed about such matters, especially for important bills, and thus realize when and how proposals have been bastardized. Examples of the president's vetoing a bill that was originally part of his program can be found in many legislative sessions. In 1974, for example, Ford vetoed a veterans' education bill as inflationary when its appropriations were increased by Congress, a revi-sion of the Freedom of Information Act amendments, and an extension of the Health Services Act. All were initially part of his legislative program. Franklin Roosevelt was known to ask his supporters for something he could veto as a reminder to the Congress that this form of policy enforcement could and would be applied.[29] Presidents are thus willing and able to deal with bills when they are altered by Congress.

Levels of Analysis

In order to facilitate the examination of the president's policy proposals and the effects of those policies on political processes and outcomes, analysis will be conducted on three levels. The first consists of a series of in-depth case studies that illustrate and exemplify the effects of the presi-dent's proposals on political processes and outcomes. The cases, which will establish detailed relationships between policy and politics, are drawn from the period between 1954 and 1974, with two exceptions to be dis-cussed later.

The second level is a summary analysis of all of the proposals compos-ing the president's annual legislative program from 1954 to 1974. The data are made up of almost fifty-five hundred separate legislative proposals drawn from the *Congressional Quarterly,* incorporating both domestic- and foreign-policy proposals. The precise criteria for the selection of these bills are discussed, along with the data, in Chapter 5. The domestic-policy proposals have been placed in the four categories that serve as the basis of analysis. This data base is not as useful as it might be, because very little information is available for each bill. For each proposal there is a one- or two-sentence description, a record of whether it was reported favorably by Senate and House committees, whether it passed on the floor of either or both chambers, and the public-law number of the bill (if it passed).

The third level of analysis is a much more detailed contextual study of 165 of these proposals. Information on differences between the House and the Senate, party support, and floor activity will all be incorporated. This level will yield a greater array of relevant data and information on the effects of policies. For purposes of commensurability, I have included only those bills that came to votes on the floors of both houses. Most of those became law.

Relying on three levels of analysis, drawn from a single data set, insures that the conclusions will be as relevant to the entire universe of legislative action as they are to the necessarily detailed case studies. This three-tiered approach should yield a thorough understanding of the policy process under investigation.

The Presidency in Perspective

The views of this study represent something of a departure from most of what has been done on the presidency. Yet the trends and perspectives in the study of the institution and the man have provided vital insights into the workings of the institution and the men who have served as chief executive. Its omissions as well as its strong points go far toward clarifying the present state of affairs. In addition to putting this study in perspective, the following discussion will provide a general organization of what has been done on the presidency, and in doing so, will back up the claims made here concerning the lacunae in the study and understanding of this institution.

Perhaps the outstanding feature of the literature on the presidency is a negative one—its lack of coherence. The Presidency has been studied from a variety of perspectives: institutional-legal, personality and style, symbolism, power and influence and roles.[30] These approaches are not only not mutually exclusive but incommensurable as well. Institutions can be a source of power, as can the use of symbols; roles can include institutional and noninstitutional elements; personality can have an impact on power, as power can have an impact on personality; and so on. While each approach seems to capture some piece of reality, it is unclear exactly what piece, and to what extent that approach can be generalized. In analyzing the presidency, this study will focus on three central activities of presidents. There is clearly overlap between the three categories below, but their purpose is to provide analytical distinctions covering the range of presidential activities.

President as Politician

This first aspect of what the president does involves activities aimed at getting into and retaining office. This heading comprises all the election-related activities: attending fund-raising dinners, delivering campaign speeches, meeting with party leaders, debating opponents, interacting with the public, and the like. Such activities are obviously most prominent in the period immediately before the election. To attempt to deal with this area would itself be a monumental task.[31] Areas of focus include parties and party systems, voting and electoral behavior, and the more specific areas of campaign finance and the media.[32] While such topics are certainly important to a proper understanding of the presidency, the primary focus of this study will be on the presidency as a functioning institution during the interelection period.[33]

President as Power Seeker

If there is one theme that pervades our understanding of the presidency, it is that the president can be best understood as an actor striving to get, keep, and use power in office. This familiar theme has been dominant since the publication of Richard Neustadt's classic work *Presidential Power.* Indeed, the presidential crises of the late sixties and early seventies produced a spate of works focusing specifically on the question of power.[34] Although the analysis of power is central to the study of politics, the ambiguous use of this notion as the key operating concept for understanding the presidency has in many respects retarded an advance in understanding since the publication of Neustadt's book. But before detailing the reasons behind this assertion, we ought to make an effort to differentiate among basic variations in the notion of presidential power.

The two basic questions around which most of the presidency literature has centered are; How much power does the president have? and How much power should the president have? Thus, works on the presidency can be classified according to two dimensions: normative-empirical, and strong-weak.[35] These two dimensions can be combined to produce four categories of presidential power attributes: is strong and should be strong; is strong but should be weak; is weak but should be strong; is weak and should be weak. Both normative and empirical elements can be found in most studies of presidential power, but the intent here is to separate analytically the normative and empirical dimensions, in order to assess each separately.

Normative-strong. Logically, there are two possible evaluations of how powerful the president should be. The first is the classic "strong-president" view, identified in modern times with Theodore Roosevelt. Also referred to as the "stewardship" role, this view, briefly stated, posits that the president has the right to engage in any activity as long as such activity is not explicitly prohibited by the Constitution (in the Constitutional Convention, James Wilson and Gouverneur Morris were among the proponents of this view). The extension of this argument is embodied in what has been called the "textbook presidency." "Presidents [are] expected to perform as purposeful activists who know what they want to accomplish and relish the challenge of office."[36] Because the president (along with his vice-president) is the only elected leader representing the entire nation, he is in a unique position to do what is necessary and best for the greatest number of people. He therefore must be given the leeway necessary to implement (execute) his progressive, purposeful activism. This is perhaps the most popular and consensual view of presidential activism.

Clinton Rossiter asserted that the president must be "a clear beacon of national purpose," especially in the face of a government that is otherwise disorganized and decentralized.[37] Louis Koenig has articulated the belief that powerful, activist presidents are good because of the necessity for decisive decision making. In this modern age of massive problems and the possibility of instant, mutually assured destruction, the nation needs a strong president capable of dealing with crucial domestic and foreign affairs.[38] A similarly articulated position argues that the imperatives of the "positive state" require a strong president to lead Congress, which by itself lacks coherence and responsibility.[39]

More recently, James MacGregor Burns has pointed out that only the president represents a national constituency, and thus a strong president is necessary in order to make Congress more efficient. Others have gone so far as to claim that "the President alone is capable of ruling."[40] The pervasiveness of this view is reflected in the writings of former congressmen who themselves decry the ineptness of their own branch and assert that a strong executive is desirable and perhaps even necessary.[41]

Normative-weak. The view that presidential power should be restrained has a similarly long history; Roger Sherman and Edmund Randolph, among others, expounded this point of view at the Constitutional Convention.[42] Theodore Roosevelt's successor, William Howard Taft, articulated the whiggish viewpoint that the job of the executive branch, and therefore of the president, was to execute the laws passed by Congress and to restrain bureaucratic excesses. As a general rule, the president should exercise only those powers and prerogatives explicitly granted to him by the Constitution.[43] Several authors writing in the late 1950s and early 1960s emphasized a restrained role for the president in his dealings with Congress. They viewed presidential power with suspicion, and they thought that the present system of checks and balances was weighted in favor of the president. They therefore proposed revising the system to reflect the view articulated by Taft. They advocated greater congressional initiatives and the restraint of presidential prerogative. Among the recommendations they offered was that a plural executive be established. This would distribute the burdens of office and thereby help to avoid the gamble they considered inherent in a solitary presidency.[44]

The general view that the president has too much power, however, did not gain wide currency until contemporary events precipitated a searching reevaluation of standard assumptions about the presidency. In the aftermath of the Johnson presidency, George Reedy, Johnson's former press secretary, articulated what he felt were the dangers of the presidents' tendency to become isolated, especially from the populace. The insularity and aloofness of a president who is able to have, on a personal level at least, anything he desires leads inexorably to popular disaffection, loss of credibility, and lack of executive responsiveness.[45]

But far more than any other event in recent years, the excesses of the Nixon administration, culminating in the Watergate scandal, precipitated a host of academic and journalistic responses, all questioning in some respect the traditional assumptions about the desirability of unchecked presidential power. The phrase "imperial presidency" was popularized by Arthur Schlesinger, Jr., a historian and political scientist who had become famous writing biographies of presidents Jackson, Franklin Roosevelt, and Kennedy, all of which extolled presidential activism. In his revisionist work, Schlesinger documented the historical appropriation of congressional powers by presidents, with the decisive impetus coming from presidential dominance in foreign affairs.[46]

Constitutional scholars have condemned presidential aggrandizement of powers beyond proper constitutional limits, especially in areas such as executive privilege and impoundment.[47] The proposal has also been made that a constitutional amendment be passed allowing Congress the option to utilize a vote of no confidence, rather than relying solely on the rusted blunderbuss of impeachment as a check on excesses.[48] Other structural and constitutional reforms have been examined, as has the longtime sop of political scientists, "party government."[49]

Empirical-strong. Most writers making the case that the president is strong have relied on the historical argument that presidential power has grown over time, whether through aggrandizement of the power of other political actors, the delegation of power to him by other branches, or the accrual of new powers and responsibilities.[50] The evolution of federal budget making is a good example of how responsibilities have shifted from the Congress, then to the president, and now slowly back toward the Congress again.[51] The establishment in 1939 of the Executive Office of the President and its subsequent ballooning (it now includes fifteen major departments) is also an often-cited indicator of the growth of presidential influence.[52]

Constitutional scholar Edward S. Corwin, in one of his most enduring works, focused on the constitutional-legal basis of presidential preeminence as evidenced by presidential accession in foreign policy and the assumption of powers and responsibilities as government moved away from laissez faire toward greater activism and reformism. Corwin observed the expansion of presidential initiative at both ends of the legislative process, that is, the submission as well as the administration of legislation. Corwin was also careful to note, as too few have since then, that a very great deal of what has been labeled presidential aggrandizement has been the product of free and willing delegation of authority to the president by the Congress, especially in the area of administrative regulation.[53] Both Arthur Schlesinger, Jr., and Raoul Berger have conducted detailed historical analyses of constitutional-legal aspects of presidential authority; Schlesinger focused on foreign policy and court cases, and Berger on the history of "executive conduct."[54]

In another vein, a number of more recent studies have looked at the relation between the mass, especially the electronic, media and the ability of presidents to control, if not manipulate, reporters of news to achieve the best possible image among the citizenry. The case has been frequently made that presidents, at least from Franklin Roosevelt to the present, have used the media to advance their own personal power.[55] This view has been extended to include the use, abuse, and cooptation of the media by would-be presidents during the campaign process.[56]

Empirical-weak. The argument that the president is not strong is based on the general argument that he is fundamentally reliant on the Congress for approval of his policies and appropriations for his programs, on the bureaucracy for implementation, on the courts for judgments as to the limits within which presidents may operate, and on journalists and public opinion for general approval.

One of the important facts about Neustadt's book at the time of publication was that it argued explicitly that the president really did not exercise power in a "power-politics" sense. For a president to attempt to exercise control by simple command was, when feasible at all, very costly in terms of the power resources expended. Neustadt contended that Harry Truman's firing of MacArthur, his seizure of the steel mills, and Eisenhower's enforcing integration at Little Rock, for example, were exceptional cases of the use of command powers by presidents and were illustrative of the costliness and limited efficacy of extreme uses of power.[57] He used these seemingly contrary cases to illustrate dramatically his theme that what has been labeled presidential power is really the power to persuade, which in practical terms involves bargaining. Therefore the degree of success a president has is greatly dependent on his degree of skill, as distinguished from his formal command authority.

An assessment of Richard Nixon's dealings with the bureaucracy during his second term makes a similar point. After being frustrated by Congress in his first term, Nixon decided to attempt to enact his programs by circumventing the Congress whenever possible. He attempted to do this by placing his own subordinates, personally loyal to him, as far down into the administrative structure as possible. This degree of tampering with administrative agencies was unprecedented, but in spite of its scope, the degree of success was minimal, Watergate notwithstanding. He was even unsuccessful in disbanding the Office of Economic Opportunity.[58]

Both Rossiter and Koenig expressed the view that the president is severely restrained regarding the achievement of policy objectives.[59] Presidential insiders, looking at the decision-making process in the White House, have observed the significant limits placed on presidential power.[60] A case study of Kennedy's successful attempt to roll back steel prices in 1962 concluded that "competitive market forces" were largely responsible for the roll-back. "These forces were much more important in bringing about abandonment of the price increase than the actions of the President. Those actions showed weakness, not strength."[61]

Despite the fact that normative and empirical assessments have not been clearly identified by most authors, the object has been to elucidate the separate trails of *is* and *ought*. In theoretical terms, the failure to acknowledge the difference between what is labeled positive theory, which explains empirical phenomena, and normative or design theory, the goal of which is to offer guidance in the design and execution of policies and institutions, results in bad theory in both instances (though the two can certainly exist together).[62] While the immediate object of most studies of the presidency is not theory per se, the importance of recognizing the distinction between *is* and *ought* stands in any context as both empirically sound and normatively desirable.

The drawbacks of not clarifying this distinction are well illustrated by one of the most widely read and theoretically ambitious books on the presidency, James David Barber's *The Presidential Character*. The core of Barber's book is the classification of presidents according to "character," which he arranges along two dimensions, the active-passive and the positive-negative. Ostensibly, Barber sets out to explain presidents' actions in terms of their character, assessed on the basis of empirical, relatively objective standards derived from psychological theory. Yet Barber is not content with assigning character traits based on his four dimensions of active-positive, active-negative, passive-positive, and passive-negative. In categorizing presidents, he offers a diagnosis for each. And he is unmistakably explicit in his disdain for active-negatives and his adulation of active-positives.[63] Coincidentally, presidents categorized as active-positives are all liberal-reform activists, including both Roosevelts, Kennedy, and Truman.

Barber implicitly assumes that presidential activism, in conjunction with a personal character that enjoys activism, is both desirable and functional for the system. Yet if one questions the normative assumption that activism per se is good in this context, one might decide that presidents such as Eisenhower (passive-negative) and Taft (passive-positive) were in many respects better, if not more successful, presidents than Kennedy, for example, who gave us the Bay of Pigs, CIA assassination attempts, and the first major escalation in Vietnam. These are questions of political judgment, based on evaluations of the desirability of activism; yet Barber recommends that citizens bend every effort to seek out and elect only active-positives.

As a final illustration, consider the twelve-page chapter on Ford. Barber concedes that "Ford came on too fast for confident prediction." One would be inclined to categorize him as a passive-positive, based on his evident enjoyment of office, combined with his (admittedly short) presidential record of willingness to use vetoes, espousal of government restraint, and Taft-like reluctance to initiate legislation. Barber, however, in his short, affectionate discussion of Ford, tentatively labels him active-positive.[64] It is not clear whether the basis of categorization is normative or empirical, or some mixture of both. The reader is left wondering if Barber's "objective" analysis is colored by his own predilections, which may have rebelled at placing Ford in the same category with Warren Harding. Barber's book, important as it is, is hurt if not crippled as a descriptive and theoretical work because of the lack of attention paid to the distinction between description and prescription.

President as Policy Maker

The study of power is essentially the study of process. To utilize a system model of politics, the study of power relations within the "black box" of governmental processes "consists of all those arrangements that regulate the way in which the demands put into the system are settled and the way in which decisions are put into effect."[65] The study of policy, however, is the study of content (outputs), referring to the products resulting from the political process. The distinction between process and content pervades political science. Obviously, no perfect dichotomy between the two exists, but it is both possible and, for scholarly purposes, desirable to focus on one as distinct from the other.[66]

This final category incorporates the president as an actor involved with substantive areas of policy. The object of study is not power or the effects of power relations, but policies themselves. Policies can be studied in one of two ways: as outputs or products of the political system and as inputs themselves.[67] The study of policy and the presidency has focused almost exclusively on the former.

Policy as outputs. References to presidential policy making, choice making, or decision making appear with frequency in writings on the presidency. These terms, while not equivalent, all describe part of the same activity. *Decision making* and *choice making* are understood to refer to individual decisions, such as Kennedy's decision to blockade Cuba during the missile crisis of 1962 or Eisenhower's to send troops to Little Rock in support of integration. Cumulatively, such decisions may constitute a policy, such as a policy toward Cuba, or a policy about racial discrimination. Thus, the term *policy making* refers to a pattern of action extending across a series of decisions.

As far back as 1898, Henry Jones Ford observed that "the agency of the presidential office has been such a master force in shaping public policy that to give a detailed account of it would be equivalent to writing the political history of the United States."[68] Various analyses have focused on the president's policy-making activities. Presidents engage in three policy-related functions: application, incorporating the traditional role of the executive as set out in article two of the Constitution ("to take care that the laws be faithfully executed") and embodying the enforcement of law principally through delegation of authority to administrative and other executive agencies; initiation, which includes the formulation of policy by the president, notably in his role as chief legislator; and advocacy, rallying public and elite opinion through press conferences, public statements, news leaks, and the like.[69] Various job descriptions of the presidential office have touched on responsibilities in the areas of foreign and national security policy, aggregate economics, and other domestic-policy functions.[70]

At least one scholar has acknowledged the importance of addressing the task of explanation through the development of models of the policy-making process. He offers three models to "explain" one aspect of policy making in the executive branch. He also notes the need to integrate those approaches with systematic explanations of presidential policy-making activities.[71] While some scholars have tried to develop models, there have been few attempts at systematic explanation and still fewer efforts to connect the two. The one other way presidents have been studied as policy makers is through case studies—and there is a proliferation of those.

The case study is one of the oldest methods of study in politics. Originally, in-depth examinations of issues or political activities were viewed exclusively as ends in themselves. The purpose in studying a case was to provide understanding of the subject matter. Such cases have been labeled atheoretical or configurative-ideographic.[72] More recently, however, theorists and researchers have recognized that case studies can be nomothetic, or theory-generating, as well.[73] Case studies can be conducted to uncover questions and problems, and possible rules for theory; they can shed light on the plausibility of propositions; and they can further contribute to the validation of propositions.[74] The great majority of case studies of the presidency, however, are ideographic-configurative in nature. Highlights of the domestic policies of presidents from Franklin Roosevelt to the present are covered by such studies.[75] There are a handful of exceptions in domestic-policy studies that attempt to do more than describe events. While these studies are not aimed explicitly at testing propositions, they do at least span presidential administrations in an attempt to look for comparative consistencies and differences.[76]

There is an important exception to this ideographic trend in the area of foreign policy and national-security policy. While a great many explicitly ideographic studies exist, others have attempted to view the evolution of foreign policy qua policy.[77] The drawback to this foreign-policy investigation is that it is limited to just that—foreign policy. There is an acknowledged qualitative distinction between the president's ascendancy in foreign policy as compared with his less dominant role in domestic affairs, at least with respect to his dealings with Congress,[78] but one is still left with more extensive knowledge of only one policy area (or group of policy areas) that the president is involved in, albeit an important one.

One other point to be made about case studies of both foreign and domestic policy is that those cases selected tend to be critical cases, and they tend to be the same ones, notably, the Cuban missile crisis, the steel-seizure case, the court-packing case, Watergate, and the like. For example, more than a dozen books, articles, and monographs have been devoted exclusively to the details of the Cuban missile crisis. While crisis decisions are both important and interesting, systematic knowledge of and ability to generalize about the presidency could be more directly advanced by focusing on the full range of more routine presidential decision and policy making.

Policy as inputs. As previously noted, policies are usually studied as outputs of the political system. There is, however, a second perspective that has received increasing notice: the study of policy as an independent variable, having its own impact upon institutions and actors within the political system. With respect to the study of the United States Congress, for example, the traditional process studies (investigations of how a bill becomes a law or of how roles and norms operate within the Congress) have been complemented by studies focusing on the significance of policy as an independent variable.[79] The study of the presidency, however, has not been subjected to the same systematic policy analysis.[80]

It is from this perspective that this study takes its cue. The analysis of policy provides a quantifiable and consistent method. It incorporates some fundamental presidential responsibilities. It establishes independent and dependent variables at the outset and in doing so reverses the standard reasoning that politics produces policy. And in focusing on the substantive nature of policies and their effects, it directly addresses the fundamental question too often neglected by studies of presidential power: power is important, yes—but power to do what?

Definitions

The first sentence of article two of the Constitution states that "the executive Power shall be vested in a President of the United States of America." It is clear, however, that executive power is held by a great many more men and institutions than the president himself. In contemporary usage, the term *executive branch* denotes a disparate array of cabinet executives, bureaucratic agencies, and presidential assistants totaling over three million civilian employees.[81] Compared to the legislative and judicial branches, the executive resembles two branches rather than one, giving rise to the notion of a fourth branch of government; "the chief executive in the American system is a product of representative government, and the executive branch is a product of bureaucratization."[82]

In order to establish the relation between the president and the rest of the executive branch, Figure 1 is offered as a diagrammatic view of the executive, based on the president as the center of the institution. It incorporates elements of both organization and influence. The term *the president* will be understood to represent the man himself, plus the departments composing the White House Office. In the President's political (and even social) life, these employees are his eyes, ears, and mouthpiece. They deal with the Congress, administrative agencies, the press, private groups, and party leaders on the president's behalf.[83] While they offer their own input to the president, they are, above everything else, the president's men and women. "The staff is the President's 'lengthened shadow.'"[84] Thus, when reference is made to "the president," two assumptions are made: that what is labeled as the president's reflects his personal preferences or preferred

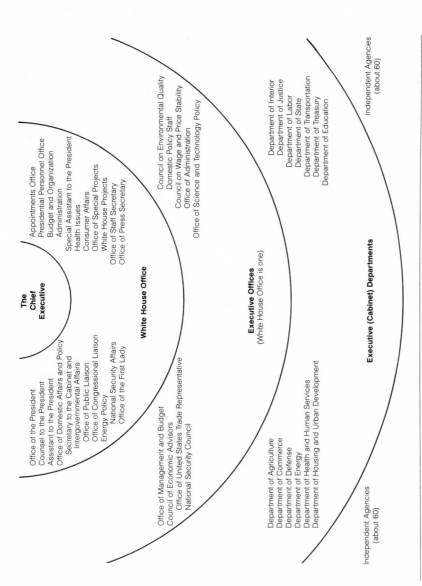

Figure 1: Copernican Schema of the Executive Universe

decisions, and that those preferences and decisions most likely involve other individuals besides the chief executive himself in statements and acts usually attributed to the president.

The terms *the presidency* will be understood to incorporate the man himself, the White House Office and the executive offices (the White House Office is one executive office). The term *executive branch* will include the chief executive, the White House Office, the executive offices, the executive (cabinet) departments, and the independent agencies. This array of agencies and departments is depicted in Figure 1 as a series of concentric circles, with the chief executive located at the center. The arrangement is presented to indicate an inverse relation between an organization's distance from the president and degree of the president's influence over it. Greater distance represents decreasing ability of the president to have control or influence over the relevant executive actor. While the chief executive's "gravitational pull" is greatest with respect to influencing the White House Office, the independent agencies "represent the most extreme point in the continuum of problems facing presidents as they try to control the bureaucracies."[85]

Outline of Presentation

Following this introduction, Chapter 2 discusses the policy theory that provides the framework for analysis of the president's domestic-policy proposals. Chapters 3 and 4 present a series of case studies that illustrate the mechanics of the policy argument in the context of some important examples of presidential legislative proposals. Chapter 5 briefly assesses existing views on the overall relationship between the president and Congress and presents the aggregate level of data analysis, incorporating the almost 5,500 legislative proposals made by presidents for the period under consideration. The emphasis here is on broad trends and patterns. Chapter 6 presents and analyzes the intermediate set of data: 165 cases (selected from the 5,500) incorporating a more detailed, contextual analysis. Chapter 7 presents conclusions, a synthesis, and some prospects for the future.

Despite variances in method, the same purpose prevails throughout: to establish the solidity of the link between type of presidential policy (the independent variable) and the nature of the political outcome (the dependent variable). The reader, however, should be aware of the fact that no direct claims are made here that the relationships discussed can be applied to time periods other than the one under consideration. Such extensions may be appropriate, but they must await further investigation.

2: Policy Typologies and Policy Theory

Our increased understanding of the Presidency will be achieved by examining presidential policy proposals. We will, however, analyze these proposals not only in a simple descriptive fashion, but also in the context of a policy framework that will in turn enhance and inform the study of the presidency. While the focus of study remains the presidency, some attention must be diverted to the conceptual framework underlying our analysis.

The avenue to be followed here is drawn from what has been broadly and, perhaps incorrectly, labeled policy theory. What this in fact refers to is a series of schemes, typologies, and taxonomies that have as their purpose the ordering of knowledge with the intent of establishing relationships amenable to the formation of hypotheses. In this chapter I will present the original version of the framework to be employed and discuss criticisms of it. Then I will introduce a refined version of the framework along with some specific rules for classifying policies and several proposed hypotheses. The refined version will be applied to the case-study and intermediate levels of data. The summary nature of the aggregate data, however, does not permit these finer distinctions to be made.

Utilizing Policy Frameworks

Typologies, taxonomies, and other schemes developed for the classification of policies abound, because they have constituted an important component of policy studies for many years.[1] A wide variety of possible categorizations has been suggested, from simple substantive categories offering organized description to more complex typologies used as tools to generate testable hypotheses.[2] But while such schemes abound, all are not equally useful. Determining a scheme's utility must rest with critical analysis and actual use. A policy framework which has undergone both substantial critical attention and application is that formulated by Theodore J. Lowi.[3] Referred to by the author as the "arenas of power," this scheme is based on the interaction of two policy characteristics: the likelihood of government coercion (remote or immediate); and the applicability of government coercion (working to affect either individual conduct or the environment of conduct).[4] When the likelihood of coercion is remote in the policy, the politics tend to be relatively consensual; when coercion is immediate in the policy, the politics tend to be more conflictual.

The two variables are crossed to produce four policy areas: distributive, regulatory, redistributive, and constituent policies. Each type of policy engenders its own unique politics and variety of government coercion. The characteristics of the policy types and some examples are provided in Figure 2. An indication of the efficacy of this approach is demonstrated not only by applications of the author himself, but by the substantial list of books, articles, and dissertations analyzing and employing this approach.[5] Substantively, it has been applied to studies of the U.S. Congress, bureaucracy, foreign policy, and cross-national studies.

The Arenas of Power

Lowi's approach to the study of policies began as a critique and synthesis of the prevailing approaches to the study of power and policy making in America, centering on the role of groups and elites.[6] The scheme is based on a three-step argument: first, that relationships among individuals are predicated upon the expectations of the participants; second, that expectations in the political realm are affected by governmental outputs or policies; and third, that political relationships are thus determined by the types of policies involved, so that each type of policy is likely to engender a different sort of politics or set of political relationships. While the causal relationship between policy and politics is not considered inviolate, it is accepted for purposes of analysis.

Policies can be examined under the typology in both sectoral and temporal respects. Policies can be evaluated and compared with each other across sectors to reveal differences and similarities among and between the types. Temporally, Lowi has observed that certain types of policies have emerged or dominated during certain historical periods. Constituent policies were the fundamental concern of the founding fathers. During the late eighteenth and early nineteenth centuries, the republic's founders were preoccupied with "state-building policies," including the establishment of public credit, the encouragement of manufactures, and the avoidance of foreign entanglements. Their efforts were bent toward

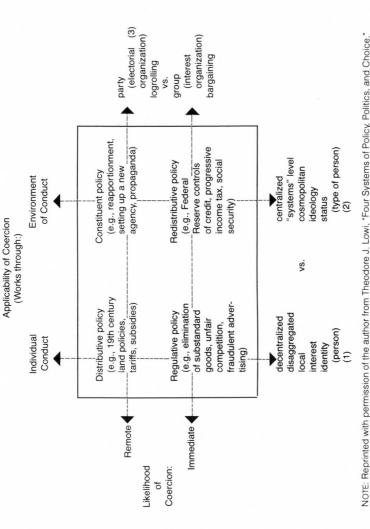

Figure 2: Types of Coercion, Types of Policy, and Types of Politics

NOTE: Reprinted with permission of the author from Theodore J. Lowi, "Four Systems of Policy, Politics, and Choice," *Public Administration Review* 32 (July–August 1972): 300.

establishing a governmental structure within which private action could take place. During most of the nineteenth century, policies at the national level were primarily distributive in character, including the development of rivers and harbors, and tariff and land-grant policies. The main aim of policy was to provide facilities and privileges. Regulatory policies became a significant national concern during the late nineteenth and early twentieth centuries. The era was ushered in symbolically by the establishment of the Interstate Commerce Commission in 1887. Redistributive policies manifested themselves most prominently during the New Deal era. The political period since the New Deal has been characterized by a confluence of all four policy types. The reasons for and implications of this evolutionary cycle are both important and interesting, but beyond the scope of this project.

In addition to this historical evolution, individual policies can themselves evolve over time. Raymond Bauer, Ithiel da Sola Pool, and Lewis A. Dexter's study of trade policy illustrates how a policy can evolve over time from distribution to regulation.[7]

Again, the point of the typology's distinctions is that each policy area incorporates its own characteristic political process, structure, elite, and group relations. A more detailed description of the policy and political characteristics of each of the areas follows.

Distributive policies. Government policies designated as distributive can be dispensed and disaggregated on a unit-by-unit basis. No direct connection exists among the recipient units or between them and any general rule. As a consequence, there is no direct political confrontation either among the groups or between them and those who do not benefit from the policy. While in the long run it seems evident that those receiving benefits are depriving others of possible benefits (a zero-sum situation), in the immediate political context the politics of distributive policies resemble a non-zero-sum situation. The immediate allocative decisions ignore limited resources. Distributive policies are often labeled "pork barrel," "patronage," or "subsidy." Standard examples include public-works projects, nineteenth-century land policies, and tariffs. Distributive policies develop a distinctive politics characterized by accommodation, noninterference and logrolling. The important decisions with respect to distributive policies involve small, homogeneous groups, each active without serious opposition in its own particular areas of interest. Political parties are important, not for ideological reasons but rather as convenient coalitions for porkbarreling. Congressional committees and administrative agencies generally serve as the centers of decision making. The politics engendered are disaggregative in the sense that very few actors are directly involved in the important political decisions. Instead, the politics are also highly stable, since the best way to create majority coalitions to insure enactment is through pacts of mutual noninterference. Part of that agreement is the assurance of support for each other's pet projects.

Regulatory policies. Regulatory policies resemble distributive policies in their individualized and specific impact. Here, however, the similarity ends. Regulation cannot be disaggregated into a series of unrelated items. Regulatory policies involve the formation and enforcement of laws that manipulate conduct, usually through the use of sanctions. They offer direct alternatives as to who will receive benefits and pay costs. The political characteristics of regulatory policies tend to resemble pluralism, insofar as a number of groups formed on the basis of similar attitudes and beliefs converge in an attempt to influence outcomes. Thus, interest groups exert proportionately more influence here than for any other policy type. Bargaining, or the granting of concessions in a common area of interest by opposing groups, constitutes the dominant political pattern (as opposed to logrolling, where agreements are made by groups having nothing in common except the desire to secure passage of their own particular programs). Because of the expanded nature of political conflict, the important decision making occurs not in congressional committees and administrative agencies, but on the floor of Congress. Political conflict expands in scope and therefore becomes less stable. The political visibility of the policy is also enhanced. Examples of regulatory policies include laws eliminating substandard goods, unfair competition, and fraudulent advertising; antitrust legislation; and public-health regulations.

Redistributive policies. Redistributive policies involve decisions that are interrelated, but the scope of impact of these policies is very broad, affecting classes of people. Governmental decisions affecting blacks versus whites, the middle class versus the poor, and big business versus small business are all characteristic of redistributive policies. The nature of redistributive policies cannot be determined by short-run effects, but rather by long-term impacts on the allocation (or reallocation) of resources among broad classes. Issues that involve redistribution resemble ideological and class conflict. This brand of political activity most nearly resembles the elitist view of politics, characterized by the struggle between haves and have-nots. Group involvement centers on peak associations (groups that speak for broad sectors of society, such as the AFL-CIO and the Chamber of Commerce). Redistributive issues usually polarize opposing groups into two sides. While issues tend thus to dichotomize political actors, the political relations remain relatively stable, if not institutionalized. Because of the centralization of conflict, the role of Congress diminishes, while the executive branch, centering on the president and his staff, flourishes.

Examples of redistributive policies include social security, monetary policy, the progressive income tax, and low-interest loan programs.

Constituent policies. The fourth area of policy was not part of the original arenas scheme but was added a few years later. Conceptually, it is the least mature of the four areas.[8] Constituent policies are the "rules of the game," or rules about rules (also referred to as "second-order policies"). They affect broad groups in society, such as voters, but their impact is relatively diffuse. Constituent policies focus on the overhead function of government; just as overhead agencies oversee other agencies, so too do constituent policies oversee the administration of governmental authority. Its politics are thus administrative in character. They involve political parties (because party concerns center on the rules and procedures that determine the nature of electoral conflict), the judiciary, and the "top officialdom" (administrative, executive, and legislative). Except for extraordinary circumstances, only the top political stratum concerns itself with, or for that matter comprehends, the rules of the game. Thus constituent policies directly involve the interaction of a few elites engaged in low-visibility activity. This often leads to accommodative, if not collusive, political arrangements, notably between leaders of rival parties.[9] Examples include reapportionment, election laws, budgeting, and departmental reorganization.

Critiques

As previously noted, the arenas-of-power typology has been extensively examined and widely applied. Although the applications speak for themselves as cases of the utility of the approach, the critiques and analyses of the framework merit attention, especially in light of the typology's importance to this project. Criticisms of Lowi's arenas approach operate on two levels: one, labeled "conceptual," questions the basic assumptions and ideas that underlie the approach; the second set of criticisms focuses on the problems with the approach as an analytical tool.

Conceptual problems. At the outset it is worth noting that the fundamental concept of the scheme, the idea that policies engender different types of politics, has won wide acceptance, even among the scheme's critics.[10] However, a major problem associated with the scheme has been that of defining and distinguishing policies in terms of the perceptions, expectations, and attitudes of relevant actors. According to Lowi, all policies may be considered regulatory, distributive, or redistributive (and presumably constituent as well) in the long run.[11] But the distinctions are maintained by virtue of the fact that political actors are usually unconcerned with the long-term cumulative effects. This perspective has led critics to focus on problems in assessing the perceptions and attitudes of political actors, notably congressmen, based on the notion that any policy can be identified with any policy area, according to how a congressman chooses to interpret that policy. Jerrold Schneider cites the example of a bill introduced into Congress that provided for the reimbursement of poultry firms that had lost millions of chickens due to pesticide contamination. The bill was successfully opposed by liberals who labeled the bill a sop to big business, since it would have set a precedent of subsidizing business losses regardless of need and responsibility. As proposed by its sponsors, the bill clearly belongs in the distributive box. From the perspective of the opponents, however, the bill is apparently perceived as redistributive, since it appears to imply the extension of government benefits to a broad class, albeit a wealthy one.[12]

This interpretation, while important and interesting as part of a case-study evaluation, is misguided in terms of both its evaluation and its use of the arenas. First, the basis of classification rests not with the type of politics, the dependent variable, but with the policy itself, the independent variable. To match up policies into the four policy areas by looking at the politics is to defeat the purpose of the scheme. Schneider's evaluation of the chicken case turns the conduct of analysis on its head by starting with the findings, that is, the type of politics, and then matching them to the policy type. Rather, the point of the analysis is to utilize the characteristics of the independent variable to predict what the politics are likely to be and then to compare the findings with the actual results. Discrepancies between the findings and the ideal characteristics can then be examined and analyzed. The scheme stands or falls on this sort of analysis, not a post hoc matching of apparently ambiguous results with one or more of the policy types, as in the chicken case. With respect to the independent variable, expectations and perceptions of relevant actors are important only insofar as they exhibit themselves in the actual product of the policy-formation process. While it is certainly neither impossible nor incorrect to deal with perceptions, the intention here is to study not political psychology but the concrete policy effects of actors in a policy-making situation. Policies are categorized according to the wording and interpretation found in the statute itself, not according to the perceptions of the actors involved. Details of how the categorization process operates in practice will be discussed in the next section.

The other primary criticism of the arenas of power as a conceptual scheme is based on the contention that there are other dimensions of governmental impact upon society that can be used in analyzing policy in addition to, or instead of, the dimensions of coercion. As noted, policy is viewed as the exercise of coercion by the state. The four policy types result from the splitting of the exercise of coercion along two dimensions, applicability and likelihood of coercion. Considerable effort has been expended by critics and others toward seeking out new dimensions that, for their authors at least, seem more appropriate for policy analysis.[13] But as we already know from policy analysis, no scheme can claim exclusivity, and the arenas of power is no exception. It does systematize and order knowledge, however, and others have found it of use in generating hypotheses.[14] Coercion as a conceptual foundation is not the only perspective, nor would anyone claim that it was. It is nevertheless an eminently acceptable alternative.

Analytical problems. Several questions have been raised regarding the analytical utility of the arenas scheme. In part, they have arisen from ambiguities in the initial description of the scheme.

The fundamental criticism has been that the categories themselves are difficult if not impossible to operationalize. For example, Wilson cites a number of cases that seem to fall equally into two or more categories.[15] Though it is clear that there are always likely to be ambiguous cases,[16] much of the confusion arises from ambiguity over selection and evaluation criteria. As indicated previously, the basis of categorization is provided by the statute itself, not its politics, nor the statements of political actors, nor the actors' cognitive processes. An often-cited example of an ambiguous case is that of a regulatory tax. Taxes in general are considered redistributive, while measures aimed at controlling individual conduct with the use of sanctions are clearly regulatory. A recent concrete example of this type of tax was a proposal offered in 1971 to adjust federal taxes on gasoline so that the price of unleaded gas would be more competitive with that of leaded gas. As the bill indicated, Congress tried to encourage the use of unleaded gas, and it hoped to do so by use of the tax. The object or main purpose was the regulation of a particular kind of conduct. The provision for the raising of revenue was the type of sanction employed in this bill (keeping in mind the fact that sanctions can be both positive and negative in character). Again, the primary purpose of the bill was to regulate conduct. That purpose can generally be seen in the organic act. The politics of this bill may have deviated from those of a pure regulatory case, such as one relying on jail terms and fines to impel conduct, but that distinction does not change the policy characteristics of the statute or, therefore, its categorization.

A second and related objection is that policies themselves change over time, both through amendment of statutes and through their interpretation or implementation.[17] In regard to the former, any amendment added to a bill at a later date may be considered a legitimate basis for reevaluation of a policy, based on statutory change, though it may not involve a shift in the main point of the original act. Bauer, Pool, and Dexter's study illustrated how a tariff policy was transformed from a distributive to a regulatory policy by statutory amendment. The alteration was accompanied by a change in the political activities surrounding the bill as well.

The execution or implementation of a statute is not irrelevant, but it plays no part in the categorization process. The activities surrounding a piece of legislation are obviously pertinent to a total picture of the legislation, but those activities are ancillary to the categorization process. A fundamental tenet of the arenas approach is that the composition of the organic statute as it relates to the four policy areas is crucial in determining what sorts of political activities occur in the later stages of policy enactment. A policy may evolve over time, but that evolution is germane to the categorization of a bill only if it occurs in the statute. Custom, interpretation, and usage, while important, are not independent variables and therefore are not relevant to the immediate categorization problems.

As this discussion implies, the arenas-of-power scheme is most directly concerned with a piece of the policy universe vis-à-vis its effects on much of the rest of that universe; it assumes that the content of statutes is of overarching importance. While this might be cited as a weakness of the scheme, it in fact proves to be a strength, because it offers the analyst a manageable yet conceptually sophisticated perspective for exploration in a field where qualifiers and delimiters are desperately needed. Moreover, this approach standardizes when and how a bill is to be compared with other bills.

Refining the Arenas

One problem that has been associated with the arenas-of-power scheme is the absence of differentiation within (and by extension among) each of the four policy areas. Clearly, some cases are "purer" than others, insofar as they possess more of the characteristics ascribed to each type. Other cases are more "mixed" in composition. Within each area, policies tend to cluster according to various subcharacteristics, and they do so with a degree of consistency. Thus, Figure 3 presents a revision of the arenas of power scheme, developed prior to the data analysis.[18]

Each box in the figure is cut in half, with the resulting inner diamond indicating the location of policies with mixed characteristics. The outer triangles in each box indicate the location of policies with more nearly pure cases. In the case of distributive policies, the pure cases located on the outside include examples such as parks, land-grant bills, and most public-works bills. The mixed cases are composed of bills that are mixed either by virtue of the nature of the bill itself, such as urban mass transit, or by virtue

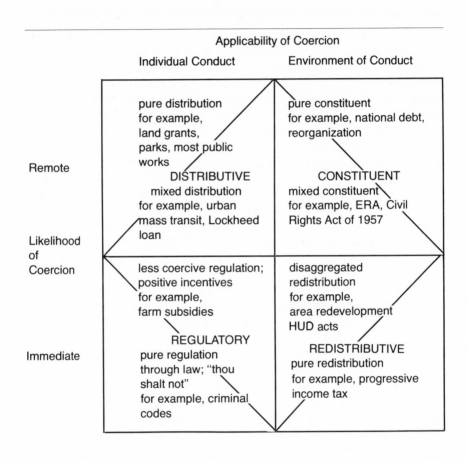

Figure 3: Revised Arenas-of-Power Scheme

of the amendments or additions made to the bill (any pure case can become a mixed case in this way).

The distinction in the regulatory category was not as clearly drawn by the cases and data presented here, but a distinction is nevertheless apparent. A case of pure regulation involves an unambiguous rule of conduct backed by a sanction ("thou shalt not"); laws related to criminal behavior or the military draft form examples. Mixed cases include those that prescribe conduct through less directly coercive means, usually via some sort of incentive, as in farm subsidies.

The fact that this distinction is not readily observable might be attributed to the difficulty of detecting the effects of an extragovernmental force on governmental outcomes. Though governmental actors (the president, members of the bureaucracy, congressional committees) are particularly important in the other policy areas, private interest groups have their greatest impact on regulatory policies, as noted in the previous description of regulatory policies and their politics. And while the actions of the important actors in the other policy areas might be more readily observable because they are in fact part of the government, the influence of interest groups may be less readily apparent because of their extragovernmental nature. While the floors of Congress are especially important for regulatory policies, that is more a statement of where influence is exerted than of by whom it is exerted.

The redistributive policy area divides itself according to disaggregation. Pure cases are those that involve direct transfers between one class and another. Mixed cases are those that involve disaggregation of the policy, as seen either in the nature of the policy itself (for example, area development) or in amendments or other provisions tacked on to the basic bill (for example, the Housing and Urban Development acts of 1965 and 1968).

Finally, constituent policies divide along lines similar to those of distributive policies. Pure cases would include reorganization, adjusting the national debt, and election law. The mixed cases involve the introduction of ourside policy elements. Examples include the Equal Rights Amendment and the Civil Rights Act of 1957.

Because of the routinely stable nature of distributive and constituent policies, the introduction of redistributive and regulatory policy elements (through introducing amendments) raises the political stakes. One manifestation of this would be increased floor activity for distributive and constituent policies. Regulatory and redistributive policies, however, may not reveal their mixed nature in such an obvious way, since these policies are already conflictual by comparison.

These clarifications of the policy categories are not proposed or conceived as fundamental alterations of the arenas-of-power concept. Rather, they provide reasonable distinctions that help to clarify apparent discrepancies among policies within the categories. The overall descriptions of policy and political characteristics still stand as descriptions of ideal cases that exemplify the four policy types.

In addition to the broad criteria associated with the characteristics already discussed for the four policy areas, a series of specific rules has been formulated which will aid in the entire classification process. Most of the rules are based on the simple idea that not only do statutes differ, but so too do parts of statutes. In many instances throughout this analysis, provisions of statutes will be considered separately. Many of these rules help distinguish between constituent and other policy characteristics.

Classification Rules

1. Individual provisions, when considered apart from an entire bill, are categorized according to the nature of the provision itself, rather than according to the bill from which it came.
2. Most bills contain constituent elements, for reasons of administration and implementation. Therefore, bills with such elements are considered distributive, regulatory, or redistributive unless the bill itself deals with purely in-house matters, or unless the administrative provision is considered separately from the rest of the bill.
3. A bill establishing an office, bureau, agency, or the like is constituent.
4. A bill establishing (extending, defining) a program is classified according to the substance of the program, even if a provision of the bill establishes an office or department. If this latter provision is considered separately from the rest of the bill, it is categorized constituent.
5. A bill dealing with relations between one governmental unit and another is constituent.
6. A bill that deals with a substantive program that happens also to involve another governmental unit is categorized according to the substance of the bill.
7. Bills that define powers and jurisdictions are constituent.
8. Bills involving relations with other nations are considered constituent (for example, immigration laws).
9. A bill that simply grants powers is constituent (for example, an act conferring the power to set fees and rates). One that grants power over a particular mandated program area or service is categorized according to the substance of the program itself (for example, a bill that authorizes a government body or official to set fees and rates according to a specific schedule imposed by the bill).
10. A policy is considered distributive if the group affected is identified by what its members do (for example, farmers, small businessmen); if the

group's members are identified on the basis of who they are (Indians, poor, elderly, veterans), the policy is considered redistributive. (The one possible exception is students; although student status is akin to a profession, policies affecting students are usually considered redistributive, because students' lifestyles, culture, and so on cause them to be identified as members of a social class rather than a profession.)

11. Bills and provisions dealing with planning and research outside of government are distributive. Planning and studying by the government in relation to a governmental program or proposed program is constituent.

12. Bills that appropriate money for a specified program or purpose are categorized according to the substance of the program or purpose. The act of budgeting, however, is constituent (for example, the vote on the total federal budget).

13. All taxes are redistributive unless the tax has another, explicitly stated, purpose (for instance, a regulatory tax—one designed explicitly to modify behavior).

The Arenas and the Presidency

After having devoted space to the discussion of a policy framework, we must return again to the presidency. We established in the last chapter the close link between presidents and the making of policy as it involves them with Congress. The task at hand is to link the logic of the arenas of power to presidential policies and policy proposals. No explicit, empirical attempts have been made to tie the two, but some possible relationships have been suggested, and experience might suggest some others. It was suggested in the discussion of the arenas that presidential and executive influence predominates in the redistributive area, while it is minimal in the distributive area and present to some extent in regulatory and constituent areas. This assessment, however, is based on an evaluation of the entire universe of legislative activity. Within the realm of the president's program, it is clear that the president is heavily involved in all four areas. However, we would expect that, due to the nature of redistributive policies and their politics, presidents would be proportionately more heavily involved in the redistributive area (without addressing for the moment the question of why this is so).

One brief assessment of the president and the policy areas concurs: because "the outcome [of distributive policies] is of no great importance for the president or for most congressmen, influence over distributive policies goes, by default, to bureaucrats, some legislators, and interest groups who do have a stake in the policy outcome."[19] The obvious inference—leaving aside the misguided reference to Congress's lack of interest in distributive policies—is that assessments of the "strong presidency" do not emanate from the president's involvement in distributive policies. His role in regulatory policies is somewhat more active, but it is primarily that of coordinator or broker among the various competing interests vying for congressional assent.[20] The president's role in redistributive policies most clearly fits the classic image of strong, activist presidents. The primary emphasis on redistributive policies in the recent era—antipoverty programs, social security, medicare, revenue sharing, and the like—has been vital in perpetuating the idea that the president is the protector of those not otherwise protected by the system and that in the long run he is protecting the interests of the nation as a whole. Given the broad scope of impact of redistributive policies, such an assessment certainly bears an element of truth. It also lends a degree of factual validity to Clinton Rossiter's simultaneous evaluation of and prescription for the presidency as "a clear beacon of national purpose." There is "a sense of importance about redistributive issues that greatly surpasses that of distributive or regulatory policies."[21] The image of Franklin Roosevelt as an activist and social democrat, for example, can be seen as emanating from the unprecedently large number of redistributive bills he sent to Congress, including such fiscal and monetary policies as suspending convertibility of dollars into gold, suspending the export of gold, the Emergency Banking Act, a broadening of authority to issue unsecured greenbacks, and authorization for the purchase of gold as well as all of the social legislation that followed these proposals.[22]

In assessing the possible outcomes among redistributive policies according to the degree to which presidents are involved, one study drew a direct relationship between degree of presidential involvement and the likelihood of passage of redistributive measures in their original form. "To the extent that the President is either opposed to the proposed redistribution or active only verbally or only sporadically or unenthusiastically the chances increase that either nothing will happen and a long-standing stalemate will persist or that the issue will be redefined, at least in part, as distributive. There are always strong natural tendencies in Congress to seek compromise through such redefinition."[23] Indeed, presidents interested in overtly distributive measures will sometimes attempt to convert the proposal into something resembling redistribution, as in the cases of Franklin Roosevelt and the Tennessee Valley Authority, and Kennedy and an emergency public-works proposal.[24] The question of policy redefinition will be examined more closely in succeeding chapters.

The above projections of the relation between policy types and presidential influence posit a progressive rise in the ability of presidents to have influence over and involvement in distributive, regulatory, and redistributive policies, with constituent policy probably placed somewhere in the middle. Although the assessment of presidential involvement in policies summarized here touches on a dimension differing from the concerns of this project, it offers a starting point from which to examine in detail the president's role as policy maker and the constraints and unique characteristics of each type of policy in determining political processes and outcomes.

Hypotheses

Case Studies. The case studies will present specific, descriptive overviews of examples of the four policy types. As such, I expect them to be consistent with the hypotheses and relationships suggested in the previous discussion and also to conform to the patterns proposed in the next section on the aggregate data. I expect that in relation to the presidency and other relevant institutions, congressional committees will have determinative influence over distributive policies, floor activity will be greatest for regulatory bills, interest groups will be most influential for regulatory bills, and the president's influence will be especially determinative over redistributive and constituent policies, and lowest for regulatory policies.

Aggregate Data. (1) Presidential involvement in policies (as measured by the number of proposals made to Congress) will be, in order from greatest to least, redistributive, constituent, distributive, and regulatory.

Redistributive is listed in first place because of two possible forces. The first, electoral in nature, suggests that presidents favor redistributive policies because they affect large groups in society that are often concentrated in the most populous states. Groups such as the poor, the elderly, blacks, and other minorities are all affected by redistributive governmental policies, and they can also cast crucial votes that swing the electoral votes of large states. Second, presidents respond to institutional forces that compel them to address and coordinate national programs affecting broad classes and segments of society. These would include not only social-welfare programs, but aggregate economic and other such redistributive policies. Constituent policies would probably come next, because of the traditional responsibilities associated with being the head of the executive branch, an office that thereby incorporates the various organizational, bureaucratic, and administrative functions. Distributive policies come third, their ranking assigned by virtue of the more particular orientation of these policies toward individual congressmen. The particularistic, disaggregative nature of distributive policies is especially important to individual congressmen because they provide readily identifiable benefits to constituents. Finally, regulatory policies, although broad in scope and applicability, are the most volatile and unstable, because of the pluralistic political activity they engender. The president is likely to involve himself least in this area, in comparison with the numbers of policy proposals in the other areas.

(2) The influence of the president over his program (success, as measured by passage rate of his proposals) will be, in order from greatest to least, redistributive, constituent, distributive, and regulatory. The reasons for the differing rates of success are similar to the reasons for his varying involvement. As previously discussed, redistributive policies have been an area where presidents have historically obtained success as the nation's leading political figure. Again, the same progression is expected from constituent, to distributive, to regulatory policy.

(3) The relative relationship among the four policy types will hold for the entire twenty-year period, regardless of who the president is, what party he belongs to, or who holds a majority in Congress. This simply states the importance of the underlying influence of policy.

(4) The number of distributive policies proposed to Congress will vary with the four-year presidential election cycle; they will be proposed most frequently immediately before an election.

This represents an extension of the logic of distributive policies, given their disaggregative characteristics, which allow individual politicians to provide and claim credit for the awarding of concrete benefits to constituents. As mentioned, distributive policies coincide closely with what politicians have traditionally labeled "pork barrel." Given that distributive policies are both concrete and disaggregable, it is reasonable to assume that incumbent politicians attempt to increase the dispensation of construction funds, jobs, grants, and the like during election years, because the recipients of these benefits are likely to support the dispenser.[25] Further, and more specific, relationships will be discussed in the relevant analysis sections. However, those relationships will also follow from previously stated hypotheses. In general, it is expected that presidential policy making will be responsive to election cycles.

Intermediate-Level Data. Since floor activity, as measured by roll-call votes, is an indication of political conflict, regulatory policies can be expected to possess the largest number of recorded votes. Substantive amendments will likely be of a regulatory nature as well, representing attempts to change the face of the bill. This indicates that conflict stems from disputes over the nature of the bill itself. One hardly expects regulatory bills to be the repository of, for example, pork-barrel provisions not directly associated with the bill. Some regulatory bills, of course, are likely to pass through without much, if any, amending, but that is consistent with the notion that regulatory bills are likely, but not required, to engender conflict. These expectations refer to tendencies, not absolutes.

Redistributive policies are expected to engender the next highest degree of amendment activity. While this might seem to contradict the hypothesis that presidents engage most actively in redistributive-policy affairs, it is in fact consistent with high presidential intervention. The most accessible point at which the president may intervene is the floor of both houses. While the president, through his aides, can exercise an important influence at the committee level, the committees' prerogatives and traditions limit direct presidential interference. The floor provides the president the opportunity to work with party and committee leaders in shaping and honing the final product. and given the broad implications of redistributive policies and the kinds of organizations and groups interested in such matters (notably peak associations), it seems logical that a greater degree of floor activity coincides with redistributive policies. However, as indicated, the president has a much firmer grip on this type of policy and the politics surrounding it, especially compared to the influence he has on regulatory policies. Substantive amendments proposed to redistributive policies are likely to be of several types. In addition to amendments designed to change portions of the bill, the tendency of congressmen to want to disaggregate these bills will probaly exhibit itself in the presence of explicitly distributive provisions tacked on during consideration on the floor of Congress.

Distributive policies are likely to reflect significantly less floor activity. On the basis of the arenas logic, this is to be expected, given that distributive policies tend to be resolved in committee. Since distributive policies are disaggregative, accommodation between the president and the Congress can be achieved in the classic logrolling fashion. Some distributive bills, however, have been subject to many roll calls. Such deviations may be the result of bills that are mixed cases, that is, bills that are not purely distributive in a non-zero-sum way.

Finally, we expect constituent policies to engender the least floor activity, given the relatively low visibility of administrative, overhead policies and functions. More conflictual cases may incorporate other than purely in-house administrative matters. A civil-service bill, for example, would not attract the degree of interest and attention in society that a bill such as the Equal Rights Amendment did. Clearly, the ERA, while constituent, is much more relevant to broad groups in society. Also, it is expected that constituent provisions and amendments will be found in bills in all four categories, because the administrative function is integral to the implementation of any policy. However, only those policies that are constituent in their overall intent are placed in this category.

As a final projection, I expect partisanship, as observed in floor voting, to exhibit itself in greatest measure in distributive and constituent policies, and less in regulatory and redistributive policies, based on the characteristics of the four policy areas (see Figure 2). The overall pattern of conflict for the four policy areas is projected to follow a progression from regulatory through redistributive and distributive to constituent. This follows also the pairing of characteristics in the headings at the sides of Figure 2. Regulatory policies are immediate in likelihood of coercion and individualized in terms of the app.icability to conduct; the sting of governmental action through regulatory policies is most directly felt. Redistributive policies are also immediate, but they affect the environment of conduct and therefore, while wide in scope, are more diffused in terms of impact. Distributive policies are remote in likelihood of coercion but relevant to the individual. Constituent policies are the most diffuse, because they are both remote and influential on the environment of conduct. Thus, the pattern, in order of degree of conflict, is immediate-individual (regulatory), immediate-environment (redistributive), remote-individual (distributive), and remote-environment (constituent). This pattern of policy characteristics, then, prescribes for the president the whats and hows of his dealings with the legislature over the matter of his annual program and the varying politics that flow from it.

The Four Presidencies

In addition to proposing relationships that will inform subsequent analysis, the above hypotheses also serve to lead into a primary theme of this study: that presidential activities in the four policy areas differ sufficiently to suggest the existence of "four presidencies." Presidential involvement in the distributive arena, characterized as it is by particularized, disaggregable policies that have clear patronage and therefore electoral-political implications, might be labeled the "special-interest presidency." Involvement in regulatory policies, dominated as it is by vigorous activity on the part of Congress and interest groups, emphasizes a "presidential broker" function, with involvement characterized mainly by mediation between and among the participants. The third category, redistributive policy, is the closest approximation to the classic "public-interest presidency." Constituent activity emphasizes the "administrative presidency" side of presidential policy activity. Obviously, these distinctions are not mutually exclusive, but they do pull presidents in different directions, leading to varying interpretations of how presidents behave, and therefore indicating distinctions worthy of further pursuit. These distinctions will be developed as analysis progresses.

Summary

Given below is a summary of the analysis to be conducted in subsequent chapters.

Case studies: relative presidential influence across policies as seen in politics of cases, in relation both to congressional activity in committee and on the floor and to interest-group activity.
Method: categorization and case description of eight presidential proposals that became law.

Aggregate: overall relative presidential interest in policy areas (policies proposed) and relative influence over outcomes (policies passed), in terms of overall congressional approval or disapproval.
Method: categorization and counts of all bills proposed by presidents (5463).

Intermediate level: ability of presidents to maintain the integrity of bills during the legislative process, as seen in the nature and amount of amending activity; how this varies for the four policy areas, and how the arenas characteristics of the amendments themselves affect the bill and therefore the outcome.
Method: categorization, counts, and content analysis of amendments (and parent bills) to 165 selected presidential proposals that reached the floors of both houses.

The chapters that follow outline in some detail the policies and policy consistencies associated with presidents. But the reader may wish to keep in mind one tenet: the presidents under consideration engaged in pursuing all four types of policies in their legislative programs. The policy characteristics differ among the four, and so does presidential behavior. But that behavior varies in consistent ways across administrations, according to the type of policy involved.

Before we proceed, a final explanatory, not to say cautionary, note is in order. In focusing on the policy characteristics outlined as they relate to the presidency and Congress, it should be made clear that the generalizability and applicability of the findings are restricted by the nature of the case under study. American politics operates within a system of separation of powers, highlighted especially by the separation of the president and the Congress (a schism accentuated in recent years). Further, the system operates with weak, ill-organized parties, whose weakness may in fact serve to strengthen the trends hypothesized. Because of these underlying conditions, no attempt is made to apply these proposed relationships to other systems or, for that matter, time periods. But the logic of the analysis may, in principle, provide a basis for these kinds of extensions.

3: Distributive and Constituent Policies: Political Stability

Not too long ago, a British citizen wrote a letter to an American magazine dealing with the subject of our president, Jimmy Carter. He expressed the opinion that Carter was the best chief executive Americans had had since the 1940s, and he could not understand why Carter was receiving so much bad press. An American editor picked up this theme and admitted that Carter was in fact doing a competent job, given the current national and world situation. Carter had clearly given major national issues "his best shot," as seen in his energy program, the SALT Treaty and the Middle East negotiations.[1]

These sentiments are worth noting because they intuitively suggest what this study is attempting explicitly to demonstrate—that there are limits to the extent to which presidential failings can be attributed to failings in the man himself. What if the gutting of Carter's energy program, for example, were found to be attributable to characteristics inherent in that particular type of policy, rather than to the loss of prestige suffered by Carter because a top aide spit a drink down a woman's dress? The example is admittedly extreme, but it is not so very different from the kinds of evaluations and analyses that haunt presidents. Presidents may indeed make effective use of their own skills and resources, but their work is carried on within the framework of policies and policy making.

In this chapter and the next, I intend to describe in case-study fashion how the fates of particular presidential proposals made to Congress are shaped by the nature of the policies themselves; I will therefore indicate how the president's political response and success is shaped by those policy characteristics. These case studies cannot be considered final and complete "proof" of the trends and characteristics already described, but they will provide important confirmation for the argument made throughout, and they will also help to illustrate the characteristics of the policy types. Some introductory remarks may clarify my procedures.

First, for purposes of organization, I have divided the eight cases to be examined (two for each of the four policy areas) into two separate chapter discussions. The present chapter will deal with distributive and constituent policy cases, and Chapter 4 with regulatory and redistributive policies. This division is based on a dichotomy previously stated, indicating relatively consensual politics for the former two policy types and more conflictual political patterns for the latter (the "likelihood-of-coercion" dimension of the arenas scheme). One would expect this "level of politics" to constitute a fundamental factor separating one group of policy types from another. I provide a table at the end of Chapter 4 to summarize the case findings.

I will, I confess, treat the cases in a summary fashion. Clearly, this entire project could be devoted to half as many cases. But the selection of eight cases facilitates comparisons within as well as among policy areas. In order to accommodate the inherent restrictions of covering eight cases in two chapters, I omit most of the anecdotes and intricate details of the cases. A few footnotes must suffice. This, of course, is a limitation, insofar as it restricts information about the cases, but it is also a virtue. By limiting discussion to the broad strokes, we reduce the likelihood of imposing unwarranted interpretations and conclusions upon the cases, because they are built upon a limited set of agreed-upon facts. Since our interest is in the overall political pattern accompanying each bill, our purposes are in fact best served by relatively brief descriptions that touch on the major characteristics of each case. The purpose of the cases, however, is not simply to describe, but also to instruct—not about the case per se so much as about the relevance of each case's basic characteristics to the larger framework. As a consequence, case descriptions serve and are treated as instruments for a larger purpose, rather than as ends in themselves. But for purposes of clarity and accuracy, I include the major facts of a case, following up with a discussion of relevant arenas characteristics.

Finally, I must acknowledge that the policy perspective employed here does not afford the only possible explanation of the configuration of these cases. There are and will always be anomalies and inconsistencies that stand in the way of accountability; these cases are no exception. Their characteristics, however, fit very well with the ideas and relationships presented in the last chapter, especially when the cases are compared with one another. This is particularly important in terms of gaining a broader understanding of presidential influence over policy making.

In the selection of cases I have followed several general procedures. First, I attempted to select cases about which relatively little secondary-source material (books and scholarly articles) was available, so that the case descriptions themselves could serve as a contribution to the existing body of case material. The one apparent exception among the eight cases is the Area Redevelopment Act of 1961. Usually I culled information on the cases themselves from contemporary news accounts and descriptions of the bills in *Congressional Quarterly.* One of the problems with selecting such cases, however, is the question of the availability of adequate source materials. Therefore I also chose cases that were prominent enough to warrant important attention at the time. Also, it was important to insure that every case represented a major presidential effort toward enactment. In each case the presidents involved were acknowledged to have a major, high-priority interest in the bills selected. And while all the bills selected were enacted into law, the importance of each derives from its political characteristics rather than the fact of its passage. I made no special effort to select pure cases beyond insuring that there were two for each of the four areas. As previously mentioned, the deviations are often as interesting and as much of an affirmation as the central characteristics. Finally, I selected cases from all the administrations covered here, plus two cases from the Carter administration. One case was from the Eisenhower years, one was from Kennedy's term, three from Lyndon Johnson's tenure, one from the Nixon years, and two from Carter's term; the Carter cases provide a more contemporary extension of the arenas logic. The actual selection was arbitrary, but it was informed by the constraints that I have mentioned.

Distributive Cases

Wilderness Areas. For a period of almost eight years in the late 1950s and early 1960s, conservation groups and their sympathizers had been pushing for legislation that would formally and finally assure a national wilderness system. In 1964 those efforts culminated in the passage of the Wilderness Areas Act. For many years federal lands exempt from normal commercial use and development had been protected under a variety of labels. National forests, which included areas designated as "primitive," "wilderness," "wild," and "canoe"; bird and animal refuges; and the national park system had all come under the federal umbrella. These ad hoc inclusions, however, had come about by administrative acts of the secretary of agriculture or the secretary of the interior. Conservationists feared that what had been done by department secretaries could just as easily be undone by future secretaries. That concern led to the pressuring of Congress to enact specific legislation to outlaw commercial exploitation of these lands. Conservationists also hoped that Congress would put aside provisions of an 1872 mining law that were applicable to much of this land.

As passed by Congress, the Wilderness Act established a National Wilderness Preservation System, composed of federally owned and administered lands (initially about nine million acres incorporating fifty-four separate tracts in fourteen states). The act also authorized the secretaries of agriculture and interior to review the addition over a period of ten years of other lands not yet incorporated into the wilderness system. In order to incorporate new lands, the president would submit recommendations to the Congress for its approval. Livestock grazing would be allowed under certain conditions, as would the extension of mining and mineral leases for a period of twenty years. The president, however, would have the right to authorize certain construction projects, such as the building of power projects and transmission lines, when it would serve the public interest. The act otherwise specifically prohibited the construction of permanent roads, use of motor vehicles and motorized equipment, aircraft, and the construction of structures or installations. Prospecting was still allowed, but only if carried on in a manner compatible with the wilderness setting.

The Wilderness Act had the strong backing of President Johnson. In his budget message to Congress, he cited the importance and necessity of wilderness legislation. On Johnson's list of thirty top-priority bills, the Wilderness Act was listed nineteenth.

Although this and other such parks legislation seem to possess regulatory elements, it is a distributive bill. The restrictions mentioned above are in fact restrictions that are inherent in any land placed under the category of wilderness land, because of the need to protect the integrity of the classification. Therefore this bill represents an act of classification rather than regulation per se. The decision for each tract of land is and can be made separately without directly affecting the project as a whole. Thus, the policy is disaggregable, allowing for the accommodation of diverse interests. It is consistent with the pattern of politics surrounding this bill.

As mentioned, the Wilderness Act called for the incorporation of federal lands (and other private lands donated to the government for this purpose) into the park system. Of the fourteen states affected, all but three (Minnesota, New Hampshire, and North Carolina) were western states. The bill was perceived as a real threat to western commercial interests, in large part because the federal government owns over 50 percent of all land in the West. The land to be included under wilderness-areas protection represented a small percentage of all federal lands (even with the addition of 5.5 million acres over the following ten years). Nevertheless, commercial interests feared the open-ended nature of such legislation.

The Senate had a record of sympathy with the conservationists. Senators, however, represent geography. Members of the House of Representatives represent people, and in the House ranchers, oil companies, lumber companies, and mining concerns found sympathy.[2] Indeed, the history of this legislation was one of sympathy in the Senate and obstruction in the House. A wilderness bill reached the Senate floor for the first time in 1961 and was passed by a vote of seventy-eight to eight. That year, the House bill never emerged from committee. In 1963 the Senate again took up the bill. The Senate Interior and Insular Affairs Committee reported a procon-servationist bill by a vote of eleven to five. The committee majority stressed that the proposal would not affect private rights already located on these public lands, and that the bill did not prohibit further exploration and exploitation of resources as long as they were considered consistent with what the president viewed as the public interest. Three senators issued a minority statement favoring the basic principles of the bill but opposing a provision of the bill that allowed the president to select lands for incorpora-tion into the wilderness system unless Congress took action to block inclusion. This procedure was supposed to make it easier to include land and was thus favored by conservationists. The Senate committee amended the original proposal, which also called for the review and inclusion of more land than did the final bill, by providing for public hearings on the question of inclusion and by further protecting the rights of private developers on such land.

Four roll-call votes were taken on the floor of the Senate. Three were sponsored by Republicans Gordon Allott and Peter Dominick of Colorado, both members of the Interior Committee. One amendment called for posi-tive congressional approval of land incorporation rather than a legislative veto. Another relaxed mining and prospecting regulations, and the third proposed the exclusion of "primitive" lands from the park system until each area could be individually investigated. Each amendment was defeated, and the final bill passed by a vote of seventy-three to twelve.

The relative ease of passage in the Senate found no counterpart in the House. The pivotal figure in the House was Wayne Aspinall, a Democrat also from Colorado, who was the chairman of the House Interior Commit-tee. Aspinall was sympathetic to the fears of commercial interests that too much land would be "locked up" under the wilderness plan. In previous years, he had been largely responsible for delaying the bill in committee. Hearings were held in 1964, however, in anticipation of some final action. Among those testifying was Secretary of the Interior Stewart Udall, the president's spokesman, who urged adoption of the administration's bill (S. 4). By way of compromise, Udall also offered to support a different version that gave Congress the right to vote on every inclusion, rather than relying on the legislative veto procedure. This represented a switch from the department's stand in 1962.

On 18 June, 1964, the Interior Committee reported out a compromise bill substantially engineered by Aspinall. The committee vote was twenty-seven in favor, one present, and five absent. The committee bill contained several concessions to commercial interests. It allowed new mineral and mining claims for a twenty-five-year period, while the Senate bill did not allow for any new claims. The bill also provided for congressional approval of each new inclusion rather than simply a presidential recommendation subject to congressional veto. The Senate bill protected eighty-seven unspoiled areas immediately, with thirty-six of these areas subject to later review. The House committee bill applied to only fifty-one areas upon enactment. Finally, the bill called for the exclusion of the San Gorgonio Wild Area in California, by allowing for the development of a ski run there. The vote in committee favoring this exemption was fourteen to eleven. Despite discrepancies between the Senate version and the House committee bill, the latter was seen as a compromise acceptable to all.

On the House floor, several of these provisions were challenged. But throughout the floor maneuverings, Aspinall was the decisive force in guiding the bill and determining compromises.[3] In fact, despite Aspinall's probusiness sympathies, the New York Times, in an editorial, lauded his deft handling of and important influence over the bill on the floor, even though the Times supported the conservationists.[4] It is important to note that the two major challenges to the committee bill on the floor were made by John P. Saylor of Pennsylvania, the ranking minority member of the Interior Committee. This indicated that, even on the floor, committee members continued to dominate the course of the bill. Saylor's first amendment, to eliminate the exemption granted to the San Gorgonio Wild Area, was adopted by the House. The other Saylor amendment deleted the provision allowing the secrtetary of agriculture to declassify areas already labeled primitive. Saylor argued that this detracted from the Congress's prerogative to decide the disposition of public lands and was therefore inconsistent with the main idea of the bill, which emphasized overall congressional control. This amendment was also adopted, though both were passed over the objections of Aspinall. A conference committee met shortly thereafter to iron out discrepancies, and the bill was signed into law on 3 September.

The Wilderness Areas Act presents a clear case of a distributive policy. The policy itself allowed for disaggregation and consideration of wild areas on a unit-by-unit basis. The dispute over the San Gorgonio Wild Area revolved around an attempt, which proved unsuccessful, to disaggregate a particular portion of the park system for private use. Though possibly important as a symbol of the fate of other wilderness areas, its fate was in no way directly tied to any of the other tracts. Despite the apparent deep cleavage between conservationists on the one hand and business interests such as the American Mining Congress, the U.S. Chamber of Commerce, and the National Association of Manufacturers on the other, accommodation came with some ease after initial jockeying. Conservationists still had their parks, and commercial interests were still able to maintain their business concerns.

Also consistent with the pattern of distributive politics was the clear dominance of congressional committees. In the Senate, the absence of vigorous dissent facilitated the committee's work. Even though several disputes were more hotly contested in the House (only one vote in the House was a recorded vote—the vote to pass the bill), the overall pattern was the same in both chambers. The committees produced bills closely resembling each other in most important respects. Both committees presented a relatively united front to their respective chambers. Though there were challenges to some aspects of the bill on the floor of both houses, all floor amendments were offered by Interior Committee members. Clearly, congressmen who were not members of that committee deferred to committee specialists. On the floor, committee leaders were credited with the important achievements and compromises. Thus, when disputes did spill out from the committee room onto the floor, they were managed there by members of that very same committee.

Significantly, the role of the president was minimal. Despite the fact that this period of legislative history was one of unprecedented presidential involvement, and despite the fact that this was considered one of Johnson's "must" bills, his influence was clearly not perceived as determinant either in committee or on the floor.

These overall impressions are generally consistent with the understanding of distributive policies and their politics. Specifically, in dealing with pure distributive proposals that are "the president's," the level of political conflict is relatively low; but at the same time, the level of presidential dominance is also minimal. Whether presidential or not, distributive policies are fundamental in keeping congressmen happy, because of the direct bearing such policies are likely to have on constituents. As a result, the subgovernment system in Congress is the dominant pattern for such policies. A clear indication of the tremendous importance of distributive policies to congressmen was illustrated in 1977 and 1978 when President Carter tried to intervene in the allocation of a series of water-resource development projects. Carter's attempt to eliminate altogether some projects that had already been authorized and funded, and were under construction, was considered absolutely unprecedented; it met the most tenacious congressional resistance.[5] In many respects, Carter's fights over the Panama Canal and SALT II treaties are relatively manageable from a political point of view, as compared with the rescinding of important congressional lollipops. Thus the fact that the president includes distributive policies in his agenda does not also mean that he can maintain tightfisted control over their shape. The president's ability to offer such legislation does not include an equivalent ability to withhold or deny the pork barrel.

The Lockheed Loan. On 9 August, 1971, President Nixon signed into law a bill, proposed by him some months before, that provided for a $250 million loan guarantee for the troubled Lockheed Aircraft Corporation.

Between the time the bill was announced on 13 May, and its signing, Congress and the administration dealt with one of the most controversial bills of the session. The wide-ranging disputes surrounding this bill are of immediate concern here, because the Lockheed bill is an example of a distributive policy. Clearly, it involved the awarding of a concrete benefit to a particular organization in society. Nothing was being denied any other group as a direct result. No immediate, decisive coercion was being employed. The purpose of the bill was simply to keep a particular company in business. How, then, can the bill's politics, at times frenetic, be explained, and how does the explanation square with classic distributive politics?

The Lockheed Aircraft Corporation was not just another company, at least from the government's point of view. It was the nation's largest defense contractor, with 95 percent of the company's work tied to federal contracts. In addition to building aircraft, Lockheed has produced major weapons, such as the Polaris and Poseidon missiles. The other primary characteristic of relevance is the company's financial standing—at the time it was on the verge of bankruptcy. Financial woes combined with highly questionable business practices had plagued Lockheed for several years. The most evident example of this was Lockheed's contract with the Department of Defense to build the C-5A cargo transport plane. Critics charged that the company had deliberately underbid to obtain the contract, knowing that the bid was unfeasibly low but hoping the government would make up the difference later, and that as a consequence it incurred large cost overruns.[6] Lockheed was finally forced to accept a $200 million loss on the C-5A, plus another $300 million in penalties for cost overruns on other defense projects.

The events that prompted Nixon to propose the "bail-out" loan for Lockheed, however, were related not to a military contract but to the company's proposed construction of a commercial passenger aircraft, the L-1011 TriStar airbus. The immediate crisis was precipitated by the company that had contracted to produce the engines for the plane, the British firm of Rolls-Royce. In November 1970, Rolls-Royce announced that the development costs of its engine, the RB-211, had more than doubled (to $344 million). On the heels of that announcement, much of Rolls-Royce's top management resigned. Then on 4 February, 1971 Rolls-Royce declared bankruptcy. These developments boded ill for Lockheed, because they caused the company to seek additional credit to finance the TriStar. A group of twenty-four banks had already lent Lockheed $400 million to complete work on the TriStar, and unfortunately they were unwilling to extend further credit. The British government was willing to prop up Rolls-Royce so that the firm could finish work on the engine, but only if Lockheed obtained an additional $250 million in credit. These were the circumstances leading Nixon to intervene by introducing a bill to guarantee the $250 million in loans to Lockheed.

The bill itself did not mention Lockheed by name. The guarantee for Lockheed was based on the dollar amount specified in the bill. If the appropriation had exceeded $250 million, it would have allowed similar help to other large companies in distress. The provisions of the bill as proposed and the final legislative outcome were virtually identical, despite all the intervening wrangling.

The bill authorized a $250 million loan for major businesses facing economic adversity. To oversee the program, it authorized the establishment of the Emergency Loan Guarantee Board made up of the treasury secretary, the Federal Reserve Board chairman, and the chairman of the Securities and Exchange Commission. The bill limited guarantees to five years with an extension of three more, required the board to assure collateral for loans, and allowed the board to make changes in company management under certain conditions, limit interest rates, and obtain from companies relevant information about their economic status.

It is argued here that the unusually active politics surrounding the bill stem from the fact that the bill opened the door to the possibility of aid to a whole class of businesses, and in so doing implied a redistribution. This implication resulted in the attempt by both sides to escalate the legislative conflict into redistributive terms in order to win. The possibility of this kind of escalation was brought out almost immediately, in fact, by Senator William Proxmire, a member of the Banking Committee (the committee to which the bill was assigned). His opposition to the loan was voiced in the immediate terms of its being a bad investment, but he also opposed the general idea of protecting big business from failure and labeled the program "welfare legislation" for a large company. The concept of offering such loan guarantees was itself important, because it represented a new effort by government to protect businesses in the private sector. The issue had previously been raised over the troubled Penn Central Railroad, but no final action was taken.

On the administration side, the loan was defended on the immediate grounds that it was important to keep Lockheed afloat because it was, despite its apparent inefficiencies, an important source of weapons and equipment for the Defense Department. The administration argued that the failure of Lockheed would leave only two major competitors, Boeing and McDonnell Douglas. Administration spokesmen, however, especially Secretary of the Treasury John Connally, also raised more sweeping economic questions. He pointed out that the failure of Lockheed would result in the ultimate loss of employment for over seventy thousand workers, including twenty-five thousand directly involved in the TriStar project. Beyond that, Connally felt that the failure of Lockheed would hinder the nation's recovery from economic recession. He was almost certainly exaggerating, but the TriStar project did involve over $1 billion in investment and production spread out across twenty-three states. As a result, many congressmen voted on this issue according to the immediate perceived effects on their constituents. Lockheed production was particularly heavy in southern California, for example, and both of California's liberal Democratic senators, John Tunney and Alan Cranston, came out in favor of the loan.

Despite the apparent support of a diverse group of congressmen, the administration quickly realized during committee hearings that the bill was in trouble. To strengthen support, they made a move that is typical of distributive politics and that would under most circumstances insure passage of the bill. They proposed to several senators on the Banking Committee that the allocation be expanded to $2 billion in order to include other companies that faced serious economic problems. In other words, they proposed tacking on additional benefits of the sort proposed to Lockheed in order to buy enough support to gain passage.[7] Meanwhile, Arthur Burns, chairman of the Federal Reserve Board, spoke for the administration in committee, urging Congress to pass permanent legislation to provide government loan guarantees for basically sound companies that had financial problems. In language that would seem more appropriate to a redistributive proposal, such as a tax bill, Burns argued that the effects of the Lockheed bankruptcy alone could be "serious" and "severe," and went on to say, "The Federal Reserve is not interested in preserving big business, as such.... We are interested in protecting the national economy."[8] As if to highlight the rhetorical, if not speculative, nature of this assertion, Proxmire suggested to Burns that any economic repercussions could be countered by more liberal policy at the Federal Reserve.

To emphasize the macroeconomic implications, the administration also sent over the deputy secretary of defense, David Packard, who testified in favor of the broader plan to the Senate, saying that the issue was not basically a defense issue, though it did appear so; it was in fact an economic issue.[9] The importance to the administration of emphasizing the broader, economic concerns in the political debate was highlighted by Packard's testimony, because he had previously testified before the House Banking Committee that he was opposed to the broader loan plan (a sentiment shared at the Defense Department). He later attempted to retract that testimony, but it was read into the record by the committee chairman.[10]

The logic of the administration's position was echoed and extended by Senator Jacob Javits of New York. He characterized the Lockheed problem as indicative of a widespread liquidity crisis in American business. In his assessment, companies with sound management had been caught in a squeeze founded in tight money and high operating costs (for labor, taxes, raw materials, and the like) plus sluggish sales and decreased profits. The result, as in the Lockheed case, was the erosion of borrowing power of businesses. This also was likely to lead to a crisis in employment. "The question is not one of bankruptcy or court reorganization nor of saving stockholders or creditors or management—but of continuing operations vital to the national interest."[11]

After lengthy hearings, the Senate committee reported out the expanded loan bill. The vote to report the bill was ten to five. Three of those opposed filed individual reports noting their objections. Action on the floor of the Senate was protracted, and debate dragged on for two weeks. A variety of unsuccessful amendments were proposed, including several attempts to expand loan coverage to small businesses, farmers, and educational and health institutions. Moves to increase congressional review procedures were also defeated. Ironically, the bill that finally passed (by a vote of forty-nine to forty-eight) was the House version, which scaled the bill back down to its original $250 million authorization.

On the other side of the Capitol, disagreement also spilled out of committee and on to the House floor. The House Banking Committee also reported out the expanded version of the loan bill, authorizing up to $2 billion in loan guarantees. The vote to report the bill out of committee was twenty-three to eleven; but no less than eighteen committee members (fifteen of whom were said to oppose the bill) issued separate statements attached to the committee report, each lodging individual complaints and qualifications.

The fate of the bill on the House floor was much the same as that in the Senate. By a vote of 192 to 189, the House passed the narrow version of the bill, authorizing the $250 million Lockheed loan only. In so doing, it rejected the committee's recommendation. A total of nine votes were taken on the House floor, three of which were recorded.

As a postscript to the Lockheed loan, it appears that the government's $250 million was money well spent—at least as a short-term balm. During the mid-1970s, Lockheed managed to extricate itself from many of its political and economic problems, in large part because of continuing defense contracts for cargo and antisubmarine planes, submarine launched missiles, and an upswing in orders for the L-1011 TriStar. By 1978, Lockheed was judged as finally being on a firm financial footing. By the early 1980s, however, its fortunes again sagged. But prospects of fat new defense contracts again offered new hope.

The overall political pattern in the House and Senate was the same. Extensive committee hearings and markup led to divisions within the committee that expressed themselves in the committee report. But divisions were not confined to the committees. Floor action was extensive in both the House and the Senate, and changes were made in committee recommendations. The major changes, however, were orchestrated by the administration toward the original proposal. The administration's lobbying efforts were especially successful in the return to the original Lockheed—only bill on the floor of both houses.

The normal pattern of distributive politics was disrupted, then, by the redistributive implications of the Lockheed bill—that is, the potential for expansion of the bill to incorporate an entire class of Lockheeds. The administration quickly realized the possibilities in the redistributive characteristics of the bill and exploited them by using important officials, especially Burns and Connally, to urge passage of the bill. Even the spokesmen for the Defense Department, Packard and Secretary of Defense Melvin Laird, were instructed to emphasize the redistributive elements of the bill at the expense of the department's immediate concerns, which were clearly more distributive (research, development, and production of weapons systems). As pointed out in previous discussions, redistributive politics tend to favor the executive. This assertion is in keeping with the political pattern of the bill.

Again, the Lockheed bill is a distributive policy, but it is a mixed case because it contains redistributive elements. As a result, the political battleground that formed tended to resemble that associated with a redistributive policy, a judgment borne out by the testimony and actions of Connally, Burns, and officials of the Defense Department. These characteristics were successfully exploited by the Nixon administration. The normal distributive response to deadlock, the addition of benefits, was unsuccessful as a response. Although the addition of benefits to the bill might have been helpful in that it could have prolonged debate until a winning coalition could be formed, it did not in and of itself contribute directly to the passage of the bill, as might otherwise be expected.

Presidential Distribution

The wilderness-areas and Lockheed-loan bills provide an interesting contrast in distributive politics. The wilderness bill was pure distribution. Committee influence dominated, and little floor activity was evident. Interest groups, while active, were accommodated without undue difficulty. Also, the president's influence was simply not a crucial part of the picture, despite the size of the shadow Johnson cast over the Congress during this period.

The mixed picture for the Lockheed bill was very different. Most important, it revealed how it is useful for a president to manipulate the politics of a bill, when the bill itself allows it, toward redistribution. It implies an expansion of the scope of conflict, as the Lockheed case illustrated, but it also prescribes the likelihood of greater presidential influence. In contrast with the previous case, conflict spilled out of committees on to the floor of the House and Senate. In its more redistributive form, the president was able to project his preferences by emphasizing the economic implications of the bill rather than the more concrete aspects of defense procurement. Nixon's problems with this bill reflected a worst-of-both-worlds syndrome. Had the bill been purely distributive, the addition of a few benefits probably would have assured a relatively uneventful passage. Had the bill been restructured as a redistributive piece of legislation, the stakes would have been higher, but so would have been the president's ability to meet the necessary challenge, including that of congressional Democrats. Instead, Nixon was caught on both flanks, attempting to pursue a strategy first in one direction (distributive), and then in the other (redistributive), while still maintaining a foot in each. The point is that Nixon's predicament arose not from his bald ineptitude (though other presidents might have handled the problem differently), but from the nature of the bill itself. Predictably, Nixon found the path of lesser resistance to be the redistributive one, other problems notwithstanding.

It is important to acknowledge that the move to redistribution, while politically helpful to a president, is not a tactic that can be adopted at will. Since the politics stem from the policy (that is, the bill), there must be some provision in the bill itself that opens the door. Admittedly, a bill can be changed or amended during the legislative process to accommodate this possibility, but the act of amending itself is discouraged by committee and overall congressional dominance. Clearly, Congress itself has no innate interest in expanding the scope of distributive bills. On a routine basis, the president need not wish to do so either. As in the case of the wilderness bill, the Congress enacted the basic proposal without a presidential strongarm because the president's wishes and Congress's interests so nearly coincided. Significantly, the patterns noted here have little direct bearing or reliance on the commonly cited fact that Nixon was a Republican president dealing with a hostile Democratic Congress, while Johnson was dealing with a friendly Congress that was overwhelmingly controlled by his own Democratic party.

Constituent Cases

Defense Reorganization. The specter of nuclear war on a grand scale profoundly affects the manner in which the nation's defense establishment handles preparation for war. Up to the end of World War II, the military was relatively decentralized, with separate military departments for each branch of the service. After the war, however, military analysts recognized the fundamental need to unify and coordinate the branches, because any major conflict in the future would almost certainly necessitate the involvement of all the branches in a coordinated effort. Similarly, it was felt that both unification and control from the top could be facilitated by placing the entire structure under the direct control of civilian leaders at the top of the defense hierarchy.

The first important attempt to unify the military services and consolidate direct civilian control was embodied in the National Security Act of 1947. Among other changes, the act established the modern Department of Defense, headed by a civilian secretary, and created the Joint Chiefs of Staff (JCS), whose function was to prepare strategic and logistic plans, establish unified commands when necessary, and serve as the chief military advisors to the president and the defense secretary. This reorganization would also—one hoped—stifle interservice rivalries. Open warfare, however, continued to break out between the services, notably in 1949, when a dispute between carrier admirals and the advocates of strategic bombing in the air force carried their fight over scarce congressional appropriations to the press and political columnists.[12] Such squabbles could only serve to weaken America's defense posture.

This continued rivalry, exacerbated in large part by jurisdictional disputes over new missile technology, plus the launching of Sputnik, spurred on President Eisenhower's attempts to hasten the reorganization of the armed forces. In his 1958 state of the union address, Eisenhower placed the matter at the top of his legislative priorities. In a special message delivered to newspaper editors on 3 April, he reiterated the need for stronger civilian control and a more responsive defense hierarchy. The product of Eisenhower's request was the Defense Department Reorganization Act of 1958.[13]

As signed into law, the Reorganization Act affirmed the subordinance of the three military departments (army, navy, and air force) to the civilian secretary of defense. More specifically, it gave the defense secretary the prerogative to assign new weapons and weapon systems to military services as he saw fit. It also provided, however, that the secretary report significant changes to House or Senate Armed Services Committee, which could veto the changes. During periods of hostility, the president was given the power to transfer and coordinate functions among the services. The bill also established the naval air force and the Marine Corps in order to insure the independent perpetuation of those branches. It gave the secretary the right to delegate authority to lower civilian heads and required subordinate civilian heads and their military counterparts to cooperate fully with the secretary and his staff. Despite these controls, the heads of the military departments and members of the JCS were also allowed to report directly to Congress. Moreover, the act called for the defense secretary to report to Congress on the progress of reorganization within the department. It increased the size of the Joint Staff of the JCS from 210 to 400 officers, allowed the JCS chairman a vote, eliminated a total of 5 assistant secretaries, created a new position of director of defense research and engineering, allowed the defense secretary the right to transfer personnel between the services, and finally, established in law the National Guard Bureau.

The Defense Reorganization Act provides an excellent example of a constituent policy. The bill is concerned exclusively with overhead, administrative matters as they relate to the Defense Department. The immediate concern of Eisenhower and Congress here was clearly intragovernmental.

The congressional response to Eisenhower's proposal was mixed. The dominant view, however, seemed to be that the bill went too far toward total unification of the branches. Sentiment favoring the maintenance of the separate identities of the services was strong in Congress, and despite Eisenhower's assurances to the contrary, some congressmen felt that the bill was intended to create total unification. The greatest congressional criticism was leveled against a provision, later dropped, that funds for defense be given directly to the defense secretary rather than to the military services. Granting the secretary this power of the purse would clearly give him greater control over the services. In order to allay congressional fears, Eisenhower drafted a bill that excluded any reference to the appropriation of funds. However, he conceded nothing more of significance. In submitting his revised draft proposal, Eisenhower also reemphasized the importance of unified strategic plans in the context of a unified defense structure.

Despite Eisenhower's firm intentions and military background, he incurred the hearty disapproval of some of the most influential members of Congress, including the two committee chairmen that headed the House and Senate Armed Services committees. Carl Vinson, the aging House chairman, not only had strong military sympathies in general but at one time had been chairman of the old Naval Affairs Committee, and he was known to have a particular fondness for the navy. Upon the introduction of the bill, Vinson took to the floor of the House and delivered an hour-long attack on it, refuting it page by page and line by line. Richard Russell, his Senate counterpart, was less vociferous, but nevertheless also entertained grave doubts about the bill. Another important sign that the bill was in trouble came from a pessimistic statement by Styles Bridges, chairman of the Senate Republican Policy Committee. A gloomy statement from one of the president's party leaders constituted a clear sign that problems lay ahead. In all, the members of the Armed Services and Appropriations committees were considered inclined heavily against the bill.[14]

The House Armed Services Committee began hearings on 22 April, and, despite misgivings within the services, the administration was careful to coordinate the full support of the military heads. The secretary of defense, the chairman of the Joint Chiefs of Staff, the army chief of staff, the chief of naval operations, the Marine Corps commandant, and the air force chief of staff all testified on successive days, generally favoring the reorganization plan. The chief of naval operations, Admiral Arleigh Burke, supported the design of the program but expressed doubts over some of the command-structure provisions, and the Marine Corps head, General Randolph Pate, expressed concern over the future autonomy of his service. Overall, however, Eisenhower succeeded in soliciting the necessary degree of consent and support from the top military officials. While unofficial, the pressure of the president on military leaders to conform to the administration line was widely acknowledged as intense.

At the same time, Eisenhower sent out several hundred letters to business leaders, urging them to support the reorganization plan. In that letter he compared his efforts to rationalize the defense system with the importance of hierarchy in the corporate structure. Apparently, Eisenhower hoped that business pressure would have a positive effect on congressional opinions.

On 22 May, the House committee reported out the bill by a vote of thirty-six to zero. Two important changes were made that were opposed by the president. One change provided that the departments be organized separately, with a chain of command running through the secretaries of each service. Eisenhower wanted the defense secretary to be able to intervene more directly in the affairs of each service. The second change gave Congress the right to disapprove the defense secretary's reorganization efforts if it so chose.

On the floor of the House, Eisenhower was unsuccessful in getting Congress to adopt suggested revisions in the committee bill. The crucial test was on a vote to recommit the bill with instructions to add the provisions desired by the White House. The move was defeated by a vote of 192 to 211. The final vote on passage, taken 12 June, was 402 to 1. These were the only recorded votes. The only change made in the bill from the committee version was the addition of an amendment to standardize and unify purchasing procedures for the services.

The Senate Armed Services Committee began hearings on 17 June. Commenting on the House version, Defense Secretary Neil H. McElroy observed that it fell short of the administration's wishes and requested that the Senate adhere more closely to the original administration version. Again, the primary dissenter among military spokesmen was Admiral Burke, who preferred the House version. After the conclusion of hearings and markup sessions, the Senate committee reported a bill closely resembling the original White House version. For example, the Senate version eliminated a provision, opposed by the administration, that required Congress to review any reorganization move at the request of a member of the JCS. The Senate's bill also restricted other mandatory congressional oversight, and it gave the defense secretary more leeway in exercising reorganization and consolidation authority.

The mood on the Senate floor was one of even greater cooperation with the president than in committee. By a unanimous vote, the Senate approved the proadministration committee bill, with little debate and no opposition. The only roll call was a unanimous vote for passage.

In conference, the administration was successful in pushing the Senate version over that of the House. Though the final bill did not meet all of the specifications originally requested, the bill was considered a major victory for Eisenhower. The two provisions distasteful to the president were kept in the final version. One allowed any service secretary or JCS member to bring complaints or other Defense Department issues directly to the Congress. Eisenhower labeled it "legalized insubordination." The other provision Eisenhower disapproved of required Congress to approve any attempts to merge, transfer, or abolish functions within the Department of Defense. However, neither concession was considered major. In all, the Defense Reorganization Act was considered the most sweeping reform in military structure since the National Security Act of 1947.

The passage of the reorganization bill illustrates several points about a president's influence over the politics of a constituent policy. First, Eisenhower was able to exert his presidential muscle over the defense establishment, a part of the executive, in order to help assure support from military sympathizers in the Congress. Such influence exerted by Eisenhower ought not to be interpreted solely as the product of his military background. Even the supposedly ineffectual Jimmy Carter was able to rally support from the Defense Department for the highly controversial SALT II Treaty. Despite its reputed influence and autonomy, the department is still a part of the executive branch and therefore subject to a certain degree of presidential dominance.

Second, it is important to note that Eisenhower was substantially successful in overriding the influence of congressional leaders to obtain congressional assent, even though the Democrats controlled Congress. In order to do this, Eisenhower had to work primarily on the floor of both houses and in conference in order to circumvent committee dominance. What floor controversy there was sprang from presidential initiatives. The right of a president to reorganize and redirect the executive departments was and is considered fundamental; it commands the respect of Congress. Again, those most directly affected by the bill, the military, were subject to presidential influence in ways that outside individuals and organizations would not be. For other types of bills, therefore, the president's influence is not necessarily so effective; this is clearly a function of type. In two of the four congressional "arenas" (Senate committee and floor), the president held sway, and the full House simply followed the recommendations of its committee. The conference committee also yielded some favorable results for the president. Despite the political rhetoric contained in early reports that the bill was in deep trouble, the reality was consistent with the nature of constituent-policy characteristics.

Civil-Service Reform. The presidential election of 1976 brought to Washington a man who had explicitly campaigned against the Washington establishment. And sitting at the center of that establishment is the federal bureaucracy, an organ that has grown over 400 percent in the last fifty years, so that it now consumes 22 percent of the gross national product. It came as no surprise, then, that in fulfillment of one of his campaign pledges, President Carter proposed a series of reorganization plans to streamline and rationalize the national administrative system. The centerpiece of that effort was the Civil Service Reform Act of 1978, formally announced in his 1978 state of the union address. The general goal of the legislation was to make the civil-service system less rigid and more responsive to its leaders. The Civil Service Act fell far short of fulfilling Carter's campaign promise to reduce the number of federal agencies from nineteen hundred to two hundred. Nevertheless, it was considered the most far-reaching reform in the federal bureaucracy since the establishment of the civil-service system in 1883. While the civil-service bill was being considered, Carter was under fire to an almost unprecedented degree for not being a sufficiently skillful and resourceful leader, especially in his dealings with Congress. Cynicism about his leadership, plus any actual failings in his political skills, were not likely to ease the passage of this bill. But despite these apparent handicaps, the civil-service bill, in its final form, gave Carter almost everything he had requested.

As signed into law, the Civil Service Act established two new agencies to replace the existing Civil Service Commission. The Office of Personnel Management would take over all personnel-management functions, while the Merit Systems Protection Board would become the new board of appeals for employee grievances (both of these new boards were first authorized in a previous reorganization plan). The act spelled out the principles of the merit system, emphasizing fair and open competition for positions based on ability, knowledge, and skill. It also prohibited certain practices, including racial and sexual discrimination and reprisals against whistle-blowing government employees. Federal managers were given somewhat more flexibility to fire incompetent workers, but the appeals process itself still provided significant protection for employees.

The act also provided for the establishment of a new Senior Executive Service (SES). These SES employees would include executive-branch jobs classified above the GS-15 level and below level 3 of the executive schedule held by top managers and supervisors not appointed by the president. Several enforcement agencies, such as the Federal Bureau of Investigation and the Central Intelligence Agency, were excluded. SES employees would have less tenure than civil-service employees, but they would be eligible for cash bonuses and could transfer more easily within or between agencies. The SES could be discontinued by Congress after five years. The bill also established merit pay for GS-13 and GS-15 employees. While these workers would still receive some automatic pay raises, merit, determined by the evaluation of individual performances, would still be the main basis for increases in salary. These employees would also be eligible for special cash bonuses. In addition, the act also established the Federal Labor Relations Authority to hear complaints of unfair labor practices from federal employees. The bill set a limit on the total number of federal employees for the fiscal years 1979 to 1981, though the president has some leeway in exceeding that ceiling. Finally, the act established in law for the first time the right of federal employees to engage in collective bargaining and join unions, although it did not allow federal employees to strike over pay and fringe benefits, nor did it allow a union to require employees to pay dues if they did not belong to the union. The one major provision sought by Carter but deleted from the bill was an attempt to reduce hiring and related preferences for veterans in filling federal jobs.

The sole concern of the Civil Service Act is the federal bureaucracy. Though it touches on the regulation of conduct (it bars discrimination in hiring and promotion, for example) and adjustment of pay scales, the bill is a constituent policy: its principal aim is to reshape the federal bureaucratic structure.

The political history of this bill would seem to illustrate clearly the truth of a lesson once stated by the playwright Edward Albee: it is often necessary for a person (or a bill) to go a long distance out of his way in order to come back a short distance correctly. From the start, the bill had both an advantage and a disadvantage. The advantage was that there was widespread popular support for some sort of reform of the federal bureaucracy, and congressmen were well aware of this sentiment. But despite the bill's elevation as a campaign issue, support for the bill was relatively shallow; it was not an issue that evoked strong sentiments among large groups of people. A related problem in terms of the Congress was the fact that, as a "good-government" issue, congressional support was difficult to mold into an enduring coalition. As Carter's chief lobbyist, Civil Service Commission Chairman Alan Campbell, observed: "To keep this moving is very difficult because there really is no group for which this is a particular goodie. It's a good government issue, and although we have broad support, it's thin support."[15]

In the Senate, the bill was assigned to the Committee on Governmental Affairs. The committee held twelve days of hearings and received testimony from over eighty witnesses. From the very start, spokesmen for the administration tried hard to sway opinions through testimony and lobbying. In fact, every member of the cabinet engaged in some sort of lobbying, because each executive department was affected by the proposed changes.

The major dispute in committee centered on the provision for giving preference to veterans, which had been included in Carter's original bill. As the system has existed, veterans have been given special preferences (automatic points added to their scores) on federal competitive examinations, protection from layoffs, and promotion preferences. Though the system of preferences does not apply to nondisabled veterans who have left the service after 1976, it still covers a pool of about 28 million veterans. The civil service employs approximately 150,000 people every year.

Women's groups and minority organizations were in the forefront of the fight to eliminate these preferences, since the overall effect favors white males. In addition, the Chamber of Commerce, Common Cause, and the Business Roundtable also registered their approval of the change. But the views of the large veterans' organizations held sway, and the Senate committee deleted this provision from the bill. The committee voted seven to nine to reject a compromise plan that would have still curtailed veterans' preferences. The committee, however, did vote thirteen to one to set up a task force to examine the problem and recommend revisions. The committee also voted to strengthen protection for whistle blowers and to place a greater burden of evidence on the agency in cases dealing with the firing of an employee.

On 29 June, the bill was approved by a vote of eleven to two. Two senators supporting the bill filed supplemental views, and the two dissenting senators, both Republicans, filed a minority report criticizing the SES, competitive examinations, and the creation of the two new agencies.

Meanwhile, action in the House followed a somewhat different path, largely because the bill was assigned to the Post Office Committee, where organized labor had much stronger ties than in the Senate Governmental Affairs Committee. Committee hearings were held throughout the spring. In May, after conclusion of the hearings, committee Democrats met in caucus to redesign the bill. Most important, the new version reflected labor unions' preferences that federal workers be given greater job protection and collective bargaining rights. Democrats on the committee, however, were themselves divided over these and other changes. This division, combined with Republican committee support, allowed supporters of the administration to carry the day on several key votes.

One important prolabor provision added to the bill in House committee was a revision of the Hatch Act. A proposed revision of that act, which would loosen governmental restrictions on political activity by federal employees, was passed in the House in 1977, but it stalled in the Senate. In large part, those who supported the revision of the Hatch Act were successful in attaching the amendment to the civil-service bill because the administration decided not to fight the issue in committee but to wait for floor consideration. The other Christmas-tree amendment added to the bill was the text of a measure designed to reduce the work week of federal firefighters, which Carter had recently vetoed as a separate bill. Several other changes and attempted changes were also considered.

By a vote of thirteen to eight, the committee adopted a motion to limit the SES program to two years and three agencies, thus making it an experimental program. This action was in part a response to representatives of the civil servants' union, who feared that the SES program could mean less job security. The committee also voted to expand the scope of bargaining rights, but Congressman Morris Udall, the bill's primary advocate in committee, was successful in watering down this provision. Udall managed to take the teeth out of an amendment that would have compelled all employees to pay union dues. The committee also added greater protection for whistle blowers and for employees accused of misconduct or incompetence. But an attempt to provide an automatic hearing for employees accused of misbehavior failed. Finally, the House committee voted to adopt a compromise version of the change in the veterans' preference provision. The compromise, backed by the administration, met defeat in Senate committee. After a month of markup, the full committee voted to report the bill by a vote of eighteen to seven. Five Republicans and two Democrats voted against the bill.

On the floor of the Senate, consideration of the bill moved smoothly, despite disputes over how much time to allot for debate and quarrels over minor provisions. The floor managers for the bill, Senators Abraham Ribicoff and Charles Percy, maintained control on behalf of the administration-committee version. Fifteen amendments were accepted, but none involved major changes. The only major concession made by the administration was the decision not to try to reinsert the change in veterans' hiring preferences. It was feared that such a fight could bring the entire bill down. On 24 August, the Senate approved the bill eighty-seven to one. Two recorded votes were taken on the floor.

In the House, a series of procedural moves designed to block the bill marred floor consideration. Unhappy with Carter's position on labor, two Democrats called for time-consuming roll calls, asked for reading of the entire bill, and employed other delaying tactics. As a result of these tactics and a variety of amendments offered to the bill, floor consideration dragged on through September. Despite the introduction of over fifty amendments, however, the administration emerged with a bill close to its preferences. The administration's supporters succeeded in knocking out the firefighter and Hatch Act provisions, and they produced a compromise on the floor concerning labor rights that was very close to the original administration version. Again, the only major defeat for Carter was the failure to change existing veterans' preferences. As an indication of final consensus, the House approved the bill 13 September by a vote of 385 to 10. In all, seven recorded votes were taken on the floor.

In conference committee, the administration was generally successful in obtaining favorable compromises. For example, the SES program was extended to five years, and the "experimental" label was dropped. After being sent back to both houses for final approval, the bill was signed into law by Carter on 13 October.

The passage of the Civil Service Reform Act was considered Carter's first really major domestic legislative achievement. And that fact is perfectly consistent with its character as a constituent policy, although it must be said that much of what Carter proposed had been unsuccessfully sought by past presidents.[16] Despite wide-ranging disputes and attempts to alter the bill drastically, Carter's forces succeeded beyond the expectations of everyone, including some of Carter's own people.[17] Only in House committee did the final product not meet the general preferences of the administration. It is important to note that, despite much disagreement and posturing, the administration ultimately had its way on every major issue related to the bill except one. Interestingly, the two areas that caused the most trouble, veterans' preferences and labor rights, were areas that are redistributive and regulatory outside of the context of this bill. In the Lockheed case, we observed an instance where a redistributive strategy was seen to help the bill. Here, however, the effect was the reverse. The resolution of this apparent contradiction rests in the fact that the Lockheed bill was distributive (politically stable, but subject to less presidential influence), whereas the Civil Service Act is constituent (stable, but most subject to presidential influence). In the latter instance, any nonconstituent policy component stands to dilute the president's initial advantage in this area.

In terms of the bill itself, the relative lack of widespread interest engendered by the bill is indicative of a constituent policy. Chairman Campbell's comment that the bill lacked "particular goodies" indicates the absence of immediate distributive or at least disaggregable benefits in the bill. Similarly, it is clear that the guiding hand of the president was considered crucial to the favorable final outcome.[18] Yet, this was a president who, by all accounts, did not command the skills, much less the respect or admiration, necessary to achieve such a coup. Possessing the knowledge of constituent-policy characteristics, however, one can easily assimilate Carter's relative ascendance in this area, and the relative absence of deep, conflictual politics on the floor or in the committes of Congress.

Constituent Patterns

As with the distributive cases, the two examples of constituent policies discussed here provide a pure and a mixed case, but both cases illustrate the ability of presidents to hold sway over constituent policy matters.

In the case of defense reorganization, the principle of presidential control over the executive was important in establishing Eisenhower's pre-emptive right to ask for the reorganization that he got. While this says nothing for the actual degree of success that presidents have in this regard, it is important in terms of defining the jurisdictions of the president and Congress.

As in the distributive pattern, the important issues surrounding defense reorganization were resolved in committee, and Eisenhower expended his greatest efforts in making modifications on the floors of both houses. Despite the tight-fisted control of Congress by southern Democrats during this period, Eisenhower achieved a notable success. And while Eisenhower's military background certainly provided him with important insights about the workings of the military, it is not clear that his success was ever directly attributed to deference to him as a result of that background. The Congress responded to him primarily as a president, not a general.

The more recent case of civil-service reform again reflected an area of relative presidential ascendancy. The more mixed nature of the bill, however, caused some controversy that spilled out onto the floors of Congress, especially in the House. The salience of differing policy characteristics is again highlighted by the nonconstituent nature of the main controversies—veterans' preferences and labor rights. Carter recognized early that a quarrel over veterans' preferences would only bog down the rest of the bill. As a consequence, he chose not to fight. Overall, however, the absence of deepseated, widespread interest in this and the defense bill contributes to an understanding of why the president is likely to have a better time with the bill vis-à-vis outside groups. The salience of these policy traits is especially pronounced when the case of Carter is assessed. While his party affiliation matches that of congressional majorities, the troubles of this novice outsider seemingly plagued his administration. Even so, the political patterns observed here can be understood in the context of basic policy forces that transcend the usual assessments of political skill and savvy. It would be a mistake to overemphasize the policy-determinative aspects of these cases, and indeed factors like political leadership, skills, effort, and agenda priorities are not simply being swept aside. The argument I seek to advocate, to restate the problem, is that a whole series of other factors operate in the policy environment, and they can in fact be used to account for the political patterns described in these chapters.

In any case, the guiding hands of both presidents were considerably important for both bills. In both instances, observers were startled at the successes achieved in the light of other presidential failings and failures at the time. The resolution can be found in making distinctions that have not been considered in the popular press or elsewhere.

4: Regulation and Redistribution: Political Conflict

Thus far we have observed the interactions of president and Congress for two relatively nonconflictual policy types. Yet presidential influence, while dominant in one (constituent), was relatively subordinate in the other (distributive). What happens when the scope of politics is broadened, as in the cases of regulatory and redistributive policies? Prior assessments would indicate that the pattern would be one of relatively low influence over regulatory policies and higher influence over redistributive ones. The cases, however, can speak quite well for themselves.

Regulatory Cases

Crime Control. Concern over crime and criminal behavior became an issue of particular public concern in the 1960s. Nixon rode the tide of that issue into the White House in 1968. But even before Nixon's ascension to the Oval Office, the incumbent president had taken steps in the direction of addressing the issue. In 1967 and again in 1968, President Johnson proposed to the Congress a sweeping crime-control bill. Congress finally consented on the day after Robert Kennedy's assassination, but the final version of the bill was far different from what the president had first proposed. At every step along the way, in the House and Senate, in committee and on the floor, the bill suffered manipulation and fundamental change.

Four major titles composed the bill in its final form. Title 1 dealt with the distribution of law-enforcement grants to states. It awarded three types of block grants to states for distribution to localities: planning grants, law-enforcement assistance grants, and training and research grants. Johnson's original proposal had called for direct or categorical grants to local governments. Direct grants allowed the federal government to maintain a degree of control over the allocation and distribution of funds. Block grants allowed each state to decide on its own how funds would be utilized on a state-by-state basis. The allocation of funds by the federal government was to be handled by a three-member panel, rather than by the attorney general, Ramsey Clark, at whom this provision was aimed. This bill was the first major program incorporating the use of the block-grant concept. Title 1 also contained the stricture that the funds be used for developing techniques to fight organized crime and to develop riot control. Neither of these requirements was part of Johnson's original bill.

Title 2 of the bill centered on the rights of the accused during interrogation—rights defined in several Supreme Court cases, including the *Mallory, Miranda,* and *Wade* decisions—for suspects accused of federal crimes. This provision of the bill attempted partially to counteract the Supreme Court decisions by allowing evidence to be submitted by the prosecution as long as the defendant responded voluntarily; it allowed for the admission of eyewitness testimony under conditions otherwise restricted by the court rulings. This title was added by the Congress during consideration.

Title 3, also added by Congress, allowed for relatively permissive wiretapping and bugging procedures for a number of specified crimes. Although warrants were usually required, police could tap and bug for a period of up to forty-eight hours if they felt an emergency existed in investigations of organized crime and national security. The administration had originally favored a relaxation of legal restrictions on bugging and wiretapping only for cases of national security.

Title 4 of the bill represented the first gun-control act passed by Congress since 1938. The provisions, however, were not as stringent as those desired by Johnson. The title called for the prohibition of the transportation of pistols and revolvers across state lines, and it forbade people to purchase handguns in stores in a state where they did not reside. But the provisions specifically excluded long-barreled weapons. The bill also contained a series of relatively minor provisions relating to legal procedures and law enforcement.

Although the face of the bill was significantly changed along the way, it started and ended as a regulatory bill. Throughout, the heart of the bill pertained to the manipulation of individual conduct through the use of the sanctions contained in titles 2 through 4.[1] The degree and type of manipulation changed in significant ways, but not the mode of the bill.

The basis of Johnson's original proposal, the centerpiece of his crime program, was derived from the findings of the President's Commission on Law Enforcement and Administration of Justice. All but one of the commission's major recommendations were incorporated into the bill. Part of the main idea of the bill, especially as embodied in title 1 was based on the notion that the best way for the federal government to help combat crime on the local level was to give aid to localities rather than mandate specific behavior in legislation. The apparently successful precedent set by the Law Enforcement Assistance Act of 1965 followed this pattern.

The House of Representatives was first to take action on the bill, which was introduced into the Judiciary Committee by its chairman, Emanuel Celler, on 8 February 1967. Not surprisingly, interest groups involved themselves deeply in the politics of the bill almost from the start. The bill's main administration spokesman was Attorney General Ramsey Clark. The U.S. Conference of Mayors, the International Association of Chiefs of Police, and representatives of municipalities spread across the nation endorsed the bill as an important step toward curtailing criminal behavior. The American Civil Liberties Union supported the bill in early committee hearings, though with some reservations about the allowance of wiretapping, even when justified in the name of national security. Groups in favor of control also spoke for the bill, but their voices were more than matched by the vociferous opposition of the National Rifle Association. The NRA proposed that the best insurance against civil disorder was the formation of armed civilian patrols. They maintained that home protection was best handled with a twelve-gauge shotgun, but they also said that "there is a good deal to be said for a sledge or ax handle."[2]

While the bill was in subcommittee, relatively few important changes were made. In the full House committee, however, the bill was significantly altered through the adoption of several proposals inspired by Republicans. As amended, the bill now allowed all local governments to be eligible for funds, rather than only areas with a population of fifty thousand or more, as originally proposed. The original bill had provided that one-third of the allotted funds could be used for local police salaries; the amended bill prohibited the use of funds for that purpose. Some significant administrative procedures were also changed. Yet the heart of the bill remained the same. In stating their opposition to various parts of the bill, eleven Republican committee members vowed in a minority report to try to alter it on the floor. They were substantially successful in their efforts.

On the floor, Republicans and sympathetic Democrats succeeded in altering the language of the bill, especially in title 1, which transferred control over program funds from the federal government and the attorney general to state governments. They also succeeded in earmarking funds specifically for riot control and prevention on the local level. Another amendment provided in title 3 for the creation of a National Institute of Law Enforcement and Criminal Justice, which would then establish regional centers to conduct research and training. A total of eight recorded votes were taken, all involving important changes in the bill. Significantly, Judiciary Committee Chairman Celler opposed the important changes, except for a clarifying amendment proposed by Celler himself. The House passed the bill on 8 August 1967, by a vote of 378 to 23. Meanwhile, in the Senate the bill's fate was even less clear.

Hearings in the Senate Judiciary Committee began in March, along with hearings on several other crime bills. The Judiciary Subcommittee on Criminal Laws and Procedures, headed by John McClellan, made several important alterations. McClellan's subcommittee called for funds to be administered by a three-man board rather than the attorney general. In response to Supreme Court decisions, the subcommittee also included sections liberalizing the use of wiretaps and admission of confessions in court. Moreover, it prohibited the applicability of title 4 of the Civil Rights Act of 1964, which allowed the government to cut off federal funds to any agency engaging in racial discrimination. The subcommittee version also barred federal courts from ruling on issues of voluntary confessions and eyewitness testimony when those issues had been ruled on in state courts. Congressmen justified these restrictions on federal courts by claiming that the Constitution granted the Congress that prerogative in article two, section two.[3] Despite these developments, action in full committee was reserved until 1968.

At the end of the session, the administration's eagerness to obtain a crime bill was suggested by a persistent story, officially denied by Ramsey Clark and the president, that they were willing to accept the wiretap and bugging provisions as the price for successful action on the bill, even though those provisions directly contradicted a prior administration bill that severely curtailed the use of electronic eavesdropping equipment. Indeed, the considerable difficulty faced by the Johnson administration in obtaining favorable action on this and other regulatory bills provoked wide discussion at the time.[4]

In the state of the union address at the start of the second session of the Ninetieth Congress, President Johnson again asked Congress for his crime bill. However, its fate in the Senate differed little from that in the House. In the full Senate committee, senators approved the White House categorical-grant approach rather than the block-grant approach by a one-vote margin. But they also approved the wiretap provisions, court review, and less restrictive gun-control measures. Then, too, they also increased the appropriation level from $50 million in the first year to $100 million, and, like the House, they emphasized the use of the funds for riot control and organized crime. While the Senate Judiciary Committee decisively altered the original bill, the diversity of views and opinions about the bill among committee members was indicated by the fact that every member of the committee, except for McClellan and Sam Ervin, filed separate, additional, and minority views. The final committee vote on approval was nine to three.

Debate on the Senate floor began in May and dragged on for almost a month, through twenty-nine recorded votes and numerous other motions. At the outset, debate focused on the wiretapping and gun-control provisions of the bill, considered the most controversial sections. An indication of the slothful floor activity was the fact that, after the first two weeks of debate and the proposal of sixty amendments, no controversial amendment relating to the major portions of the bill had yet been brought to the floor. Later in the month the Senate rejected a series of administration-backed amendments designed to strengthen firearms regulation. Included in those was an amendment proposed by Edward Brooke to outlaw the purchase of machine guns, bombs, hand grenades, and related weaponry.

The next major debate centered on the section of the bill dealing with criminal rights. Against administration wishes and after much acrimonious debate, the Senate kept in provisions that countered the *Miranda, Mallory,* and *Wade* cases for trials in federal courts. They did, however, delete the sections that would have limited federal-court jurisdiction, including a section that would have prevented federal courts from reviewing state-court convictions on a writ of habeas corpus. Following the resolution of this dispute, administration attempts to tighten up restrictions on the use of wiretapping were also defeated on the floor. And finally, as if to consolidate the administration's loss of control over the bill, the Senate minority leader, Everett Dirksen, succeeded in changing the Senate committee's recommendation to maintain categorical grants in title 1 by utilizing block grants to states instead (as in the House version). On 23 May, the Senate approved the bill by a vote of seventy-two to four.

Final action on the bill came in early June. The House had to vote to decide whether to accept the Senate version or send the bill to a conference committee. As a final irony, the House voted for the Senate version, with the key vote coming within twelve hours of the death of Robert Kennedy. Emanuel Celler and other supporters of the administration failed in their attempt to send the bill to conference, where they hoped it could be softened.

Many urged Johnson to veto the bill. For example, Alexander Bickel, a constitutional scholar, commented that the bill " has been so mangled by the Senate Judiciary Committee as to be an abomination."[5] Disregarding such advice, however, Johnson signed the measure into law on 19 June, stating that the bill had more good provisions than bad.

The politics of this bill exemplify the characteristics associated with regulatory policies. Both House and Senate committees made significant changes in the bill, but floor activity was very extensive as well. In many instances, committee recommendations were overturned on the floor. The almost complete inability of Congressman Celler, the otherwise influential House Judiciary Committee chairman, to alter the outcome, either in committee or on the floor, exemplifies the volatile nature of regulatory politics. More centrally, the administration itself was blocked at almost every turn. Johnson's panoply of problems with this bill stands in stark contrast with his notable successes in other areas. The mandatory emphasis on riot control, the absence of pressure to integrate local police forces, the broad wiretapping provisions, the weak gun control, and the limits placed on the rights of the accused were all provisions that ran counter to Johnson's expressed desires. Clearly, he could have vetoed the bill, especially since by June he had announced his intention not to run for reelection. But he accepted the political realities of the moment, swallowed his pride, and signed the "compromise bill."

One other interesting pattern is worth noting. Congress exhibited a disaggregative trend in its handling of title 1 funds. In relying on the block-grant principle and opening up eligibility to communities of any size, the Congress was moving in a direction that could only serve to benefit its members' own interests at home. Clearly, Johnson did not have enough political control over this regulatory bill to counter their move.

Airline Deregulation. At the beginning of his administration, President Carter was advised by his aides that he could register an early and easy victory in Congress by advocating the deregulation of airlines, in large part because Congress had spent considerable time exploring the matter in the previous term. Carter finally did get his deregulation bill, but it arrived on his desk the last day of the session, and the political costs proved to be far more extensive than his aides had anticipated at the start of 1977. For the Carter administration, the effort to deregulate the airlines began not with a piece of legislation, but with the Civil Aeronautics Board (CAB) and its head, Alfred Kahn.

Since its creation in 1938, the CAB's history has been one of protecting airlines from competition by restricting the routes and fares of air carriers. The appointment of Kahn in early 1977, however, marked a change from that tradition. Kahn directed his efforts at deregulating the commercial-flight industry by allowing automatic entry into the market and by permitting airlines to compete by changing their fares. Automatic entry allows an airline to start new routes without the prior approval of the CAB. Not surprisingly, this plan attracted both fierce support and vehement opposition. Within the industry itself, support for deregulation came from the very large carriers (primarily United Airlines, the nation's largest) and other, smaller carriers that were looking for the opportunity to enter markets previously closed to them. The notable support for deregulation from United was attributed to its size. It had grown as much as it could under present regulations, and because of its size, it could enter new markets and drive out competitors after deregulation was implemented.[6]

Carter's legislative effort was essentially an attempt to reinforce the CAB's moves by providing a firmer legal grounding. As passed by Congress, the Airline Deregulation Act followed up on Kahn's work at the CAB. Most important, the act provided for automatic entry by allowing airlines to begin service on one new route each year from 1979 to 1981, without formal approval from the CAB. Also, each airline could designate one route per year as exempt from automatic-entry competition. In addition, the bill allowed the air carriers to lower rates as much as 50 percent or raise them up to 5 percent above what was considered the standard industry fare, again without CAB approval. The CAB, however, did have the option to regulate what it considered to be an exorbitant fare. In addition to these major provisions, the deregulation bill called for the gradual elimination of the CAB itself. Unless otherwise directed by Congress, the CAB would lose its authority over domestic routes at the end of 1981 and over mergers and acquisitions at the end of 1982, and it would cease to exist by the end of 1984. Also, the bill directed the CAB to simplify and speed up many of its procedures, to place maximum reliance on competition, to impose on charter airlines restrictions that were no more rigid than those placed on other air carriers, and to approve airline consolidations, mergers, purchases, leases, and acquisitions. In the case of consolidations, the burden of proving the absence of competition was specifically placed on the party challenging the action. The act also exempted interstate airlines from state regulation of rates and routes, required commuter-airline craft to conform to the safety standards imposed on larger passenger craft, and made commuter and intrastate airlines eligible for a federal loan-guarantee program.

The individual provisions and overall intention of this act spell out a regulatory policy, founded in its fundamental emphasis on the manipulation of individual (airline) conduct. It does have some important constituent and distributive elements, notably the abolition of the CAB, and a loan-guarantee program, but these elements are all in support of and subordinate to the bill's attempt to recast airline regulation in America.

Action on airline deregulation in Congress extended back to 1977. The Senate Commerce Committee led legislative consideration of this matter, though the bill itself met with something less than enthusiam.[7] The committee's chairman, Warren Magnuson, complained that consideration of this bill had taken more time than any piece of legislation in memory. It was plagued by intense lobbying by the airlines and labor, a high absentee rate among committee members, and the generally complex nature of the bill itself. Compromises and alterations were frequent. The committee chairman himself was reluctant to embrace the bill, and its main advocate turned out to be the chairman of the Aviation Subcommittee, Howard Cannon. In all, the bill went through twenty markup sessions over a period of four months. The final committee product represented a heavily amended and rewritten fourth draft of the original bill. This protracted effort assumes special significance in light of Carter's repeated efforts to expedite the bill. His attempts to provoke action included a meeting at the White House with executives of the airline industry and reporters.

In committee hearings, representatives of most of the major passenger airlines and several cargo carriers testified as to the desirability and effects of deregulation. United and Eastern, two of the largest carriers, endorsed a change in regulatory procedures along the lines of those proposed in the bill. Most of the other carriers, however, including Delta, Southwest, Western, Continental, Federal Express, and American, voiced strong opposition. Representatives of the Air Line Pilots Association and the International Association of Machinists and Aerospace Workers also expressed doubts about the move to deregulate; they feared for the long-term job security of airline employees.

Controversy in Senate committee centered around several particular issues. The question of automatic entry was of major importance to the reliance on market forces, central to the deregulation concept. The automatic entry provision constituted the core of the bill, because without it, an airline with a monopoly over a route could raise its fares to an artificially high level without fear of competitive retribution. Most air carriers feared automatic entry, viewing it as the provision most likely to wreak havoc within the industry. A compromise was worked out that generally favored automatic entry, after the bill's supporters beat back several attempts to gut this provision along with the bill itself. Controversies also developed in committee over labor protection and what was termed "public need." The former centered around the fear that the bill could conceivably lead to massive layoffs if many companies were driven out of business. Senator John Danforth proposed that the bill include a provision insuring financial guarantees for workers in case of large-scale layoffs. The amendment carried after a weaker version failed. The other controversy concerned new routes. The bill provided that the legal burden of proof as to whether a new route was consistent with public interest and need rested with the airline opposing the application. Senator John Melcher proposed that the burden of proof rest instead with the applicant. On the initial committee vote, the amendment was defeated by an eight-to-eight tie vote. On reconsideration, however, it was adopted.

In the House, hearings were held during 1977 by the Committee on Public Works. Similar controversies plagued consideration there, and markup was postponed until 1978.

By 1978 the Carter administration had stepped up its efforts to see the bill through Congress, as it was considered the centerpiece of Carter's attempts to minimize federal regulation. After further wrangling, the Senate Commerce Committee reported out the bill but delayed floor consideration until after debate over the Panama Canal Treaty. The administration expressed its disappointment over the number of compromises required in order to obtain the Senate committee's approval. The vote to report the bill out of committee was thirteen to three, but five senators who voted for the bill filed separate statements, and each of the three who voted no also filed separate views.

Meanwhile, the House Aviation Subcommittee began 1978 with a version different from the original proposal. After spending several days marking up the revised bill, they rejected it altogether at the last minute and substituted for it a bill that did not contain deregulation at all. Both the subcommittee chairman, Glenn M. Anderson, and the administration were taken completely by surprise. After six days of markup sessions incorporating sixty-eight proposals for revision, forty-two of which actually came to a vote, the subcommittee voted (fourteen to nine) to report the bill. The compromise measure reincorporated the automatic-entry provision and some of the other provisions that had been previously eliminated. The administration had suffered a severe blow, but with the help of the subcommittee chairman they were able ultimately to recoup their losses.

During this time, the Senate was moving ahead on its own. On 22 April the Senate approved the basic deregulation bill, by a final vote of eighty-three to nine. The only major change from the original version was a strengthening of deregulation. It was considered an important victory for Carter. A number of attempts were made, however, to alter the bill on the Senate floor; the effects of those changes would have been to weaken automatic entry and labor protection in particular. Interestingly, Senator Cannon thought that the active lobbying of the airline industry had had a reverse effect on the chamber, hardening senators' attitudes in favor of deregulation. In all, eight recorded votes plus several voice votes on suggested changes were taken.

Passage in the House turned out be be less smooth than in the Senate. Indeed, the fate of the bill itself was in doubt right up to the end. A member of the Aviation Subcommittee, Elliott Levitas, sent a letter to the White House, warning Carter that he ought not to push for automatic entry if he hoped to see the bill enacted. The coalition supporting the bill was considered to be very fragile, and Levitas played on that theme in his communication with Carter. For Carter to have accepted that compromise, however, would have meant accepting a bill that would not have served his purposes. After further discussions, and despite the efforts of Levitas and a few others, the House Public Works Committee on 15 May approved a bill by a vote of thirty-six to four. Though still a compromise, the measure did allow air carriers to add a new route in the first year without CAB approval and also permitted airlines to cut fares up to 50 percent, or raise them up to 5 percent, also without CAB approval. The automatic entry provision was retained as well.

On the floor, several attempts were made to alter the bill. One successful attempt was an amendment that made it easier for carriers to add new routes. In all, three roll-call and four voice votes were taken. The final vote for passage, taken 21 September, was a lopsided 363 to 8. This seems to indicate a high degree of support for the bill, but much of that support was cautious, if not lukewarm. As evidence, Speaker of the House Thomas P. O'Neill gave a list on 9 August of top-priority bills, including many administration proposals. Airline deregulation was not among them.

Even at this juncture, however, final approval of the bill was still in doubt. The Senate's version was more strongly committed to deregulation than the House's, and the conference committee offered no immediate hope to the president's supporters. Part of the interchamber tension came from reports that House leaders were unwilling to compromise on deregulation unless the Senate approved a bill calling for federal subsidies for airplane-noise abatement. The House, however, did not follow through in its threat to hold the deregulation bill hostage. In fact, the conference committee concluded its negotiations within a few days. The final bill reflected several concessions by the House in favor of the stronger Senate version, including beefing up the automatic-entry provision. On 24 October 1978, President Carter signed the bill into law.

The importance of this bill was readily observable in terms of the behavior of the air carriers. The bill's signing led to an immediate scramble for new routes (Braniff Airlines, for example, applied for 626 new routes). It also spurred several merger efforts, such as the successful one of Western and Continental airlines. Clearly, this regulatory bill had a significant effect on the affected carriers and thus on passengers as well.

The heavily conflictual pattern of politics customarily associated with regulatory policies was very much in evidence. Congressional leaders were reluctant to deal with the issue at all, even at the strong urging of the White House. Indeed, Carter's best efforts were barely successful in keeping the bill on track. This is all the more significant in the light of the successes and popularity that then surrounded Alfred Kahn and the CAB. The bill's blueprint had already been shown to be feasible, at least in the short run, by CAB actions. Thus, it was all the more surprising that congressmen were so hesitant to identify themselves with the bill until the very end—though that surprise loses its mystery in the context of regulatory-policy characteristics. Interestingly, the constituent and distributive elements of the bill were not sources of controversy, and while the pattern of politics of the bill was dominated by that associated with regulation, the presence of these other, less conflictual policy provisions may have contributed to the overall success of the bill (especially when compared with the crime bill). Constituent elements were an especially important part of the bill.

Interest-group activity, although relatively limited in scope (mostly the airlines and labor versus administration spokesmen, especially Kahn, Transportation Secretary Brock Adams, and their supporters), was vigorous from the start. Ironically, the heavyhanded presence of the airline lobby probably helped more than hurt the bill's chances at crucial times.

Although the committees were clearly important in terms of resolving many major disputes, important changes were made all the way through, right up to and including the conference committee. More important, committee politics at times were akin to open warfare, and committee leaders had all they could do trying to limit changes in the bill.

Congress's caution and relative disorganization probably facilitated the President's intervention and influence. The volatile nature of the politics engendered by this regulatory bill, however, made it difficult for any political leader to maintain a firm grasp on the bill. Despite the bad reputation Carter has acquired in terms of his dealings with Congress, there were not many stumbles or slipups on his part. Yet, ultimate success seemed to rest less with Carter than with strategic mistakes by the airline lobbies, general public support, and the proven successes of Alfred Kahn and the CAB.

Regulatory Patterns

The pattern for these regulatory cases is very much in line with that previously delineated. A classic strong president, Johnson, was all but completely ineffectual in maintaining the crime-control bill as originally proposed. From the very start, it was substantially altered and disaggregated in committee and on the floor. That Johnson's supporters advised him to veto the bill clearly indicates how fundamental those changes were.

Carter's airline-deregulation bill encountered similarly stiff resistance, and significant alterations were made both on the floor (though more on the House than the Senate floor) and in committee. It is important, however, to note that the "weak" Carter emerged with a bill closer to his original request than had the "strong" Johnson. This may be attributable in part to the broader scope of the crime bill and the significant constituent characteristics of the deregulation bill. But what is most important to note is the basic congruity of the political patterns surrounding both bills. Interest groups were vigorously and pluralistically involved in both instances, and congressional leaders themselves had a difficult time managing the bills. Most important, both presidents, despite their best efforts, could not prevent the long and exhaustive struggles and basic changes imposed on the bills. The volatility of the politics of regulatory policies, combined with the tenacious involvement of interest groups directly affected by bills that manipulate conduct on an individual level, combine to produce a level of political pluralism that inhibits presidential influence and effectiveness, even when congressional leaders share the president's sympathies.

Redistributive Cases

Area Redevelopment. In the late 1950s the nation's economy entered a recession. As is always true, the areas and sectors with the most precarious economic standing are those most likely to feel the pinch of hard times. Statistics compiled by the Department of Labor showed a steady rise in the number of areas across the country with "substantial labor surplus." Thus, throughout this period, a rising chorus of voices called for a governmental remedy to aid those areas of the country hardest hit by chronic unemployment and related problems. In the Congress the liberal voice of Senator Paul Douglas led this chorus. Since 1955 Douglas had been the prime mover behind an act designed to aid depressed areas of the country. The idea was to bring new, permanent jobs to economically depressed areas by helping to finance industrial development and public works needed to support industry.[8] Despite yearly efforts by Douglas, his bill never became law. In 1955 and 1957 it died in committee, in 1956 and 1959 it died in the House after Senate approval, and in 1958 and 1960 the measure was vetoed by President Eisenhower. During this time, Eisenhower claimed to favor an area-redevelopment bill, but because he was never satisfied with the version Congress produced, he was in large part responsible for the bill's failure to pass. Republican opposition itself became an important campaign issue in the late 1950s.

During the 1960 presidential campaign, John Kennedy pledged in a speech in West Virginia to push for a redevelopment act. The pledge was not a case of expedience, however; as a young senator, Kennedy had been an important floor leader for the redevelopment bill, especially in 1956. After the election, area redevelopment was listed as one of the administration's top five legislative priorities. The passage of the Area Redevelopment Act on 1 May 1961 marked the first major legislative victory of the Kennedy Administration.

As signed into law, the bill provided for $394 million in aid to depressed areas over a four-year period. Specifically, it granted assistance to urban areas where the unemployment rate was at least 6 percent and had averaged at least 6 percent in the recent past. Areas in question also had to have unemployment rates a certain percentage above the national average for certain periods of time (the act borrowed the Department of Labor's classification for areas with "significant labor surplus"). The program's administrator was allowed to designate equivalent rural areas as in need of help based on comparable employment and income standards. The program itself allowed for the establishment of a revolving fund from which loans could be drawn for industrial redevelopment, rural redevelopment, and the contruction of public facilities. The degree of federal participation in these programs was set at a maximum of 65 percent of the total cost, with minimum participation rates set at 10 percent for state and local governments and 5 percent for private investors. In addition to loans, the act provided for outright grants for public facilities for areas unable to repay federal loans. It also provided technical assistance, vocational-training programs for the unemployed, and subsistence payments for those being trained for new jobs. Finally, the act called for the creation of an Area Redevelopment Advisory Policy Board, a National Public Advisory Committee on Area Redevelopment (made up of state and local officials) and an overall administrator who would serve under the secretary of commerce.

The conception of this act is redistributive in its aim to aid chronically depressed areas. The bill was criticized by some for granting the program administrator too much discretion in designating areas as eligible for redevelopment aid,[9] but it clearly set out an accepted formula for determining aid. The program may have had the effect of granting benefits to industry and related business interests, but in its conception the program was directed at chronic unemployment.

Action on Kennedy's proposal began even before the president-elect took office. In early December 1960 Kennedy appointed a panel, chaired by Senator Douglas, to investigate the problem of depressed areas and issue a report. On 1 January the panel issued a report calling for redevelopment legislation. Four days later, Douglas introduced a bill, designated S. 1, with the cosponsorship of forty-three other members of Congress. The bill actually introduced by Douglas, however, varied slightly from the administration's version. The latter placed the proposed Area Redevelopment Administration under the Department of Commerce, rather than maintaining it as an independent agency, as Douglas preferred; it provided that funds would be appropriated on a yearly basis by Congress, rather than through "back-door" financing, which allowed administrators to spend money without going through the Appropriations committees; finally, the administration version provided for up to 100 percent support from federal loans, rather than 65 percent. These first two differences were the main bones of contention in Congress.

Support for the bill outside of Congress stemmed from an amalgam of liberals, labor unions, economists, and progressive farm interests. Opposition stemmed primarily from business groups such as the Chamber of Commerce and the National Association of Manufacturers. To back up the voices of labor and other supporters, Kennedy sent three of his department heads to testify before committees in support of the bill: Commerce Secretary Luther Hodges, Labor Secretary Arthur Goldberg, and Agriculture Secretary Orville Freeman.

In the Senate the Banking Committee took expeditious action. By a vote of eight to seven, it placed the Area Redevelopment Administration under the Commerce Department, but with the director responsible to the president. Douglas had been concerned that hostile interests in the Commerce Department would paralyze the program. The move to change funding from "back door" to direct appropriations was defeated, however. After several more minor alterations and some unsuccessful attempts to water down the bill, it was reported out of committee. Three members registered objections to it, and two others expressed displeasure with a few provisions.

As considered and passed by the Senate, the bill was basically the same as that approved by the Senate committee. A total of fourteen amendments were offered to the bill, several of them duplicating the committee's efforts to restrict the size and scope of the bill. All those attempts, however, were beaten back. The closest vote on the floor came in an effort to reintroduce direct appropriations rather than back-door financing; the motion was defeated by a vote of forty-five to forty-nine. Also on the floor, the program was limited to a period of four years, and its director was made responsible to the Secretary of Commerce. The final vote to pass was sixty-three to twenty-seven. A total of seven roll-call votes were taken.

House Banking Committee hearings at the other end of the Capitol highlighted the testimony of Kennedy's three cabinet secretaries, in addition to the usual array of elected officials and corporate and union representatives. Congressman Wright Patman offered the trenchant observation that the bill would have a difficult fight because many congressmen had supported it during the previous administration only because they knew that Eisenhower's opposition prevented its enactment.

After a month's consideration, the bill was approved by the committee by a twenty-to-six vote. The House committee version, while very similar to the Senate version, did differ in several respects. It provided for financing through regular congressional appropriations and set no time limit on the program. It also was more restrictive in forbidding the use of funds to help businesses to relocate, and in addition it provided for 100 percent federal financing. Eight members of the committee, all Republicans, filed a minority report, stating their preference for a program employing accelerated tax amortization in order to facilitate business growth.

Floor consideration was a matter of some concern to the bill's supporters: they feared a fatal alliance of Republicans and southern Democrats. But the designers of the bill had anticipated this coalition when the bill was drafted. The provision that provided for aid to depressed rural areas happened to favor southern states heavily. To drive this point home, supporters set up a large map in the lobby of the House Speaker's office, showing that the designated rural areas were primarily in border and southern states. In addition, the money for depressed rural areas could be used for industrialization or tourism, according to local discretion. One southern congressman, Albert Rains of Alabama, aptly referred to the "vote-getting proclivities" of the bill.[10]

The Republicans offered a substitute for the administration-Douglas bill, but it excluded aid to rural areas. The vote to recommit and substitute the Republican version met decisive defeat, 139 to 242. Only one Democrat voted for the Republican substitute. In all, seven amendments were offered, three of which required roll-call votes. However, the full House by and large accepted the committee version.

After passage of the House version on 29 March, a conference committee convened to iron out discrepancies between the House and Senate bills. After weeks of deliberation and compromise, the conference committee agreed on a final version. Most important, Douglas won the day on financing by gaining acceptance for financing directly through the Treasury Department rather than through congressional appropriations. The passage of this resolution was facilitated when the White House sent a message announcing its willingness to accept back-door financing. This method of financing, however, cost the bill about twenty-five votes in the House. Conferees accepted the Senate's four-year termination date for the program. Also eliminated from the final version was the 65 percent limit on federal contributions to localities. House approval came less easily, however, because of unhappiness over back-door spending. But the bill was approved by a 224-to-193 vote, and sent to the president on 1 May.

As a final note, the financing issue came back to haunt supporters of the bill late in the session. In a move that caught them off guard, the Congress nullified direct Treasury financing in a supplemental appropriation bill for fiscal year 1962.

As noted, the Area Redevelopment Act was aimed at depressed areas. The bill, however, contained disaggregative characteristics in its composition and implementation, elements fundamental to its passage. The aid itself was not aimed directly at the poor and the unemployed, with the exception of the minor provisions for job training and subsistence payments ($10 million for subsistence payments and $4.5 million for vocational retraining). The lion's share of the funds went to local governments and private industry in what was essentially a two-step aid process. In addition, the program as set out in the bill gave administrators and recipients considerable discretion, within the bounds of the statute, to spend funds as they saw fit. The existence of this discretion could only facilitate disaggregation.

If this case illustrates anything, it is the importance of the presidential seal of approval. Area redevelopment had been Senator Douglas's favorite project since 1955, as it was in 1961. But it was the heavy hand of the Kennedy administration that assured passage, after Eisenhower had held up the bill almost singlehandedly for six years.

In Congress passage was itself relatively smooth and expeditious. The major disputes over financing and degree of federal support were secondary insofar as they did not affect the basic nature of the bill, and in fact they did not engender acrimony either in committee or on the floor. Even though the bill had been voted upon favorably in the past, the Kennedy administration was faced with a precarious majority in both houses, and the important block of southern Democrats cast a shadow over every administration proposal. Regardless of the partisan composition of Congress, however, I argue that presidents have relatively high success with redistributive proposals. When those proposals incorporate disaggregation, the likelihood of passage is greatly enhanced.

Housing. Nineteen sixty-five was the high point of the halcyon years of Lyndon Johnson's Great Society. In grand fashion Johnson quoted from Aristotle during his major address to announce his forthcoming program to deal with urban problems, as if to imply that the ancient Greek's words would soon be realized by congressional enactment of a presidential proposal: "Men come together in cities in order to live, but they remain together in order to live the good life."[11] Beneath the high-sounding rhetoric and promises of an aristotelian urban life, several bills nestled, including a housing bill that was firmly grounded in political reality.

Since the New Deal era, the federal government has assumed some responsiblities in the area of housing. Up until the 1960s, however, the federal government never involved itself in the financing and construction of more than half of the housing units constructed in any year. In his housing message in early 1965, Johnson emphasized the need for the federal government to intervene more actively in an exploding housing market, primarily through the coordination, construction, and rehabilitation of housing in urban areas. His bill, the Housing and Urban Development Act of 1965, was an amalgam of proposals, with the rent-supplement program by far the most important (and most controversial). The major battle centered on who should be eligible for the subsidies. The original proposal held that persons eligible for supplements should be those too poor to afford decent private housing but also too well off to be eligible for public housing. Thus the act excluded people eligible for public housing. The Congress changed this restriction, however, to include only those eligible for public housing, though the upper income limit was ambiguous. In addition to setting these income requirements, the bill also required the recipients to be sixty-three years of age, physically handicapped, displaced by government actions, or currently living in substandard housing. The ambiguity of this last criterion caused many people, especially proponents of public housing, to label the program excessively discretionary and therefore available to too wide a range of families above the poorest groups in greatest need.[12]

In addition to the rent-supplements provision, the bill, both as proposed and as passed, provided a hodgepodge of other housing and housing-related provisions. It extended and increased a variety of existing housing programs affecting moderate- to low-income families and the elderly. It created a new program under the Federal Housing Administration to insure commercial loans for land development in neighborhoods. It authorized an additional housing program for veterans by providing an extension and funding increase for urban renewal programs, expanded enforcement of the urban-renewal code and rehabilitation, provided payments to businesses moved by urban renewal, and home-repair grants to low-income homeowners in urban renewal areas. The bill also increased funding for college housing loans. It authorized matching grants for sewer and water facilities, the construction of neighborhood health, recreation, and community centers, parks, playgrounds and urban beautification. Finally, the act insured housing loans for rural areas and broadened the eligibility requirements for existing rural housing loans.

Despite the grab-bag nature of the bill, it presents itself as a clear case of a redistributive policy. It provides for assistance to a broad class of people, mostly the urban lower-middle class and the poor.[13] I will discuss the act's quilted composition in due time.

As mentioned, the rent-supplements program provided the main source of controversy surrounding the bill. Liberals felt that, as originally proposed, the provision slighted the poor. Conservatives viewed the program as one more step in the advance of creeping socialism and the indiscriminate mixing of lower and middle classes. To blunt much of the criticism, Johnson sent Robert C. Weaver, the administration's top housing official, to testify before the House and the Senate Banking committees. (Weaver, a black man, would soon be named to head the new Department of Housing and Urban Development). Before the Housing Subcommittee of the House of Representatives, Weaver strongly defended the extension of aid to those falling into the gap between poor and middle incomes. Moreover, he stood his ground on a proposal in the bill that called for the creation and development of new, planned communities in outlying areas to deal with urban sprawl.

Despite the social-welfare function manifest in the bill, many felt that an important aim of the bill was also to allow private capital to play a larger part in low-income housing. This was indicated by the support the bill derived from the real-estate industry, the American Bankers Association and other business organizations. But other business interests, such as the National Association of Manufacturers, opposed the bill. Housing authorities in big cities were dissatisfied with the original rent-supplements program because it did not help them in the search for more low-rent public housing.

In early May, after a month of testimony and consideration, the Housing Subcommittee approved the bill in revised form by a vote of ten to one. Two weeks later the full Banking Committee approved the bill by a vote of twenty-six to seven (all dissenters were Republicans). The full committee adopted the subcomittee recommendations in toto. The bill was changed in three major respects. First, eligibility for rent supplements was changed to include low-income families. Second, the new-towns proposal, admittedly an experimental program, was dropped. Finally, the provision covering grants for construction of water and sewer facilities was broadened to include all communities, instead of just growing communities, and the federal share for construction was increased from 40 to 50 percent. The subcommittee also lowered the effective interest rate for loan programs and expanded the veterans' mortgage-insurance provision.

In the committee report, eight Republicans issued a minority report. They limited their dissent to one part of the bill—the rent-subsidy program, which they termed "a wide-open, socialistic subsidy formula." Despite disagreement over this part of the bill, overall support was relatively strong.

The disputes that arose in committee also emerged on the floor of the House. Debate over the rent-supplements program at times became acrimonious, and at one point Republicans nearly succeeded in recommitting the bill over this provision. However, the expanded committee version was adopted after the key vote not to recommit the bill (202 to 208). A variety of other amendments were successfully attached to the bill. None of them changed its basic complexion, but they were significant because they were aimed at programs and parts of programs that had the effect of expanding benefits for congressmen's constituents.[14] In all, twenty amendments were voted on during floor consideration. Only four were recorded votes.

In the Senate, consideration followed a similar path. After soliciting testimony, the Housing Subcommittee approved the administration bill on a voice vote. The only major change was the elimination of the new-towns proposal. The full Banking Committee, however, made some additional changes. It adopted the House version of the rent-supplements program by incorporating those poor enough to be eligible for public housing, rather than emphasizing lower-middle income groups. Moreover, the committee approved a cut in interest charges for the elderly, the handicapped, the displaced, and low- to moderate-income families. On 28 June, the committee reported the housing bill favorably by a vote of ten to four. As in the House committee, the minority was composed of Republicans. Among those Republicans voting for the bill was conservative John Tower. But Tower signed the minority report, explaining his vote for the bill by saying that the bill had a number of meritorious provisions aside from the rent supplement, of which he disapproved. In fact, it was Tower who sponsored an amendment on the floor of the Senate to delete the rent-supplements program (the vote to delete was defeated, forty to forty-seven). As in the House, the main dispute on the floor centered on the rent-supplements program. Republicans claimed that the program represented a move toward socialism, while Democratic proponents argued that the program represented a move away from socialism because it encouraged low-income families to seek out and refurbish private housing rather than live in public housing projects. Echoing the fears of conservative colleagues, Tower voiced concern over the effects of "socioeconomic integration" and the indiscriminate mixing of low- to high-income groups in the same setting. On 15 July, after almost forty amendments, five of them roll calls, the bill passed in a form similar to that of the House version by a vote of fifty-four to thirty.

Despite basic similarity in the House and Senate bills, a conference committee met to work out minor differences. It agreed on a total authorization of $7.5 million over a four-year period. The committee also assented to most of the new programs and provisions tacked on in each house.

On 10 August Johnson signed the housing bill, hailing it as a major achievement. And clearly, it represented an important victory for the Great Society. The reason can be found in the bill itself.

Johnson's redistributive housing bill was a package that was carefully designed from the outset to achieve congressional approval. From the start, it resembled a Christmas tree. It was surely no accident that provisions dealing with veterans, schools, sewer construction, and payments to private businesses were all included in a bill dealing with rent supplements. In policy terms, Johnson anticipated Congress's disaggregative and allocative tendencies by adding on to the core program a series of goodies that would appeal to Congress. The success of this approach can be gleaned from the behavior of John Tower, who though philosophically opposed to the rent-supplements idea, nevertheless backed the bill in committee. He carried the fight over rent supplements to the floor, but it was in the context of a bill for which he had already registered his approval.

While Johnson anticipated the need to pursue this coalition-building strategy, both the House and the Senate, as noted, tacked on additional measures that had the effect of handing out benefits to local concerns. In addition, they expanded the scope of existing provisions, such as eligibility for water and sewer projects, and they increased the proportion of the federal burden for those costs. However, it bears noting that the crucial battle was over rent supplements and the definition of who could benefit from them. The powerful housing lobby, plus a variety of civic, labor, and business groups (all fundamentally Johnson supporters) came down heavily on the side of aiding more people in the lowest income brackets. Although this represented a change in the direction of the redistribution, it was a change the Johnson administration could live with and did. The housing bill constituted a major success, despite the Christmas-tree provisions, because Johnson was able to buy support for a relatively daring social program by using those extraneous provisions without seriously compromising the core of the bill itself. Johnson's political skills came into play when he anticipated in his original proposal the kinds of measures that were likely to insure passage. Redistributive policies may encourage congressional deference, but they do not come with any guarantees. In the context of other battles Johnson was fighting at the time, his anticipation of the disaggregative, distributive tendencies of Congress, especially on this redistributive measure, gave him the insurance necessary to see the bill through. Despite the changes and conflicts along the way, the housing bill passed through Congress with relative ease.

As a final twist, Congress denied the funds for this bill in 1966. The move, which caught the administration by surprise, was justified on the grounds that the FHA was being allowed too much discretion in providing for assistance to an unduly wide group of people. While this justification might not seem consistent with the Congress's disaggregative tendencies, it could in fact be understood in that light if one realized that when funds are spent by the FHA for groups beyond the original intent of the legislators, the money may not go to groups and individuals for whom the bill was carefully crafted. Congressmen can continue to protect their interests even after a bill becomes law.

Redistributive Patterns

The two cases of redistribution follow several very similar patterns. The Area Redevelopment Act, while apparently favored by Congress for several years, nevertheless engendered significant controversy and floor activity. Unlike the regulatory cases, however, that conflict was kept within manageable limits, and the president got what he requested. This was in part due to the disaggregative nature of the program itself, in terms of the benefits it provided for businesses and local leaders, and the accompanying discretion it allowed.

The housing bill, also broadly conceived, was again managed successfully by the President and his congressional sympathizers. Disaggregation was also in evidence here, in part related to the questions of eligibility for housing subsidies, but more centrally related to the long list of additional provisions that were part of the original bill. Additional disaggregation by Congress occurred in the expansion of community eligibility for water and sewer-construction funds, and in related increases in the proportion of federal aid. Johnson's success might be attributed in part to the fact that he was dealing with the famed Eighty-ninth Congress, but he achieved an even greater and easier success in housing in 1968 with the passage of that year's Housing and Urban Development Act (considered even more far-reaching than the 1965 act), despite a substantially hostile Congress and public.

The redevelopment and housing cases clearly indicate presidential ascendancy. But they also indicate that that ascendancy usually comes with a price tag imposed by Congress and, to some degree, interest groups as well. Though a redistributive, aggregative element helped the president in the distributive Lockheed case, a distributive, disaggregative element helped presidents in the redistributive cases. No contradiction exists: political actors seeking winning coalitions often must reach beyond limited bounds to seek additional support. This simply illustrates that in political life, nothing comes easily or for free. But in relative terms, the costs to the president and his programs are likely to be significantly less, and the outcomes more favorable, than for other policy types—certainly more so than with regulatory policies.

Summary

In following the important details of eight examples of successful legislative efforts by presidents, the last two chapters have illustrated the ways in which policy types affect the president's ability to get what he wants from Congress in the format he wants. The usual factors associated with political patterns and political success—party consonance, ideological dispositions, bargaining skills, reputation, and the like—while certainly still important, have not entered into the political equations in any major respect. And most important, the variations observed are consistent with the distinctions laid out in Chapter 2. Table 1 summarizes the case findings and in so doing presents a convenient format for comparison of the eight cases.

Table 1: Summary of Case Studies

	No. of Votes Recorded:		Attribute:				
	House	Senate	President	Interest Groups	Committees	Floor Activity	Overall Stability
DISTRIBUTIVE:							
Wilderness Act 1964	1	4	passive-ineffectual	moderate	determinative	consensual	high–very high
Lockheed Loan 1971	3	9	coordinative	moderate	creative	contentious	moderate
CONSTITUENT:							
Defense Reorganization 1958	2	1	legislative	low	conduit (Senate), lobbyist (House)	consensual	very high
Civil Service Reform 1978	7	2	legislative	high	lobbyist (Senate), creative (House)	contentious (House), consensual (Senate)	moderate
REGULATORY:							
Crime Control 1968	3	29	passive-ineffectual	high	creative	creative	low
Airline Deregulation 1978	3	8	supplicative	high	creative	contentious (Senate), creative (House)	moderate

REDISTRIBUTIVE:							
Area Redevelopment 1961	3	7	legislative	moderate	conduit	consensual	high
Housing Act 1965	4	5	legislative-coordinative	moderate	lobbyist	contentious (Senate), consensual (House)	high

Key (all are listed from high to low influence)

PRESIDENT
legislative: determinative
coordinative: active refereeing
supplicative: entreating, requesting
passive-ineffectual: no significant influence

INTEREST GROUPS
very high: if prominent and creative in legislative, executive, and grass roots
high: if prominent and creative at any point
moderate: if only prominent
low: if no evidence of anything

COMMITTEES
determinative: responsible for and originative
creative: originative
lobbyist: influence in advisory capacity
conduit: channel for legislation

FLOOR:
creative: if evidence of alteration
contentious: a lot of debate, little bill alteration
consensual: little debate, alteration

STABILITY
very high, high, moderate, low

SOURCE: Altered and adopted from Theodore J. Lowi, "Four Systems of Policy, Politics, and Choice," *Public Administration Review* 32 (July–August 1972): 305.
Used by permission from *Public Administration Review*, © 1972 by The American Society for Public Administration, 1225 Connecticut Avenue, N.W., Washington, D.C. All rights reserved.

If it appears to the reader that we have slighted the president thus far—the phone calls made, the backs slapped, the arms twisted, the promises made and broken—be reminded that our emphasis is on variations in overall political patterns springing from policy types. The whole point is to concentrate on those factors external to the president that determine what happens to his bills. Our concerns are substantially larger than simply what deals were made by whom for whom. Rather than focus on individual decision points, we have scanned the entire process in search of the summary shape of politics. The cases demonstrated how the policy approach operates. In the next two chapters, we will examine the scope of these policy patterns.

5: President and Congress: The Policy Connection

I have described in some detail how presidential interactions are affected by the scope and characteristics of policies themselves, and the eight cases have provided some important confirmations. My present object is to expand the logic of this policy application to the full range of policies offered by presidents to Congress during the period under study. Before doing so, however, I will discuss the standard evaluations of relations between the president and Congress, including the few existing empirical studies. In considering the full range of presidential policy proposals, it is important to establish and, if possible, reconcile existing paradigms. Critics may always treat a handful of cases alone as anomalies.

The second part of the chapter consists of an analysis and discussion of the 5,463 bills proposed to Congress by presidents from 1954 to 1974. After I discuss the sources and nature of the data, my analysis presents the overall distribution of bills (policies) proposed to Congress by the president and then the proportion passed according to the four categories. I discuss relative trends within the four policy areas across the twenty-year period, including correlations between increases and decreases in the percentages across policy areas. The percentages are then averaged for each administration and are compared. In addition, the percentages (of both proposals and successes) are averaged according to presidential electoral cycles. Finally, I will examine the bills according to the number previously proposed to Congress but not passed (again by policy area). These data arrays thus provide a fairly wide-ranging look at the overall scope of the president's policy program as proposed to Congress.

The President and Congress

In general, there are three basic models or, perhaps more correctly, ideal types for characterizing presidential-congressional relations. Like studies of presidential power, they mix normative and empirical elements.

The first variant is the executive-supremacy model. It posits simply that the president is and should be the primary initiator and implementer of legislative proposals. Congress can modify and ratify, though it has an obstructionist streak the president must overcome. The old axiom that "the president proposes and the Congress disposes" accurately conveys what many feel is and should be the relation between the executive and the legislative.[1] Many presidents have been characterized as having fulfilled the executive-supremacist role, but none exemplifies that approach better than Franklin Roosevelt. While not original, Roosevelt's approach to legislation as an integral part of a package designed to cure the nation's ills, labeled the New Deal, set a pattern and a precedent that almost every successor has followed. Even the titles of his successors' programs are similar: Fair Deal, New Freedom, Great Society, New Federalism, New Foundation.

A second view of the relations between the president and the Congress has been labeled the Whig or strong-Congress model. Simply stated, this approach contends that primary legislative initiative does or should rest with Congress—or, that "the primary business of the legislature in a democratic republic is to answer the big questions of policy."[2] The Congress legislates, and the president executes the laws. The primary problem the legislative branch faces vis-à-vis the other branches is the breakdown of traditional checks and balances as evidenced by usurpation of legislative functions. The president, the bureaucracy, and the courts all threaten to usurp the Congress's prerogatives. The strong-Congress view was dominant both early in the nineteenth century, especially during the heyday of Henry Clay, Daniel Webster, and John C. Calhoun, and late in the nineteenth century, during the "reigns" of the House Speakers Thomas Reed and Joseph Cannon.

The third variant of presidential-congressional relations is the responsible-party or party-government model. The primary theme of responsible-party advocates is that both the president and members of Congress should take their cues from their political parties, based on clear-cut, programmatic, specific, and ideologically coherent programs emanating from the parties.[3] When the electorate votes for the president and members of Congress, it can do so on the basis of party performance. Presidential policy leadership is still important, but it is the operation of party behind the two institutions that distinguishes this view from the other approaches. Probably the closest example of this in history is the presidency of Woodrow Wilson, particularly during his first term. Like most political scientists of the day, Wilson admired the parliamentary system, especially that of Britain, which most nearly approximated the responsible-party ideal. After he became president, Wilson worked hard to pattern his administration after the British system. During the congresssional elections of 1914 and especially 1918, he stumped the country for Democratic candidates in an attempt to seek an affirmation of his programs and policies by tying the election of local Democrats to approval of his program. His short-lived success is itself an adequate commentary on the practicality of this approach.

The general consensus on the state of presidential-congressional relations since the New Deal era is that, with the possible exception of a few of the Eisenhower years, the president has dominated the legislative process by being the prime source of legislative initiative, the most important lobbyist, and the frequent regulator of legislative outputs through the use of the veto. In the years after Vietnam and Watergate it has been widely felt that Congress has done much to reassert its authority through such legislation as the Case Act on Executive Agreements (1972), the War Powers Resolution (1973), and the Budget and Impoundment Control Act (1974). The long-term impact, however, of these and similar actions is still difficult to gauge and generally falls beyond the time period under consideration.[4]

The three overall approaches to presidential-congressional relations are easily reconcilable with the "four-presidencies" argument. In assessing entire presidencies as strong, weak, or party-oriented, we make summary judgments that obfuscate the evident fact that "strong" presidents are frequently ineffectual, while "weak" presidents frequently succeed in getting what they seek, despite apparently adverse circumstances. We have seen that presidents are more likely to have consistent successes when dealing with constituent and redistributive policies than when dealing with regulatory policies. It may thus be the case that "strong" presidents are so labeled because of the frequency with which they engage in certain types of policies over others. But this is getting ahead of ourselves. Clearly, the standard divisions provide crude, undifferentiated assessments that mask important distinctions such as those made here.

Past Empirical Studies

A few empirical attempts have been made to gauge the degree of presidential influence in policy making. Since they anticipate this study by their method, I should mention their findings. The first and most detailed was executed by Lawrence Chamberlain. Chamberlain conducted an extensive case study analysis of ninety major pieces of legislation passed by Congress from 1870 to 1940. He found that for nineteen of the ninety bills passed, presidential influence was preponderant; congressional influence was dominant for thirty-five; joint influence was important for twenty-nine;

Table 2: Responsibility for Passage of Major Legislative Proposals

	President	Congress	Joint	Pressure Group	Totals
1870–1910	17% (5)	53% (16)	20% (6)	10% (3)	100% (30)
1911–30	12 (4)	48 (16)	27 (9)	12 (4)	99 (33)
1931–40	37 (10)	11 (3)	52 (14)	0 —	100 (27)
1945–54	33 (12)	17 (6)	44 (16)	6 (2)	100 (36)
1955–64	56 (15)	4 (1)	41 (11)	0 —	100 (27)

Note: Variations from 100 percent are due to rounding error. Data taken and readjusted from Lawrence Chamberlain, "The President, Congress, and Legislation," reprinted in *The President: Roles and Powers*, ed. David Haight and Larry Johnson (Chicago: Rand McNally, 1965), pp. 301–3, and William Goldsmith, *The Growth of Presidential Power,* New York: Chelsea House, 1974), 3: 1398—99. Goldsmith claimed to use the same evaluation standards and techniques as Chamberlain. Data from 1870 to 1940 from Chamberlain study. Data from 1945 to 1964 from Goldsmith study.

and pressure-group influence was dominant for seven bills.[5] Chamberlain's primary conclusion was "not that the president is less important than generally supposed, but that Congress is more important."[6]

Two more recent studies have revised Chamberlain's study by analyzing legislative case studies roughly using the criteria set forth by Chamberlain. Ronald Moe and Steven Teel concurred with Chamberlain's conclusion that Congress has been underrated as an independent policy-making institution. But they went a step farther by challenging "the conventional wisdom that the president has come to enjoy an increasingly preponderant role in national policy making."[7] They based their data on the analysis of secondary sources for the period 1940–67. Another author, relying on the Moe and Teel data, concluded that the presidential title of "chief legislator" was a paper one.[8]

William Goldsmith also replicated the Chamberlain study, basing his work on major legislation enacted into law between 1945 and 1964. On the basis of an analysis of sixty-three bills, he came to conclusions rather different from those of Moe and Teel: "the President has indeed become a major partner in the legislative process, and...very little significant legislation is now passed that either does not emanate from the Executive branch, or is not significantly influenced by executive action at some stage of its legislative history."[9] Goldsmith found this to be true for Republican and Democratic administrations alike.

What appears on the surface to be a series of contradictory evaluations turns out in fact not to be when examined in depth. The empirical data offered by Chamberlain and Goldsmith can be reordered along a temporal dimension, as appears in Table 2. When this is done, it is possible to see how the role of each actor varies over time. Despite relatively small Ns, the important variations occur over time. From 1870 to 1964, the primary responsibility for passage generally increases for the president, just as it steadily decreases for Congress, and increases somewhat for joint action. This runs directly counter to Moe and Teel's analysis. Because an exact bill count cannot be extracted from it, a comparable treatment of the Moe and Teel data was not carried out. For example, in their discussion of economic legislation, they offer the following evaluation: "Both Congress and the executive have exhibited initiative in this field; the Area Redevelopment Act of 1961 [and the Employment Act of 1946 are] largely attributed to congressional initiative while much of the 'Great Society' economic legislation is a product of the executive."[10] Such vagueness in presenting data makes it impossible to weigh executive influence—how can one accurately assess influence over "much of the 'Great Society'"? Moe and Teel and most of the other writers attempt to make a general statement about relations between the president and Congress when in fact their data have severe temporal and conceptual restrictions that must be taken into account.[11]

The bills incorporated in the empirical assessment summarized above could be categorized according to the policy types if more than their titles were available. Such an effort, however, would involve an expansion of this study far beyond its existing data base and time frame. Our sole concern is with the president's proposals, whereas these studies have selected bills according to their overall importance regardless of source. The data are presented in the format in Table 2 to illustrate that the apparently conflicting findings of those studies can be reconciled when other factors are introduced. The main finding of the table (that presidential influence over legislation has increased since the early 1900s) is not disputed here. Indeed, it is perfectly consistent with the policy argument.[12]

These and most other such studies contain one important bias that deserves attention at this point: they analyze only successful legislative proposals. It is evident that the number of successful legislative proposals is but a small portion of the total number of legislative efforts. And it is surely as important to understand why proposals fail as it is to understand what succeeds and why. In this chapter I will address that imbalance, at least for presidential programs.

Presidential Boxscores

The analysis offered herein, involving an aggregation of 5,463 bills over a twenty-one year period, is taken from *Congressional Quarterly's* Presidential Boxscore.[13] The Boxscore is the best readily available aggregation of presidential legislative proposals. It incorporates only the specific legislative requests contained in the president's messages to Congress and other public statements. The Boxscore does not include proposals advocated by officials of the executive branch but not by the president, bills endorsed by but not specifically requested by the president (*CQ* tabulates these in its Presidential Support Scores), nominations, and routine appropriation requests. Appropriation requests for specific programs are incorporated if they are tied directly to some element of the president's program. *CQ* does not differentiate between more and less important pieces of legislation, though more important legislative proposals are likely to be broken up into several bills in the Boxscore and in that way given greater weight. Finally, *CQ* evaluates legislation that has been altered from the original proposal to determine whether compromises amount to approval or disapproval of the president's requests.

It should be explicitly stated that the four policy categories are not without gaps, and there was some ambiguity in bill assignment. However, the categorization process was in part a collective effort to insure a greater likelihood of validity.[14] The bills composing the Boxscore represent the clearest subset of bills representing the president's legislative program. There will always be some proposals from which he will withdraw his support, even though they are a part of his program, and some that he will push hard for even though they were not a part of his program. Overall, however, such possible anomalies should not affect the aggregate totals.[15] Coding procedures and examples are discussed in the Appendix.

Given the limited amount of information available for each bill, it would be a mistake to make too much of the data by attempting to extract more from them than can be reasonably obtained. Therefore, I will address two broad questions: What does the president propose? and What does the president get? These two questions will be addressed on two levels. The first breaks down the data by administrations after presenting summaries, and the second breaks it down by electoral cycles.

Data By Administrations

Table 3 presents the percentage of bills proposed each year by presidents according to each of the four categories as a percentage of all domestic legislation. The residual category of foreign policy is also given as a percentage of all policy proposals. It is labeled residual because it is an amalgam of policies, including treaties, foreign aid, national defense, and trade.

The general hypotheses stated in Chapter 2, it will be recalled, posit that: presidential involvement in policies (number of bills proposed by him) will be greatest for redistributive proposals, followed by constituent, distributive, and regulatory; presidential influence over his program (success, measured by passage rate of his proposals) will also be greatest for redistributive, followed by constituent, distributive, and regulatory; the

Table 3: Bills Proposed in the President's Annual Legislative Program, Grouped by Policy Areas

	Domestic Policy Areas[a]				Foreign Policy as % of All Proposals
	Distributive[b]	Regulatory	Redistributive	Constituent	
1954	22.3% (46)	25.7% (53)	35.0% (72)	17.0% (35)	11.2% (26)
1955	24.1 (40)	14.5 (24)	25.3 (42)	36.1 (60)	19.4 (40)
1956	35.5 (71)	12.0 (24)	24.0 (48)	28.5 (57)	11.1 (25)
1957	25.2 (40)	15.7 (25)	21.4 (34)	37.7 (60)	22.4 (46)
1958	18.4 (38)	18.4 (38)	20.8 (43)	42.5 (88)	10.8 (25)
1959	22.3 (41)	19.0 (35)	27.2 (50)	31.5 (58)	18.9 (43)
1960	29.9 (43)	9.7 (14)	31.9 (46)	28.5 (41)	20.4 (37)
1961	26.4 (76)	4.9 (14)	43.1 (124)	25.7 (74)	17.7 (62)
1962	38.3 (97)	20.9 (53)	24.9 (63)	15.8 (40)	15.1 (45)
1963	30.4 (107)	9.4 (33)	35.8 (126)	24.4 (86)	12.0 (48)
1964	35.0 (63)	10.0 (18)	38.9 (70)	16.1 (29)	16.7 (36)
1965	33.2 (143)	12.5 (54)	31.1 (134)	23.2 (100)	7.9 (37)
1966	20.8 (63)	22.0 (67)	29.4 (89)	27.7 (84)	17.9 (66)
1967	14.9 (55)	27.3 (101)	36.5 (135)	21.4 (79)	13.1 (56)
1968	29.8 (108)	22.3 (81)	29.5 (107)	18.5 (67)	10.4 (42)
1969	14.0 (19)	16.2 (22)	32.4 (44)	37.5 (51)	20.0 (34)
1970	17.2 (30)	27.6 (48)	28.2 (49)	27.0 (47)	16.7 (35)
1971	21.5 (35)	28.8 (47)	30.7 (50)	19.0 (31)	17.7 (35)
1972	40.6 (26)	18.7 (12)	25.0 (16)	15.6 (10)	40.7 (44)
1973	24.8 (28)	34.5 (29)	26.5 (30)	14.2 (16)	37.6 (68)
1974	13.1 (14)	20.6 (22)	37.4 (40)	29.0 (31)	31.8 (50)
Mean	25.6 (1183)	18.6 (824)	30.2 (1412)	25.6 (1144)	18.5 (900)

Source: Congressional Quarterly, "Presidential Boxscore," *Congressional Quarterly Almanac*, 1954–74.
[a] Domestic policy area percentages figured as percentage of all domestic policies per year.
[b] Distributive policy average without presidential election year peaks and 1962 is 21.9 percent.

number of distributive policies proposed to Congress will vary with the four-year presidential cycle, with the greatest number of proposals occurring during election years; and the relation among the four policy types will hold for the entire twenty-year period.

As the mean precentages indicate, redistributive policies predominate as compared with the other areas. Over the years there are variations, to be sure, that appear to militate against the overall trend. In Table 4 the percentages are broken up according to presidential administrations (see Table 3 for data by year). During the four periods, redistributive policies predominate, except for the Eisenhower years, when they compose the second largest category. In three of the four periods, regulatory policies compose the smallest category, while distributive-policy activity is substantially greater than anticipated. (For a summary comparison of the rank orderings for all years for both proposals and success rates, see Table 8. It confirms the existence of basic trends across policy types.)

The predominant concern with redistributive policies is consistent with the assumption of presidential responsibility for policy considerations that involve broad classes and groups in society (public-interest presidency). The exception of the Eisenhower administration indicates an evidently greater concern with affairs relating to the structuring and functioning of government. The Eisenhower case study in Chaper 3, dealing with Defense Department reorganization, is thus characteristic of the primary policy concern of his administration (as measured by number of proposals). Perhaps it also reflects that the 1950s, falling between the New Deal period of Roosevelt and Truman and the New Frontier–Great Society of Kennedy and Johnson, was a time of relaxation in certain types of social-welfare programs. The assumption, however, that Republicans invariably deemphasize redistributive policies is contradicted by the Nixon years.

The one exception to the hypothesized rank ordering of presidential policy proposals is the inversion of the distributive and constituent categories. This inversion can be accounted for in several ways. First, the proposing of distributive policies may involve a larger number of discrete legislative proposals than do other policy types (for example, a bill for a dam in Utah, a bill for roads development in New York, a bill to create a national park in California). Second, the averages for distributive policies are inflated by election-year peaks (I will discuss this point later). The situation also points to a related matter, namely, that presidents can and do respond in their proposals to congressional needs and by extension to their own needs, because presidents need the assent of Congress, as well as that of constituents everywhere in America. Similarly, constituent policies offer little in the way of immediate rewards to Congress. While presidents have an interest in reorganization and other administrative, overhead

Table 4: Averages of Bills Proposed in Policy Areas, Grouped by Presidential Administrations

| | Distributive | Domestic Policy Areas | | Constituent | Marginal Totals | Foreign Policy as % of All Proposals |
		Regulatory	Redistributive			
1954–60	25.4% [3]	16.4% [4]	26.5% [2]	31.7% [1]	(1266)	16.3% (242)
1961–63	31.7 [2]	11.7 [4]	34.6 [1]	22.0 [3]	(893)	14.9 (155)
1964–68	26.7 [2]	18.8 [4]	33.1 [1]	21.4 [3]	(1647)	13.2 (237)
1969–74	21.9 [4]	24.4 [2]	30.0 [1]	23.7 [3]	(757)	27.4 (266)
Average of four administrations	26.4	17.8	31.1	24.7		17.9

NOTE: Data summarized from Table 3. Numbers in brackets are rank orderings of percents for each period. Numbers in parentheses are absolute numbers. For average of all years, see Table 3.

programs because they are heads of the executive branch (the administrative presidency), such policies usually do not yield the sort of attention that, say, redistributive policies do.

Finally, the lower overall attention to regulatory policies is consistent with the fact that regulatory policies engender a great deal of pluralistic floor activity involving a wide array of interest groups. It thus indicates a reluctance, if not an inability, to initiate much regulatory legislation. That is consistent with the general idea of high political costs combined with low concrete rewards for this kind of legislation. The exception during the Nixon years would reflect his administration's greater concern, expressed in the 1968 and 1972 campaigns, with issues such as crime control, selective service, the environment, and consumerism. As these issues imply, matters of regulatory policy can themselves take on electoral (popular) significance.

As indicated by the rank orderings, the data in Table 4 show a relatively high degree of consistency among the various policy types across administrations. Such regularity lends credence to the simple presumption that much is to be gained by seeking out fundamental similarities in presidential policy making that to a large degree transcend the standard factors usually associated with variations in presidential activity. This conclusion is important in large part because it runs counter to the pervasive presumption, previously outlined, that each president presents a new case and that, as a consequence, it is not possible to produce meaningful generalizations that span administrations. Yet even if we maintain the validity of wide variances in presidential behavior from one administration to another, as in "strong" versus "weak" presidents, within each presidency one may still observe the same kind of uniformity in policy. The level of politics may vary, but the characteristics of the "four presidencies" remain. The point about the president's involvement in the four areas is not only that it exists, but that the quality of his involvement varies across the policy areas. These variations, however, or differences that exist *across* policy types, are not inconsistent with the existence of consistencies *within* policy types across administrations.

As the graph of Figure 4 makes clear, the percentage of distributive policies proposed by presidents reaches high points during the congressional session immediately preceding each presidential election. The single exception occurs in 1962; this, however, is consistent with a political fact of history. Kennedy campaigned heavily in 1962 for congressional candidates to bolster the slim Democratic margin in Congress, and, in fact, the Democrats lost fewer House seats during that midterm election (four) than the president's party had since the midterm election of 1934. When the election-year high points plus 1962 are removed and the remaining years averaged, the mean is still greater than that for regulatory policies. With

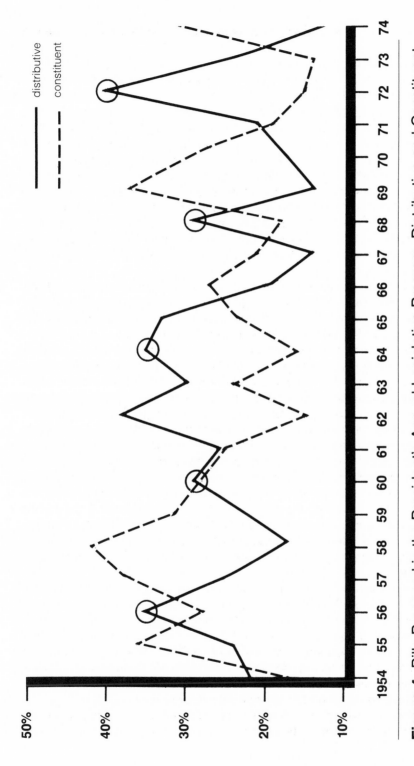

Figure 4: Bills Proposed in the President's Annual Legislative Program, Distributive and Constituent Policies

respect to redistributive policies, it is also interesting to note that the Kennedy administration exhibits the highest percentage of redistributive policy proposals (43.1 percent in 1961; see Table 3), surpassing Johnson's efforts with a more friendly Congress. However, as Table 7 indicates, Johnson's success rate is greater.

To further flesh out the interrelation among bills proposed in the four policy areas, Table 5 presents relative variations using correlations and paired comparisons. Correlations among the four areas for the twenty-year period indicate the highest negative correlation between distributive- and constituent-policy proposals.[16] The relationship can be easily seen in Figure 4, where the two are graphed. When more distributive bills are proposed, fewer constituent are, and vice versa. The relationship is confirmed by the use of paired comparisons, also presented in Table 5. The paired-comparison percentages simply report the percentage of percentages that vary directly and inversely between the two sets of numbers.[17]

This high negative correlation clearly suggests that constituent activity by presidents, administrative in nature as it is, is viewed as having the least electoral and therefore popular significance, in contradistinction to distributive proposals.[18] Nevertheless, it is a function fundamental to the running of the office. The next highest negative correlation, distributive with regulatory policy, provides a similar indication of the absence of electoral-political benefits to be extracted from regulatory policies. However, while constituent policies facilitate presidential administration, regulatory policies offer no such evident benefit or tool for presidents. And the political costs associated with regulatory policies are certainly very high. The lowest correlation, observed between distributive and redistributive policies, suggests that for the president redistributive policies themselves can possess a degree of benefits similar to those associated with distributive policies; that is, redistributive policies can be thought of as benefits distributed to broad classes with rules attached, rather than to discrete units without rules or guidelines. But there are still important, even fundamental differences between distributive and redistributive policies. As noted, the tendency of Congress is to want to disaggregate redistributive policies in order to obtain immediate, identifiable benefits for constituents. The president, however, is generally the primary force in opposition to Congress, for both electoral reasons and institutional and policy reasons. According to the president's disposition, he can forcefully promote redistribution, as in the case of much of the Great Society legislation, or he can "go with the flow" of Congress and its parochialisms, and allow (or encourage) disaggregation, as in the cases of Nixon's revenue sharing and the Elementary and Secondary Education Act amendments of 1974.

In both of these situations, relating to redistributive policies, presidents seem to be responding to two types of forces. The first, electoral (founded

Table 5: Bills Proposed in the President's Annual Legislative Program: Relations between Domestic-Policy Areas, 1954–74

Policy Areas	Pearson Correlations[a]	Proportion of Paired Instances (Comparisons) Where Percentages Vary:	
		Directly	Inversely[b]
Distributive-Regulatory	−.408	31.9%	62.8%
Distributive-Redistributive	−.173	40.0	55.2
Distributive-Constituent	−.477	30.5	65.2
Regulatory-Redistributive	−.255	42.8	52.4
Regulatory-Constituent	−.334	37.1	58.1
Redistributive-Constituent	−.317	40.0	55.7

[a]Correlations are derived from the percentages in Table 3. Percentages were correlated rather than raw numbers so that the correlations would not be affected by small Ns in some years—that is, fewer bills proposed. The concern is with the *proportion* (percentages) of bills offered in each category in relation to the other categories.

Since simple correlations are employed, the question of possible seriality (hidden recurring patterns) might be raised. As noted, however, the effect of other policy areas is accepted and understood. In any case, the actual data in Table 3 can be readily inspected for any recurring patterns. As the data under examination represent a population from 1954 to 1974, no tests of significance were applied. (Even though the bills examined here might be considered a sample of all bills proposed by presidents, no question of randomness is appropriate, because the data were not selected as a sample of all presidential proposals across time. Logical inference would suggest that the arguments and hypotheses proposed would extend beyond the twenty-one year period under study.)

[b]Difference between sums of direct and inverse pairs and 100% for each variable due to tied pairs. No relation between variables is indicated when the percent of direct and inverse pairs is 50% for each. The short span of time does not permit running correlations among separate administrations.

in the president's nationwide constituency), is based on the tie between populous industrial states with large, concentrated, absolute numbers of poor, and the presence of substantial electoral votes in those states. Clearly, however, there is no direct link between redistributive policies, at least insofar as numbers are concerned, and the electoral cycle of presidents (see Table 3). The second force to which the president responds is institutional. The president is expected to coordinate national programs, to provide comprehensive alternatives through central planning and coordination. As detailed in this and previous chapters, this function has become part of the job. The expectations and responsibilities tied to the office compel presidents to adopt as their own problems of redistributive policy more than any other type. It is a responsiblity which, in its purest form has fallen squarely on the president.

A widely accepted axiom posits that it is necessary in national policy making for presidents to provide a guiding hand. It is a function of the office, not ideology or even direct electoral pressures, although how a president substantively responds in his programs may be a function of either ideology or more immediate political concerns, as the Great Society versus revenue-sharing cases imply, since ideological or electoral concerns (or both) dictate who is most likely to benefit. The data enforce the emphasis on institutional rather than immediate electoral concerns for redistributive policies.

However difficult it may seem, presidents are forced by modern circumstances to provide policy leadership, especially in Congress, "even though what Lord Chesterton once said of 'sexual congress' applies equally well to his [the president's] job: 'the pleasure is temporary, the position ludicrous, and the expense is damnable.'"[19] In no area is this leadership more important than in redistributive policy. Demands on the institution compel this sort of action more than action in other areas; idealized views of the presidential office extol the virtues of positive social and economic action; and empirically, the presidents under consideration have responded in suitable fashion.

The other general factor of which the aggregate data allow consideration is the percentage of the president's legislative proposals that are successfully passed by the Congress. The use of aggregate success percentages, however, would seem to pose some problems that might affect the accuracy of the findings. Most important, the arenas categories are not designed to predict final outcomes; that is, to know that a policy is redistributive is not to know that the policy will be enacted into law. It may have a bearing on the likelihood of passage, but without examining a whole series of additional factors related to the politics of (in this case) redistributive policies, it is not clear to what degree the nature of policy types in and of themselves is responsible for the existence or liklihood of a favorable legislative outcome. Therefore, simple aggregations of success rates must be treated with caution and are offered here to suggest some likely overall trends to inform future analysis. Yet, despite these restrictions, some interesting trends appear. Table 6 presents straightforward percentages indicating average yearly passage rates. (See Table 7 for an overall summary of the percentage arrays by policy area.)

Again, the overall percentages of success indicate a predominance of redistributive policies, followed closely by distributive, then constituent and regulatory policies. When considered by administration (see Table 8) percentages of success for redistributive policies are highest for the two Democratic administrations and second highest for the two Republican administrations. Similarly, passage rates for distributive policies rank first for the Republican administrations and second for the Democratic administrations (though the difference in success rates in Kennedy's administration between distributive and redistributive policies is only .1 percent). This high rate of success for distributive bills would seem to indicate the

Table 6: Rates of Success for Bills Proposed by the President in His Annual Legislative Program

	Domestic-Policy Areas				Foreign Policy
	Distributive	Regulatory	Redistributive	Constituent	
1954	80.4% (46)	47.2% (53)	69.4% (72)	60.0% (35)	65.4% (26)
1955	47.5 (40)	33.3 (24)	33.3 (42)	43.3 (60)	85.0 (40)
1956	60.6 (71)	16.7 (24)	60.4 (48)	19.3 (57)	72.0 (25)
1957	35.0 (40)	8.0 (25)	38.2 (34)	23.3 (60)	76.1 (46)
1958	63.2 (38)	26.3 (38)	32.6 (43)	48.9 (88)	76.0 (25)
1959	24.4 (41)	57.1 (35)	40.0 (50)	24.1 (58)	67.4 (43)
1960	25.6 (43)	35.7 (14)	19.6 (46)	26.8 (41)	59.5 (37)
1961	55.3 (76)	28.6 (14)	46.0 (124)	25.7 (74)	75.8 (62)
1962	33.0 (97)	39.6 (53)	49.2 (63)	35.0 (40)	80.0 (45)
1963	32.7 (107)	9.1 (33)	27.0 (126)	16.3 (86)	47.9 (48)
1964	49.2 (62)	27.8 (18)	60.0 (70)	58.6 (29)	77.8 (36)
1965	67.1 (143)	59.3 (54)	85.8 (134)	52.0 (100)	75.7 (37)
1966	69.8 (63)	35.8 (67)	66.3 (89)	45.2 (84)	60.6 (66)
1967	27.3 (55)	22.8 (101)	65.9 (135)	51.9 (79)	57.1 (56)
1968	47.2 (108)	51.9 (81)	61.7 (107)	56.7 (67)	66.7 (42)
1969	52.6 (19)	45.5 (22)	38.6 (44)	27.5 (51)	20.6 (34)
1970	33.3 (30)	58.3 (48)	40.8 (49)	38.3 (47)	57.1 (35)
1971	20.0 (35)	4.3 (47)	26.0 (50)	16.1 (31)	40.0 (35)
1972	46.2 (26)	33.3 (12)	62.5 (16)	30.0 (10)	52.3 (44)
1973	35.7 (28)	10.3 (29)	10.0 (30)	31.2 (16)	45.6 (68)
1974	57.1 (14)	18.2 (22)	35.0 (40)	29.0 (31)	40.0 (50)
	(1183)	(824)	(1412)	(1144)	(900)
Average Yearly Passage Rate—Unweighted	45.9	31.9	46.1	36.2	61.8
Average Passage Rate—Weighted by Ns	53.0	43.0	58.2	42.7	65.1

SOURCE: "Presidential Boxscores," *CQ Almanac*, 1954–74. Percentages based on bills successfully passed divided by bills proposed for each area for each year.

NOTE: Formula for weighted average: $\frac{\Sigma(y\% \times y_n)}{\text{total } n}$

y_n = absolute nos. for each year $y\%$ = percents for each year   total n = total absolute numbers for each year

Table 7: Number of Years Where Policies Are Ranked Highest to Lowest

Proposals (from Table 3)	Rankings per year			
	First	Second	Third	Fourth
Redistributive	10*	9	2	0
Distributive	5	5	5.5	5.5
Constituent	5	3	7	6
Regulatory	1	4	6.5	9.5

Success rates (from Table 6)	Rankings per year			
	First	Second	Third	Fourth
Redistributive	8	8	2.5	2.5
Distributive	10	4	4	3
Constituent	0	7	9	5
Regulatory	3	2	5.5	10.5

*For example, of the twenty-one years under consideration, more redistributive policies were proposed than any other type of policy for ten of those years.

Table 8: Averages of Success for Bills Proposed Annually by the President, Grouped by Presidential Administrations

	Domestic-Policy Areas				Foreign Policy
	Distributive	Regulatory	Redistributive	Constituent	
1954–60	49.5% [1]	34.7% [4]	44.5% [2]	35.1% [3]	71.9%
	(319)	(213)	(335)	(399)	(242)
1961–63	38.9 [2]	28.0 [3]	39.0 [1]	23.5 [4]	68.4
	(280)	(100)	(313)	(200)	(155)
1964–68	54.9 [2]	39.2 [4]	69.3 [1]	51.8 [3]	65.8
	(432)	(321)	(535)	(359)	(237)
1969–74	37.5 [1]	27.4 [4]	33.6 [2]	29.0 [3]	43.2
	(152)	(190)	(229)	(186)	(266)
Average of four administrations					
	45.2 [2]	32.3 [4]	46.6 [1]	34.8 [3]	62.3

NOTE: Based on data from Table 6. Numbers in brackets are rank orderings of percentages for each period. Absolute numbers given in parentheses below percentages. For average of all years, see Table 6.

tendencies of congressional preferences to conform to presidential proposals. The high distributive-policy success rate surely reflects Congress's basic, if not primordial, interest in particularistic, disaggregable, concrete policy benefits.

As we would expect from the previous discussion, constituent policies are next in order, with regulatory policies possessing the lowest success rate. One other very predictable outcome is that presidential success rates are higher for foreign policy than for any of the other policy areas.

One other trend that emerges quite clearly is the Johnson redistributive hump from 1964 to 1968. It far surpasses that of any other area or time period, in comparison with success in other policy areas during the same period and in other time periods. Figure 5 clearly reveals as much. What the figure illustrates is that, except for distributive policies during the peak year of 1965, Johnson's unusually high legislative success rate occurred primarily in the redistributive policy area. This is an important observation simply as a refined description of the Johnson years. If the primary cause of Johnson's success as president during these years was his widely touted ability to manipulate congressional leadership, an ability based on political expertise gained during his years as majority leader, then how does one account for the startling variations among the four areas? The political-skill argument makes no allowance for these evident differences. They are in fact consistent with the logic of the "four-presidencies" argument, insofar as they reveal that, within a classic "strong-president" administration, greatest policy success occurred in the redistributive area, and least success occurred in the regulatory area. No one denies Johnson's political acumen, but it is clear that, in terms of sheer results, that acumen manifested itself disproportionately in one policy area (Johnson's successes are also greater in the other policy areas—but not in the same degree). Political skill is not being ruled out as an important factor; rather it is being displaced as the independent variable by policy type. For all his celebrated skill, the fact that Johnson's success was so much more pronounced in one policy area lends additional credence to the logic of making policy the causative agent. There is no accounting in the conventional wisdom for these marked trends.

As noted, presidential success is greatest in the area of foreign policy. While the concern here is with domestic policies, the fact that such a consistent trend in foreign policy exists is in and of itself consistent with the notion that the type of policy has an effect on processes and outcomes. While presidential dominance in foreign policy has long legal, constitutional, and traditional roots which in themselves are important factors, it would be a mistake to reject the policy argument out of hand for foreign policy.[20]

Electoral Cycles

Up until now, the data examined have been broken up by the standard parameter of presidential administration. Another dimension suggests

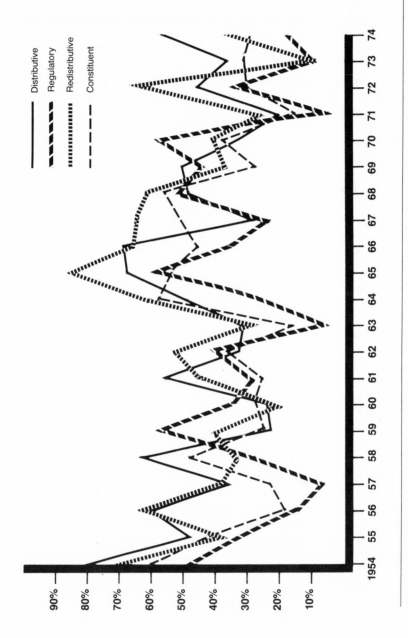

Figure 5: Rates of Success for Bills Proposed by the President in His Annual Legislative Program by Domestic Policy Areas, 1954–74

itself, however, and it is related to the president's electoral cycle. A recent study has posited a direct relation between a year's political importance to the president and his administration's attempts to stimulate the economy, as measured by changes in unemployment and real disposable per capital income.[21] While the focus of that study is on substantive changes in certain aggregate economic and social policies (largely redistributive), rather than on the overall importance of those types of policies as a portion of a total policy program of presidents, the study is useful in suggesting a rank-ordering of years according to their electoral importance to the president. In descending order of importance they are (including the years incorporated in this study): (1) on-years, incumbent president seeking reelection (1956, 1964, 1972); (2) midterm congressional elections (1954, 1958, 1962, 1966, 1970, 1974); (3) on-years, incumbent president not seeking reelection (1960, 1968); (4) odd-numbered years (all odd years from 1955 to 1973).

Using this scheme, I have arrayed policies across these four time categories for each of the policy areas, plus foreign policy. Again these characteristics are examined for policies proposed to the Congress by presidents and policies passed. The results provide some important additional confirmations.

Table 9 summarizes the findings for bills proposed. The distributive category shows the greatest percentage of proposals during presidential reelection years (as in Figure 4) and second highest during years when the incumbent retires. Such distributive activity when the incumbent is not seeking reelection would indicate an effort to help the nominee of the president's party, since ties are often made between the administration and the new presidential aspirant of the same party. The lowest percentage in the distributive category falls during midterm elections, indicating the absence of a tie between the president's distributive policy activity and that of the Congress. This increase in distributive proposals during times of the president's reelection is consistent with the standard wisdom that elected public officials, now including presidents, try to aid their reelection chances by "passing out the pork."

The regulatory-policy pattern is the reverse of the distributive pattern, insofar as the two lowest percentages occur during presidential-election years. This is indicative of the conflictual, nonbenefit (in the distributive sense) nature of regulatory policies.

Interestingly, the one category for which there is no signifcant variance across types of election years is the redistributive area. Indeed, there is a slight (1.7 percent) increase in the number of redistributive policies proposed. This provides a very clear indication that the frequencies of redistributive policies do not follow the electoral cycle, thereby further

Table 9: Average Percentage of Bills Proposed, Arrayed by Years in Electoral Cycle, 1954–74

	Distributive	Regulatory	Redistribution	Constituent	Foreign Policy
1. President a candidate	37.0% (160)	13.6% (54)	29.3% (134)	20.1% (96)	22.8% (105)
2. Midterm	21.7 (288)	22.6 (281)	29.3 (356)	26.5 (325)	17.2 (247)
3. New president	29.8 (151)	16.0 (95)	30.7 (153)	23.5 (108)	15.4 (79)
4. Odd years	23.7 (584)	18.3 (394)	31.0 (769)	27.1 (615)	18.6 (460)

SOURCE: Data drawn from Table 3.
NOTE: 1: 1956, 1964, 1972
2: 1954, 1958, 1962, 1966, 1970, 1974
3: 1960, 1968

Table 10: Average Percentage of Bills Passed, Arrayed by Years in Electoral Cycle, 1954–74

	Distributive	Regulatory	Redistribution	Constituent	Foreign Policy
1. President a candidate	52.0% (160)	25.9% (54)	61.0% (134)	36.0% (96)	67.4% (105)
2. Midterm	56.1 (288)	37.6 (281)	48.9 (356)	42.7 (325)	63.2 (247)
3. New President	36.4 (151)	43.8 (95)	40.6 (153)	41.7 (108)	63.1 (79)
4. Odd years	39.8 (584)	27.8 (394)	41.1 (769)	31.1 (615)	59.1 (469)

SOURCE: Table 6.
NOTE: 1: 1956, 1964, 1972
2: 1954, 1958, 1962, 1966, 1970, 1974
3: 1960, 1968

discounting the electoral explanation for presidential involvement in redistributive policies. Redistributive policies are indisputably important to
presidents in their legislative-policy agendas. But there is no indication that
this importance stems from or is related to the election cycle. This conclusion is consistent with my description of the "public-interest presidency."

The category of foreign policy reveals the greatest activity during periods when the incumbent is a candidate for reelection, but unlike distributive policies, the low point for foreign-policy activity occurs during
presidential-election years when the incumbent is not running for reelection. Evidently, the electoral benefits that are perceived to accrue from
foreign policy are not considered to be as readily transferable to the party's
new candidate as are distributive benefits, which if nothing else are concrete and directly felt in their impact on voters.

Table 10 is similarly provocative. Under the distributive category, the
highest passage rates are for midterm-election years (Congress, after all,
votes one way or the other on all of the president's proposals), and
presidential-reelection years. The lowest percentage of success for presidents in the distributive category and the highest success rate in the
regulatory category are the same for each—those presidential-election
years during which the incumbent is not running (the third category of
elections). The widely acknowledged characteristics of the lame-duck
president in his last year in office seem to be borne out here by the decline
of distributive-policy success, and the rise in regulatory success. The
presence of this higher passage rate for regulatory policies may reflect
lame-duck attempts to enact policies which, though viewed as necessary,
do not possess concrete electoral or other benefits. A lame duck is beyond
fearing retribution and therefore perhaps feels free to serve higher political
ideals by tackling policies that are important but highly conflictual and
therefore costly. Similarly, the least amount of success in the regulatory
area occurs during presidential reelection years.

The percentages in the redistributive-policy area are, along with foreign
policy, the only figures that do follow the expected pattern of decline
according to years of electoral importance to the president. Yet this is
perfectly consistent with the logic of the analysis. While the constancy of
the redistributive percentages in Table 9 shows the president's consistent
commitment to redistributive policies regardless of electoral situation, the
success rates indicate fluctuations in policy achievement consistent with
his own likely pattern of efforts. That is, the high point occurs during years
when the president was a candidate for reelection (in all three cases, 1956,
1964, and 1972, the incumbent won handily), and the low point occurs
during the lame-duck years. Thus, while institutional forces promote redistributive commitments in terms of numbers of proposals, electoral

forces or, more properly, the cycle of the presidential term, influences the actual rate of success.

Finally, the area of foreign policy follows the redistributive-policy trend and therefore adds additional credence to the notion that these two areas reflect greatest presidential ascendancy (historically true for foreign policy), as seen in the correlation of the declining percentages with the electoral importance of the year for the president. It is logical that presidents would expend their resources to obtain passage of policies during years of greatest electoral importance to them, especially for the purpose of credit claiming. Both foreign-policy and redistributive-policy issues make the president appear most "presidential." While concrete rewards may accrue for presidents from distributive policies, there is little glory and stature as a national leader to be gained by claiming credit for a dam in Georgia or an office building in Minneapolis, outside of those districts. A trip to China, a SALT treaty, medicare, a supplemental social-security program, or a tax cut, however, all yield a much more direct credit-claiming function for the president. This evident similarity between redistributive policies and foreign policy in the data imply a certain commonality that might be traced to the more broad and sweeping nature of these kinds of policies. Thus, the political characteristics associated with the "public-interest presidency" for redistributive policy may be equally applicable to foreign policy as well.

As a final, more general point, we observe that the cycles summarized in Tables 9 and 10 do in fact reflect presidential, rather than congressional, cycles. The marked dissimilarities between percentages in the first three categories would not distribute themselves as they do if control of the president's involvement in legislating was dependent solely upon the good graces of the Congress. Quite the reverse is true. The president is, at least for this time period, the senior partner, and certainly he is largely in command of his own programs.

Resubmission of Bills

Related to the issue of the proposal and passage of bills is the question of resubmission. That is, how many of the president's legislative requests were previously submitted to Congress (by his own, not a previous, administration) but denied passage? This can be construed both as a measure of effort (much resubmission meaning persistence on the president's part), and success (little resubmission implying early resolution of an issue, either through success or abandonment). Given the president's across-the-board interest in his legislative agenda, one would expect the greatest

Table 11: Percentages of Bills Previously Submitted by the President to Congress and Denied

	Distributive	Regulatory	Redistributive	Constituent	Foreign Policy
1954	13.0%	0%	1.4%	5.7%	0%
1955	7.5	12.5	21.4	20.0	10.0
1956	23.9	33.3	37.5	61.4	4.0
1957	40.0	56.0	32.4	46.7	6.5
1958	7.9	31.6	25.6	31.8	16.0
1959	14.6	25.7	18.0	58.6	9.3
1960	30.2	71.4	50.0	43.9	29.7
1961	....	....	....	....	....
1962	9.3	0	41.3	7.5	0
1963	12.1	27.3	14.3	22.1	10.4
1964	36.5	44.4	35.7	17.2	11.1
1965	4.2	9.3	7.5	7.0	0
1966	23.8	9.0	12.4	6.0	0
1967	3.6	14.9	6.7	3.8	1.8
1968	17.6	42.0	15.0	13.4	7.1
1969	....	....	....	....	....
1970	16.7	22.9	24.5	25.5	2.9
1971	22.9	27.7	42.0	35.5	28.6
1972	0	8.3	6.2	10.0	4.5
1973	0	0	0	0	0
1974	14.3	4.5	7.5	12.9	0
1954–60	20.1	35.0	24.5	39.3	11.2
1961–63	10.8	13.6	23.3	17.5	5.4
1964–68	15.0	21.2	13.3	8.1	3.4
1969–74	11.3	15.5	20.0	20.7	5.6

SOURCE: "Presidential Boxscores," *Congressional Quarterly Almanac,* 1954–74.
NOTE: Formula for percentages: number of bills previously submitted and denied divided by the total number of bills proposed per policy area. For *N*, see Table 3. 1961 and 1969 excluded from averages.

degree of resubmission in conflictual policies, especially regulatory policies, and the least degree of resubmission for nonconflictual policies, especially distributive policies. This is in large part a reflection of relative success in these areas. The data are presented in Table 11 and Figure 6.[22]

As the pictorial representation in Figure 6 shows, across policy areas bills are most frequently reintroduced at reelection time for the incumbent and at the end of the administration. Though Nixon's term ended two years early, an upward trend is evident in 1974. Successful reelection is probably interpreted by the incumbent as a mandate to embark on new policy ventures, while the end-of-term upsurge indicates the incumbent's final

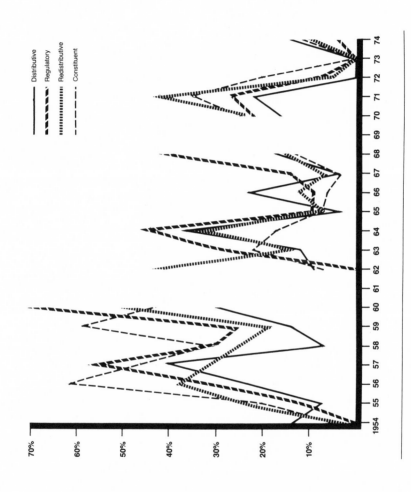

Figure 6: Percentages of Bills Previously Submitted by the President to Congress and Denied, 1954–74

push to enact previously failed pieces of legislation. Although the percentages for the four policy areas differ, they follow the same general pattern of upward and downward movement.

The graph seems to indicate that the largest degree of redundancy, aside from foreign policy, occurs in the distributive category, and indeed this proves to be the case for three of the four presidential administrations. It may be interpreted as an additional testament to the stability and success of logrolling politics. But there is no consistency as to which category maintains the highest degree of redundancy.

Perhaps the most significant observation to be drawn from this particular datum is the confirmation it adds to the notion of seeking out similarities across presidential administrations. While the policy categories do not present any startling consistencies aside from the distributive policy area, the similarity of the overall trends across presidencies is consistent with the posited existence of like patterns that span the administrations under study.

From the data presented thus far, the outlines of "four presidencies" are evident, based on the case descriptions in chapters 3 and 4, and the aggregate data presented here. The "special-interest presidency" engages in porkbarreling and logrolling through the judicious use of distributive policies as they bear on electoral realities. The "presidential broker" is reduced to that role by virtue of the highly conflictual nature of those policies. Of the four areas, distributive policies are certainly the political hot potato. Though total avoidance might be the easiest path, the use of regulation at times cannot be avoided. The president's involvement in this area thus seems to reflect his more limited influence here, as well as the greater political costs associated with successful passage of regulatory bills.

The "public-interest presidency" reflects both the assumption of national responsibilities vis-à-vis the deference other political actors bestow in the area, and the symbols and related benefits the president receives from being identified as protector of the poor, defender of the dollar, and champion of courses of action that, in affecting broad classes of Americans, seem to be derived from the perspective of "national interest" shared by no other political actor. Finally, the "administrative presidency" responds to organizational and overhead functions associated with the title of chief administrator. Presidential response in this area seems to reflect the lack of immediate political ramifications outside of governmental circles, at least for the period under consideration. Succeeding discussion will serve to further clarify these distinctions.

6: Policy Patterns and Congressional Floor Activity

In Chapter 5 I attempted to provide an overview of presidential policy making in the congressional arena by looking basically at the president's input (proposals) and the output (bills successfully passed). We have seen the policy areas in which the president is most likely to propose and obtain bills. But in focusing on rates of proposal and rates of success in the last chapter, I have omitted a critical aspect of the legislative process: What happens to bills between the time they are proposed and the time they are passed? How and in what ways are bills changed, if at all? What are the characteristics of those changes? What is the nature and degree of support for and opposition to the president's proposals? And most important for this study, how do all these things vary according to the type of policy being proposed by the president? Following the logic of the "four presidencies," one expects that the political characteristics associated with these proposals will vary in ways I have articulated in Chapter 2.

The reader should keep in mind the fact that, while the previous analysis examined the total number of bills, my concern here is with the relative political fates (degree of controversy) of selected bills across policy types. Thus, the previous empirical analysis was quantitative; the present is more qualitative. The present discussion may be less exhaustive than the case studies, but it is more inclusive.

The discussion and analysis will delve more deeply into the process of legislating in Congress, but it should be remembered that these are still "the president's proposals." In very large measure his reputation and ultimate fate as a president hinge on the outcome of these bills. The assessment of his success in the legislative sphere is as fundamental to the president's standing in the polls as it is to his standing in the Washington community. What follows is an account of what happened to some of the president's bills, as considered from the perspective of the policy framework.

After I discuss the sources and nature of the data, I will turn to the degree of floor activity to which the president's bills were subjected. Specifically, I shall consider the degree to which attempts were made to change bills by roll-call votes across policy areas by administration in the House and Senate. An additional measure of floor activity is employed by looking at the number of bills for which no roll calls were taken. The difference between House and Senate roll-call activity is also examined for each bill (by policy area) to observe differences between the House's and the Senate's treatment of the president's bills. I will also examine the matter of relative floor activity by considering the degree of controversy in voting patterns for each roll call. Moreover, I will analyze the possible existence of varying degrees of party voting across policy areas. And finally, I will conduct a detailed substantive analysis of the 165 cases under examination.

In all these instances, my aim will be to subject some of the president's bills to various analytical techniques in order to observe whether and in what ways policy type affects the fate of the president's bills on the floor of Congress.

Selecting the Bills

I selected the subset of bills to be examined here, composed of 165 cases over the same twenty-year period, in order to facilitate more detailed comparison. The selection of a subset of cases allows a degree of in-depth analysis not feasible for the full set of bills and also an element of representativeness not to be found in a handful of cases. In selecting these cases, I followed several criteria. First, I chose only bills that had at least come to a vote on the floors of both houses. While such a procedure excludes a wide array of bills that died in committee, this criterion insures that the comparisons made between bills will be commensurable. This procedure may introduce a bias,[1] but it also serves a positive function related to the second criterion of selection. I also selected cases on the basis of the availability of information about them.[2] This was important because of the need to insure the existence of continuing presidential support for each bill under consideration. Further, this selection procedure has the effect of weeding out less important bills, because it omits bills that the president and his congressional supporters abandoned (a likely reason for failure), either because of lack of interest or because excessive costs were associated with support of a bill. Using these selection criteria, I found it unnecessary to winnow out any bills in order to establish a manageable number of cases. Finally, I made no attempt to select cases that were more or less easily classifiable into the four arenas of power. Though some bills are clear cases and others are mixed, all but a handful of cases were classified.[3] Far from obscuring the analysis, the mixed cases should put the arenas theory to a stern test. There was also no conscious attempt to select cases that were in any sense representative of the policy types or of important proposals generally.

The Committee and the Floor

The ideal approach to studying the effects of the congressional process on the president's legislative program across policy areas would involve a before-and-after analysis of the president's bills in the legislative process. All bills introduced into Congress must be introduced by congressmen. It is customary, however, for the president's supporters in Congress to introduce on his behalf those bills and versions of bills that he favors. Thus, all of the bills examined here reflected his preference at the time they were introduced. The quantity and quality of the changes the bills undergo as they run the legislative gauntlet indicate the nature of the type of policy and therefore affect the final complexion of the president's program.

In the context of the legislative process, there are two fundamental arenas of activity in each house where bills are likely to be altered. The first is in committee, and the second is on the floor. The ideal comparison, then, would involve an assessment of each bill as introduced (and then sent to committee), compared with the version of the bill as it is reported out of committee. Then the committee bill would be compared with the final version after it has been considered on the floor of each house. In some instances, House and Senate versions differ enough to warrant conference-committee action and then a vote on the revised bill in each house. But the critical work on bills generally occurs in regular standing chamber committees and on the floor.

The conduct of this kind of detailed analysis on a broad scale poses a problem, because it could extend well beyond the scope of a single or even several chapters. This is a particular problem in the analysis of committee action, since there is no readily quantifiable source of information on committee activity. Therefore I have seen fit to make an analytical compromise; I have omitted information pertaining to committee action on bills.[4] It turns out, however, that such omission represents less of a compromise than might be anticipated; committee action and floor action on a bill are in fact closely related to each other.

Every bill that reaches the floor of the House and Senate has already been subjected to at least a minimum of scrutiny in committee hearings, executive sessions, debate, and markup sessions. Changes may be cosmetic or substantial, but the procedures of scrutiny are generally followed. This is indicative of the standard assessment of congressional committees, prevalent since the time of Woodrow Wilson:[5] they "provide the fundamental structuring for the division of legislative labor."[6] As such, they constitute "the great baronies of congressional power."[7] Institutional norms of seniority, specialization, reciprocity, and accommodation all contribute to the stability of the institution and more specifically to the dominance of committees in the shaping of legislation.[8]

There are times, however, when important work on a bill is done on the floor of the House or Senate; this is called "floor creativity."[9] According to the arenas-of-power scheme, the existence of high or low floor creativity is one factor that varies according to the type of policy (see chapters 3 and 4). Thus, if a bill passes both houses without being challenged or amended in any significant way on the floor, it is evident that the committee is responsible for the major input into the bill. If serious attempts to amend a bill occur on the floor, however, then it can be said that some floor creativity is present, and that its presence indicates the inability of the relevant committee to resolve all of the major issues surrounding the bill. This is all the more important given the general trend of committee dominance as reflected in the rules that govern Congress: "The general impact of the rules in both the House and the Senate is the same: the rules protect the power and prerogatives of the standing committees of the House and Senate by making it very difficult for a bill that does not have committee approval to come to either floor and by making it very difficult to amend bills reported from committee (this is particularly true of the House). Thus the centrifugal impact of stable standing committees is enhanced and perpetuated."[10] The presence or absence of floor creativity (as seen in the amending process), then, also reflects upon the ability of committees to deal with and resolve the important issues surrounding a given bill. Whether amendments are successfully added is secondary to the crucial question of whether the major issues surrounding a bill have been resolved.

Differences between the House and the Senate

Because I will be including action in both the House and the Senate, I ought to acknowledge the relevant differences between House and Senate procedures. As compared with the Senate, the House is more restrictive and hierarchical in its floor procedures. In large part, the greater strictness stems from its greater size and smaller constituency units. The rules of the House reflect the need for maintaining greater rigidity. Debate on most bills is severely limited. Some bills are considered on the floor under a closed rule, which does not permit substantive amendments except (under some instances) by members of the committee that reported the bill. This is important because the closed rule, enacted at the request of the relevant committee, helps protect the sanctity of the committee's prerogatives and jurisdictions. As a result, the few House bills included here that were considered under a closed rule will be treated no differently from those under an open rule, since the presence of a closed rule reflects a success-ful effort by a committee to conclude substantive work on a bill before it reaches the floor.[11] The same can be said of bills that come to the floor under an open rule but are not amended on the floor. When an open rule is allowed, amendments must normally be germane to the bill. In the Senate, members possess greater personal prerogatives. Debate is likely to be extended, closed rules are not used, nor is there a requirement that amendments be germane. Thus, it is evident that amendments and related floor activity are much more likely to appear on the floor of the Senate than the House.[12]

The analysis and discussion in this chapter will again center around the president's policy proposals (in this instance, 165 cases) spanning the period from 1954 to 1974, according to the four policy areas. The principal focus will be on floor activity—specifically, all roll-call votes for each bill, including substantive and procedural votes, votes on passage, and con-ference reports. While some bills under consideration involved no roll-call votes, these cases were also included, because the absence of recorded votes for a bill is as significant as the presence of these votes. The emphasis on recorded votes also helps us to avoid giving unwarranted attention to more frivolous amendments.

Following a general description of the overall amendment activity (at-tempts to amend bills in recorded votes) and degree of partisan support for the full set of bills, I will examine the bills in each policy category separately according to the content of the amendments themselves. The data in all cases will be considered according to presidential administra-tions. In addition to revealing differences between administrations, such a procedure will be especially helpful in distinguishing trends in congres-sional behavior that are not related to presidential activity, such as the general decline in party voting and the increase in the number of recorded votes in Congress over time.

Floor Activity

Before discussing the 165 cases, I must remind the reader of the hypoth-eses mentioned in Chapter 2. I posited that: (1) Regulatory bills would possess the largest number of roll calls, compared with the other three categories. Substantive amendments will probably be regulatory as well, representing attempts to change the face of bills. Therefore, conflict will stem from the content of the bill itself. (2) Redistributive bills will exhibit the next highest level of amendment activity, and those amendments will be of varying policy types. (3) Attempts to amend distributive bills will be fewer, because disputes are more likely to be resolved in committee, and the proposed amendments will be of various policy types. (4) Constituent bills will exhibit the least amount of floor activity, given the low visibility of administrative, overhead policies and functions. Conflict that does arise on the floor will probably spring from amendments that are not constituent, just as conflicts arising for distributive bills are likely to have their source in nondistributive amendments. (5) Partisanship will exhibit itself on the floor in greatest degree for distributive and constituent bills, and less for regulatory and redistributive bills, as Lowi posits in his scheme.

The bills that make up the list of presidential proposals under consideration are listed in Table 12 according to the four policy categories. There are forty distributive, thirty-seven constituent, thirty-one regulatory and fifty-seven redistributive bills. The numbers roughly represent—though not by intent—the actual distribution of proposals made by presidents during this period as outlined in Chapter 5. In addition to giving the bills' titles or descriptions, Table 12 also gives their bill numbers and public-law numbers, when appropriate, and the number of roll-call votes taken on each bill in each house. The list covers the gamut of domestic policies, and though some types of bills recur (such as measures to support farm prices and proposals to extend tax rates) both within and between administrations, each bill represents a new case and a new opportunity for the political actors involved. Listed chronologically, the bills were numbered before they were separated into the four categories. It is interesting to note that of the eight bills that did not become public laws, four were regulatory (the smallest category numerically), and all of those bills died on either the House or Senate floor.

Tables 13 and 14 present summary information on amendments by the four categories, broken up by administrations. The mean for all years for both House and Senate follows the pattern previously hypothesized, with attempts to amend regulatory bills occurring most often and attempts to amend constituent bills occurring least often. When broken up by administration, the pattern varies somewhat. In all cases but one, however, a clear dichotomy appears between distributive and constituent policies on the one hand, and regulatory and redistributive policies on the other. This division parallels the "likelihood-of-coercion" dimension of the arenas scheme (see Figure 2), because it is consistent with the notion that distributive and constituent policies are remote in terms of their coercive effects,

Table 12: List of 165 Bills Categorized by Policy Areas

			No. of Recorded Votes for Each Bill	
Distributive			House	Senate
1973	6.	Federal Aid Highway Act of 1973; S. 502, P.L. 93-87	3	10
	7.	Alaska Pipeline; S. 1081, H.R. 9130, P.L. 93-153	9	20
	8.	FLood Disaster Protection Act of 1973; H.R. 8449, P.L. 93-234	1	1
1972	12.	Federal Aid Highway Act of 1973; S. 3939, H.R. 16656[a]	2	5
	13.	Emergency Highway Relief; H.R. 15950, S. 3796, P.L. 92-361	0	0
1971	20.	Emergency Loan Guarantee (Lockheed); H.R. 8432	3	9
	21.	Amendment to Rural Telephone Electrification Act of 1970; S. 70, H.R. 7, P.L. 92-12	1	0
1970	26.	Extension of National Foundation on the Arts and Humanities; H.R. 16065, S. 3215, P.L. 91-346	2	0
	27.	Urban Mass Transit Aid; S. 3154, H.R. 18185, P.L. 91-453	2	6
1969	34.	D.C. Mass Transit Funds; S. 2185, H.R. 11193, P.L. 91-143	2	0
	35.	Airport Development Act of 1970; H.R. 14465, S. 3108, P.L. 91-258	2	8
1968	42.	Extension of National Foundations on the Arts and Humanities; H.R. 11308, P.L. 90-348	3	0
	43.	Extension of Corporation for Public Broadcasting; S. 3135, H.R. 15986, P.L. 90-294	1	0
1967	50.	Partnership for Health Amendments of 1967; H.R. 6418, S. 1131, P.L. 90-174	3	0
	51.	Desalting Plant; S. 270, H.R. 207, P.L. 90-18	1	0
	52.	San Rafael Wilderness Park; S. 889, H.R. 5161, P.L. 90-271	1	0
1966	59.	Federal Aid Highway Act of 1966; H.R. 14359, S. 3155, P.L. 89-574	3	1
	60.	Cape Lookout National Seashore; S. 251, H.R. 1784, P.L. 89-366	0	0
1965	70.	Highway Beautification Act of 1965; S. 2084, P.L. 89-285	2	5
1964	80.	Urban Mass Transit Act; S. 6, H.R. 3881, P.L. 88-365	3	15
	81.	National Wildlife Preserve; S. 4, H.R. 9070, P.L. 88-577	1	4
1963	87.	Higher Education Facilities Act of 1963; H.R. 6143, P.L. 88-204	2	6
	88.	Health Facilities Construction; S. 1576, P.L. 88-154	2	2
	89.	Health Professions Educational Assistance Act; H.R. 12, P.L. 88-129	2	4
1962	96.	Trade Expansion Act; H.R. 11970, P.L. 87-794	3	11
	97.	College Academic Facilities and Student Assistance Act; H.R. 8900, S. 1241[a]	2	5
1961	102.	Emergency Feed Grains Program; H.R. 4510, S. 993, P.L. 87-5	3	2

Table 12, continued

1960	110.	Sugar Quota Act; H.R. 12311, S.J. Res. 217, P.L. 86-592	1	2
	111.	Federal Highway Act of 1960; H.R. 104-95, P.L. 86-657	0	1
	112.	Small Business Investment Act Amendments; S. 2611, H.R. 10886, P.L. 86-502	0	0
1958	126.	Trade Agreements Extension Act; H.R. 12591, P.L. 85-686	2	6
	127.	1970 Winter Olympics; S. 3262, P.L. 85-365	2	0
1957	134.	Small Business Association Loan Authorization; S. 637, P.L. 85-4	0	0
	135.	Export-Import Bank Lending Authority; H.R. 4136, P.L. 85-55	0	0
	136.	Drought Aid; H.R. 2367, S. 511, P.L. 85-25	1	0
	137.	Extension of Small Business Administration; H.R. 7963, S. 2504, P.L. 85-120	1	0
1956	144.	Colorado River Project; S. 500, H.R. 3383, P.L. 84-485	1	2
1955	151.	Reciprocal Trade Extension Act; H.R. 1, P.L. 84-86	2	4
	152.	Highway Construction; S. 1084, H.R. 7474[b]	2	2
1954	160.	D.C. Public Works; H.R. 8079, P.L. 83-364	0	2
			71	133

Regulatory

1973	9.	Endangered Species; H.R. 4758, S. 1983, P.L. 93-205	1	2
	10.	Extension of Economic Stabilization Act of 1970; S. 398, H.R. 2099, P.L. 93-28	1	14
1972	14.	Equal Educational Opportunities Act; H.R. 13915, S. 3395[c]	8	3
	15.	West Coast Dock Strike; S.J. Res. 197, H.J. Res. 1025, P.L. 92-235	1	2
1971	22.	Extension of Military Draft; H.R. 531, P.L. 92-129	12	56
	23.	Extension of Economic Stabilization Act; H.R. 11309, P.L. 92-210	4	23
1970	28.	Comprehensive Drug Abuse Prevention and Control Act; H.R. 18583, P.L. 91-513	1	5
	29.	D.C. Court Reform and Criminal Procedure Act of 1970; H.R. 16196, S. 2601, P.L. 91-358	2	1
	30.	Clean Air Amendments of 1970; H.R. 17255, S. 4358, P.L. 91-604	1	3
1969	36.	Amendment to Selective Service Act of 1967; H.R. 14001, P.L. 91-124	1	0
1968	44.	Gun Control Act of 1968; H.R. 17735, S. 3633, P.L. 90-618	5	11
	45.	Civil Rights–Open Housing; H.R. 2516, P.L. 90-284	1	30
1967	53.	Omnibus Crime Control and Safe Streets Act; H.R. 5037, S. 917, P.L. 90-351	3	29
	54.	Consumer Credit Protection Act; S. 5, H.R. 11601, P.L. 90-321	2	1
	55.	Railroad Strike; S.J. Res. 81, P.L. 90-54	1	5
1966	61.	Civil Rights Act of 1966; H.R. 14765, S. 3296[c]	6	2
	62.	Traffic Safety Act; S. 3005, H.R. 13228, P.L. 89-563	3	3
	63.	Fair Packaging and Labeling Act; S. 985, H.R. 15440, P.L. 89-775	2	5

Table 12, continued

Year	No.	Description		
1965	69.	Food and Agriculture Act of 1965; H.R. 9811, P.L. 89-321	3	8
	71.	Voting Rights Act of 1965; H.R. 6400, S. 1564, P.L. 89-110	8	29
	72.	Repeal of Taft-Hartley Act; H.R. 77[b]	2	7
1964	79.	Cotton and Wheat Farm Bill; H.R. 6196, S. 1511, P.L. 88-297	3	17
1962	95.	Food and Agriculture Act of 1972; S. 3225, H.R. 12391, H.R. 11222, P.L. 87-703	4	16
1960	109.	Farm Surplus Act; S. 2759, H.R. 12261[b]	2	7
	113.	Civil Rights Act of 1960; H.R. 8601, P.L. 86-449	3	18
	114.	Regulation of Bank Mergers; S. 1062, P.L. 86-463	0	1
1959	117.	Labor-Management Reporting and Disclosure Act; H.R. 8342, S. 1555, P.L. 86-257	4	18
1958	143.	Omnibus Farm Bill; H.R. 10875, P.L. 85-540	5	7
1956	145.	Bank Holding Company Act of 1956; H.R. 6227, S. 2577, P.L. 84-511	1	3
1955	153.	Selective Service Extension; H.R. 3005, P.L. 84-118	3	0
1954	159.	Omnibus Farm Bill; H.R. 9680, S. 3052, P.L. 83-690	1	16
			94	342

Redistributive

Year	No.	Description		
1974	1.	Elementary and Secondary Education Act Amendments; H.R. 69, S. 1539, P.L. 93-380	12	21
	2.	Public Service Jobs; H.R. 16596, S. 4079, P.L. 93-567	3	1
	3.	Extension of Unemployment Benefits; H.R. 17597, P.L. 93-572	1	1
1972	16.	Expansion of Child Nutrition Program; H.R. 14896, P.L. 92-433	1	4
	17.	Amendment to Older Americans Act of 1965; S. 1163, H.R. 5017, P.L. 92-258	1	2
1971	24.	Welfare Reform; H.R. 1, P.L. 92-603	3	29
	25.	Revenue Act of 1971; H.R. 10947, P.L. 92-178	1	78
1970	31.	Food Stamp Act Amendments; H.R. 18582, S. 2547, P.L. 91-671	3	3
1969	37.	Food Stamps Authorization; H.J. Res. 934, P.L. 91-116	0	0
1968	46.	Housing and Urban Development Act of 1968; S. 3497, H.R. 17989, P.L. 90-448	4	8
	47.	Revenue and Expenditure Control Act of 1968; H.R. 15414, P.L. 90-364	2	20
	48.	Vocational Education Act Amendments of 1968; H.R. 18366, P.L. 90-576	1	6
1967	56.	Economic Opportunity Amendments; S. 2388, P.L. 90-222	4	13
	57.	Social Security Benefits; H.R. 12080, P.L. 90-248	2	25
1966	64.	Fair Labor Standards Amendments of 1966; H.R. 13712, P.L. 89-601	6	13
	65.	Economic Opportunity Amendments of 1966; H.R. 15111, S. 3164, P.L. 89-794	5	7
	66.	Suspend Investment Tax Credit; H.R. 17607, P.L. 89-800	4	4
	67.	Allied Health Professions Personnel Training Act; H.R. 13196, P.L. 89-751	1	0

Table 12, continued

Year	No.	Description		
1965	73.	Elementary and Secondary Education Act of 1965; H.R. 2362, S. 370, P.L. 89-10	2	12
	74.	Social Security Amendments; H.R. 6675, P.L. 89-97	3	13
	75.	Housing and Urban Development Act of 1965; H.R. 7984, S. 2213, P.L. 89-117	4	5
1964	82.	Economic Opportunity Act of 1964; H.R. 11377, S. 2642, P.L. 88-452	4	10
	83.	Social Security Amendments of 1964; H.R. 11865c	2	3
	84.	Food Stamp Act of 1964; H.R. 10222, P.L. 88-525	2	0
	85.	National Defense Education Act Amendments; S. 3060, H.R. 11904, P.L. 88-665	2	0
1963	90.	Area Redevelopment Act Amendments; S. 1163, H.R. 4996	1	3
	91.	Vocational Education Act of 1963; H.R. 4955, P.L. 88-210	4	4
	92.	Maternal, Child, Mental Retardation Planning Amendments of 1963; H.R. 7544, P.L. 88-156	0	0
	93.	Manpower Development and Training Act Amendments; H.R. 8720, P.L. 88-214	0	6
1962	98.	Standby Public Works Act; S. 2965, H.R. 10113, P.L. 87-658	1	11
	99.	Public Welfare Amendments of 1962; H.R. 10606, P.L. 87-543	3	3
	100.	Revenue Act of 1962; H.R. 10650, P.L. 87-834	2	18
1961	103.	Area Redevelopment Act of 1961; S. 1, H.R. 4569, P.L. 87-27	3	7
	104.	Fair Labor Standard Amendments of 1961; H.R. 3935, P.L. 87-30	4	9
	105.	Housing Act of 1961; S. 1922, H.R. 6028, P.L. 87-70	3	20
	106.	Temporary Extended Unemployment Compensation Act of 1961; H.R. 4806, P.L. 87-6	2	4
	107.	Aid to Dependent Children; H.R. 4884, P.L. 87-31	0	0
1960	115.	Tax Extension; H.R. 12381, P.L. 86-564	1	12
1959	118.	Federal Aid Highway Act of 1959; H.R. 8678, P.L. 86-342	1	5
	119.	Bond Interest Rate Increase; H.R. 9035, P.L. 86-346	2	2
	120.	Tax Rate Extension Act of 1959; H.R. 7523, P.L. 186-75	0	9
	121.	Veterans Pension Act of 1959; H.R. 7650, P.L. 86-211	0	3
1958	128.	Temporary Unemployment Compensation Act of 1958; H.R. 12065, P.L. 85-441	2	7
	129.	Tax Rate Extension; H.R. 12695, P.L. 85-475	1	9
	130.	National Defense Education Act of 1958; H.R. 13427, S. 4237, P.L. 85-864	2	5
1957	138.	Housing Act of 1957; H.R. 6659, P.L. 85-104	0	6
1956	146.	Housing Act of 1956; S. 3855, H.R. 11742, P.L. 84-1020	1	4
	147.	Highway Revenue Act of 1956; H.R. 10660, P.L. 84-627	1	7
	148.	Social Security Amendments H.R. 7225, P.L. 84-880	1	6
	149.	School Milk Program; H.R. 8320, P.L. 84-465	2	1
	150.	Extension of Tax Rates; H.R. 9166, P.L. 85-458	1	0
1955	154.	Extension of Tax Rates; H.R. 4259, P.L. 84-18	3	2
	155.	Housing Amendments of 1955; S. 2126, P.L. 84-345	3	2
	156.	Minimum Wage; S. 2168, H.R. 7214, P.L. 84-381	1	0

Table 12, continued

1954	161.	Internal Revenue Code of 1954; H.R. 8300, P.L. 83-591	4	11
	162.	Omnibus Housing Act of 1954; H.R. 7839, S. 2938, P.L. 83-560	4	2
	163.	Unemployment Aid Extension; H.R. 9719, P.L. 83-767	2	0
			128	456

Constituent

1974	4.	Health Planning; H.R. 16204, S. 2994, P.L. 93-641	1	1
	5.	Established Council on Wage and Price Stability; H.R. 16425, S. 3919, P.L. 93-387	2	4
1973	11.	Extension of Aid to Handicapped; H.R. 8070, S. 1875, P.L. 93-112	2	1
1972	18.	Equal Rights Amendment; H.R. Res. 208	2	10
	19.	Debt Limit, Spending Ceiling; H.R. 16810, P.L. 92-599	3	9
1970	32.	Federal Employees Salary Act of 1970; S. 3690, H.R. 16844, P.L. 91-231	2	4
	33.	Postal Reorganization; H.R. 17070, S. 3842, P.L. 91-375	4	10
1969	38.	Amendment to Voting Rights Act of 1965; H.R. 4249, S. 2507, P.L. 91-285	2	22
	39.	Civil Service; S. 3225, P.L. 91-187	0	0
	40.	Executive Reorganization Act; S. 1038, P.L. 91-5	1	0
	41.	Establishment of Commission on Population Growth and American Future; S. 2701, H.R. 15165, P.L. 91-213	1	0
1968	49.	Establish National Water Commission; S. 20, P.L. 90-515	1	0
1967	58.	Establish Corporation for Public Broadcasting S. 1160, H.R. 6736, P.L. 90-129	2	0
1966	68.	Establishment of Dept. of Transportation; H.R. 15963, S. 3010, P.L. 89-270	3	1
1965	76.	Establishment of Dept. of Housing and Urban Development; H.R. 6927, P.L. 89-174	2	1
	77.	Amendment to Immigration Law; H.R. 2580, S. 500, P.L. 89-236	3	1
	78.	Establish National Foundation on the Arts and Humanities; H.R. 9460, S. 1483, P.L. 89-209	1	0
1964	86.	Raise Federal salaries; H.R. 11049, P.L. 88-246	1	11
1963	94.	Extension of National Debt; H.R. 6009, P.L. 88-30	2	2
1962	101.	Extension of National Debt; H.R. 11990, P.L. 87-512	2	2
1961	108.	Peace Corps Act; S. 2000, H.R. 7500, P.L. 87-293	2	1
1960	116.	D.C. Transportation System; S. 3193, H.R. 11135, P.L. 86-669	0	0
1959	122.	Hawaiian Statehood; S. 50, H.R. 4221, P.L. 86-3	1	1
	123.	TVA Bonds; H.R. 3460, S. 931, P.L. 86-137	2	1
	124.	Amend Atomic Energy Act; S. 2568, H.R. 8755, P.L. 86-373	0	0
	125.	Tighten Regulatory Enforcement; S. 726, P.L. 86-107	0	0
1958	131.	Alaskan Statehood; H.R. 7999, S. 49, P.L. 85-508	4	6
	132.	Dept. of Defense Reorganization Act of 1958; H.R. 12541, P.L. 85-599	2	1
	133.	Amendment to Civil Defense Act of 1950; H.R. 7576, P.L. 85-606	0	0

Table 12, continued

1957	139.	Civil Rights Act of 1957; H.R. 6127, P.L. 85-315	2	13
	140.	Airways Modernization Act; S. 1856, P.L. 85-133	1	0
	141.	Amendment to Immigration and Nationality Act of 1952; H.R. 8123, S. 2792, P.L. 85-316	1	1
	142.	St. Lawrence Seaway Borrowing Authority; H.R. 5728, S. 1174, P.L. 85-108	0	0
1955	157.	Federal Pay Raise; S. 67, P.L. 84-94	1	0
	158.	Congressional Pay Raises; S. 67, P.L. 84-94	2	4
1954	164.	St. Lawrence Seaway; S. 2150, P.L. 83-358	2	3
	165.	Civil Service Benefits; S. 2665, H.R. 2263, P.L. 83-763	0	0
			57	110

NOTE: Bills selected from overall lists of presidential proposals. Each bill was examined individually from detailed bill descriptions in *Congressional Quarterly Almanac*, 1954–74.
aBill died in conference.
bBill defeated on House floor.
cBill defeated on Senate floor.

while regulatory and redistributive policies are immediate and therefore spur greater controversy over exactly who is being coerced, and how. The exception is the average number of amendments for redistributive bills in the House during the Kennedy years, 1961-63 (Table 13). But even that average is only slightly lower than that for distributive and constituent policies. The Senate average for the same policy type and same time period does conform to the expected pattern (Table 14). Of the eight averages for regulatory policies in Tables 13 and 14, seven are highest and one is second; of the eight for redistributive policies, six are second highest, one is highest, and the other lowest; of the eight distributive averages, three are second lowest, four are lowest, and one is second highest; and for constituent policies, three are lowest and five are second lowest. As expected, the average number of roll calls for Senate bills is consistently much higher than for House bills. This holds true with the single exception of constituent policies from 1961 to 1962 (these means are based, however, on only three bills).

Tables 15 and 16 focus on bills not involving roll calls. Table 15 gives the number of bills for which no roll-call votes were taken in either house. The pattern is as expected, with no such bills in the regulatory category (that is, every regulatory bill under consideration required at least one roll call in at least one house), three bills with no roll calls in either house in the redistributive category (5.3 percent), and five in the distributive and constituent categories (12.5 and 13.5 percent respectively). Table 16 presents the same information, except that the counts here are made by chamber (that is, we tabulated the number of bills with no roll-call votes in each house).

Table 13: List of 165 Bills, Categorized—Number of Roll Calls, Number of Bills, and Means for Bills in House

	Distributive	Regulatory	Redistributive	Constituent
1969–74				
No. Roll Calls	27	32	25	20
No. Bills	11	10	9	11
Mean	2.5	3.2	2.8	1.8
1964–68				
No. Roll Calls	18	40	48	13
No. Bills	10	12	16	7
Mean	1.8	3.3	3.0	1.9
1961–63				
No. Roll Calls	14	4	23	6
No. Bills	6	1	12	3
Mean	2.3	4.0	1.9	2.0
1954–60				
No. Roll Calls	12	19	32	18
No. Bills	13	8	20	16
Mean	0.9	2.4	1.6	1.1
All Years				
No. Roll Calls	71	95	128	57
No. Bills	40	31	57	37
Mean	1.8	3.1	2.2	1.5

NOTE: The mean equals the number of roll calls divided by the number of bills for each administrative period.

The projected pattern is followed for the Senate and the House, though the trend exhibits itself more clearly in the Senate. The Senate numbers are too small to allow meaningful statements about individual administrations.

One can observe some salient trends when comparing House-Senate roll calls bill by bill. Although the averages clearly indicate a greater number of roll calls for Senate than for House versions, that tendency varies when individual bills are examined by arenas.

Table 17 compares House versus Senate votes for each bill to determine which bills actually have more House than Senate roll calls. For constituent bills, House versions of bills had more roll-call votes than the Senate versions by a ratio of more than two to one. That is, for every constituent bill that had more Senate than House roll calls, two constituent bills had more House than Senate roll calls. (Ties were placed in the House-more-than-Senate categories because of the Senate's greater floor flexibility. However, when ties are removed, the basic patterns remain. See Table 17.) Among distributive bills, twenty-one had more (or equal) roll-call votes in

Table 14: List of 165 Bills, Categorized—Number of Roll Calls, Number of Bills, and Means for Bills in Senate

	Distributive	Regulatory	Redistributive	Constituent
1969–74				
No. Roll Calls	59	109	140	69
No. Bills	11	10	9	11
Mean	5.4	10.9	15.6	5.5
1964–68				
No. Roll Calls	25	147	139	14
No. Bills	10	12	16	7
Mean	2.5	12.3	8.7	2.0
1961–63				
No. Roll Calls	30	16	85	5
No. Bills	6	1	12	3
Mean	5.0	16.0	7.1	1.7
1954–60				
No. Roll Calls	19	70	93	31
No. Bills	13	8	20	16
Mean	1.5	8.7	4.6	1.9
All Years				
No. Roll Calls	133	342	457	111
No. Bills	40	31	57	37
Mean	3.3	11.0	8.0	3.0

NOTE: The mean equals the number of roll calls divided by the number of bills for each administrative period.

the House, as compared with nineteen bills having more Senate than House votes per bill. The ratio is almost two to one favoring more Senate amendments than House amendments per bill for redistributive bills, and more than three to one in the same direction for regulatory bills. The administration-by-administration breakdowns follow these trends overall as well. A question might be raised concerning the possibility that this trend is due to bills' being passed in the House but killed in the Senate, and that this division thereby favors the House over the Senate in number of votes. Only three bills, however, fall into that category, and all are regulatory; two of those three have more House than Senate votes. These variations would seem to stem primarily from the wider fluctuation in numbers of Senate amendments to bills, which is attributable to the greater rigidity of the House rules. Thus when floor activity for the president's bills is greater, as for regulatory and redistributive bills (in comparison with constituent and distributive bills), that floor activity is more likely to manifest itself in the Senate than in the House. Again, these trends indicate that the president's regulatory and redistributive bills are engendering greater

Table 15: Number of Bills with No Roll-Call Votes in Either House (by Bill)

	Distributive	Regulatory	Redistributive	Constituent
1969–74	1	0	1	1
1964–68	1	0	0	0
1961–63	0	0[a]	2	0[b]
1954–60	3	0	0	4
	5 12.5%	0	3 5.3%	5 13.5%

NOTE: Number of bills in each category: 40, 31, 57, and 37, respectively.
[a]Based on one bill
[b]Based on three bills.

Table 16: Number of Bills with No Roll-Call Votes in One House

	Distributive		Regulatory		Redistributive		Constituent	
	House	Senate	House	Senate	House	Senate	House	Senate
1969–74	1	3	0	1	1	1	1	3
1964–68	1	6	0	0	0	3	0	3
1961–63	0	0	0[a]	0[a]	3	2	0[b]	0[b]
1954–60	5	6	1	1	3	3	5	8
	7	15	1	2	7	9	6	14
	(17.5%)	(37.5%)	(3.2%)	(6.5%)	(12.3%)	(15.8%)	(16.2%)	(37.8%)

NOTE: Number of bills in each category: 40, 31, 57, 37, respectively.
[a]Based on one bill.
[b]Based on three bills.

conflict and therefore are subject to greater attempted alterations on the floor. Whether the changes are for or against his wishes (and they are far more likely to be against his wishes for regulatory bills, as previously indicated), they indicate heightened political maneuvering by the participants, which means a greater effort by the president either to make more changes or prevent more changes than he would have to do for distributive and constituent policies.

One other way of looking at the degree of relative floor conflict in the House and Senate for the president's bills is to consider the roll calls on each vote. All roll-call votes were divided into two categories, controversial and noncontroversial, according to the degree of unanimity exhibited in each vote.[13] Tables 18 and 19 present the percentages of noncontroversial votes by administration for each house. More importantly, the mean per-

Table 17: Comparison of the Numbers of Roll-Call Votes in the House and in the Senate, Bill by Bill

	Distributive		Regulatory		Redistributive		Constituent	
	House Equal, More than Senate	Senate More than House	House Equal, More than Senate	Senate More than House	House Equal, More than Senate	Senate More than House	House Equal, More than Senate	Senate More than House
1969–74	5	6	3	7	4	5	5	6
1964–68	7	3	3	9	4	12	6	1
1961–63	2	4	0	1	4	8	3	0
1954–60	7	6	1	7	8	12	12 ·	4
Total	21	19	7	24	20	37	26	11
Totals minus Ties	13	19	6	24	11	37	16	11

NOTE: Bills with equal numbers of amendments in the House and Senate were placed in the House-more-than-Senate category because of the wide array of institutional and other informal factors that encourage greater floor activity in the Senate than in the House. Thus, when the House and Senate are equal in recorded votes, it indicates proportionately more activity in the House.

centages for both tables show distributive policies to have the largest number of noncontroversial votes and regulatory the smallest. However, the percentages by administration range more widely. This is another indication of the distinction between the low floor activity for distributive policies and the high floor activity for regulatory policies (constituent and redistributive policies present more mixed patterns). Though it is evident that the percentage of vote is a measure much more sensitive to the influence of extraneous factors than the number of amendments as a measure, the finding is nevertheless consistent with the differences between distributive and regulatory policies. When votes are more controversial, the president must pay greater attention to the outcome if he has any concern for the content of his bills while they are being dealt with on the floor of Congress.

The preceding analysis serves as an entree to a more detailed, substantive examination of the bills in each category. But before embarking upon that case analysis, I will consider the matter of partisanship.

Partisan Support

The president is traditionally considered to be the head of his political party, and by extension the leader of his party in Congress. Party is thus

Table 18: Percentage of Noncontroversial Recorded Votes in the House

	Distributive	Regulatory	Redistributive	Constituent
1969–74	29.6% (27)	12.5% (32)	23.1% (26)	35.0% (20)
1964–68	20.8 (18)	26.5 (40)	16.7 (48)	7.7 (13)
1961–63	5.6 (14)	0[a] (4)	17.4 (23)	0[b] (6)
1954–60	10.0 (12)	27.3 (19)	31.2 (32)	11.1 (18)
Mean—all years	22.5 (71)	16.8 (95)	21.7 (129)	17.5 (57)

NOTE: Noncontroversial recorded votes are those where the vote is at least 90% either in favor or in opposition. Numbers in parentheses are numbers of amendments.
[a]Based on a single bill.
[b]Based on three bills.

Table 19: Percentage of Noncontroversial Recorded Votes in the Senate

	Distributive	Regulatory	Redistributive	Constituent
1969–74	23.7% (59)	15.6% (109)	13.6% (140)	16.4% (61)
1964–68	6.0 (25)	10.7 (147)	11.5 (139)	14.3 (14)
1961–63	6.5 (30)	0[a] (16)	5.9 (85)	0[b] (5)
1954–60	6.1 (19)	12.5 (70)	11.8 (93)	16.7 (30)
Mean—all years	17.3 (133)	10.2 (342)	11.2 (457)	15.5 (110)

NOTE: Noncontroversial recorded votes are those where the vote is at least 90% either in favor or in opposition. Numbers in parentheses are numbers of amendments.
[a]Based on a single bill.
[b]Based on three bills.

usually considered an important factor in explaining congressional support for the president's program, and congressional behavior in general.[14]

The object of this section, however, is not to assess the absolute level of partisan support for the president's program, but rather to see *if* the degree to which members of the political parties exhibit partisanship in Congress varies from one policy area to another—whatever the level of partisan support might be. The question, then, is, Do policy types have differing effects on partisanship as observed in votes on the president's proposals? If the answer is yes, then that will certainly have an impact on the kind of political role the president plays, vis-à-vis his party, depending on the policy. When greater party discipline is in evidence, the president's job should be made easier, because that discipline provides an immediate base of support for his programs in Congress, whether he is a member of the majority or minority party (if he is a member of the minority party, the

Table 20: Index of Likeness for Recorded Votes in the House

	Distributive		Regulatory		Redistributive		Constituent	
1969–74	85.1%	(10)	81.1%	(10)	86.7%	(8)	77.4%	(10)
1964–68	74.0	(9)	70.8	(12)	63.3	(16)	62.4	(7)
1961–63	56.9	(6)	24.3	(1)	43.1	(9)	33.3	(3)
1954–60	77.1	(8)	61.3	(7)	75.3	(17)	77.1	(10)
Mean—all years	75.0	(33)	70.5	(30)	67.5	(50)	69.4	(30)

NOTE: The numbers in parentheses are the number of index scores, tabulated on a bill-by-bill basis, for each administrative period given in the lefthand column. A single index score was averaged for each bill based on its recorded votes, and those averages were averaged to produce the percentages here. The index of likeness is arrived at by subtracting the percentage of yes votes of one party from the percentage of yes votes from the other party, and then subtracting that percentage from 100.

Table 21: Index of Likeness for Recorded Votes in the Senate

	Distributive		Regulatory		Redistributive		Constituent	
1969–74	76.7%	(7)	74.0%	(9)	81.9%	(8)	83.2%	(8)
1964–68	65.6	(4)	74.6	(12)	63.4	(13)	81.2	(4)
1961–63	63.7	(6)	33.7	(1)	51.3	(10)	42.5	(3)
1954–60	77.2	(7)	67.7	(7)	58.1	(17)	83.2	(8)
Mean—all years	71.7	(24)	71.3	(29)	62.1	(48)	77.5	(23)

NOTE: The numbers in parentheses are the number of index scores, tabulated on a bill-by-bill basis, for each administrative period given in the lefthand column. A single index score was averaged for each bill based on its recorded votes, and those averages were averaged to produce percentages here. The index of likeness is arrived at by subtracting the percentage of yes votes of one party from the percentage of yes votes from the other party, and then subtracting that percentage from 100.

president has other resources he can marshal to obtain a voting majority). The arenas-of-power scheme suggests that party voting is more likely to exhibit itself in distributive and constituent policies, as compared with the other two policy areas. As mentioned, the degree to which party members vote with each other, and therefore differ with members of the opposite party, is examined here for recorded votes across the four policy areas in order to determine variations in partisanship as it relates to the president's program. For what types of issues is the president most likely to get single-minded support from his own party and opposition from the opposing party? In order to measure partisanship, I will employ a simple measure called the index of likeness.[15] The formula involves subtracting the percentage of yes votes cast by one party from the percentage of yes votes cast by the other party for a given roll call, and then subtracting that percentage from 100. The index thus ranges from 0 to 100, with high percentages indicating low party voting, and low percents indicating high party voting.

Tables 20 and 21 summarize the index-of-likeness scores for all recorded votes. A summary score was averaged for each bill, and those scores were then collapsed into the administration periods given in the tables. The purpose is to observe the degree to which partisanship varies from bill to bill in the four categories. The bill itself was used as the basic percentage unit rather than the individual recorded vote in order to control for the likelihood of a few bills with lots of recorded votes dominating the percentage.

Some basic trends not related to the arenas are evident. First, the Kennedy years exhibit the greatest overall degree of partisanship (lowest percentages). The Nixon years show the lowest level of partisanship, followed by the Eisenhower years. Thus it appears to be the case that party voting is most likely when the president is of the party that holds the majority in Congress. Second, when the percentages in the House are compared with the corresponding Senate percents for each box, it turns out that the actual amount of partisanship matches closely for both houses. Of the twenty pairs of percentages (including the percentages of all years) compared across chambers, all but two pairs (constituent, 1964—68; redistributive, 1954—60) differ less than 10 percent from each other. When the percentages are compared across policy categories within each house, they vary only a little more than 10 percent on the average for each time period, indicating generally that partisanship is not especially salient when broken up by policy area.

When looking for relative partisanship across policy categories, few clear patterns emerge. Constituent policies show the greatest amount of partisanship in the two top categories for the House, but in the Senate the corresponding percentages plus the overall mean show the least partisanship. Three of the four percentages (plus the overall mean) in the distributive category in the House show the least degree of partisanship, as does one of the distributive percentages in the Senate. The greatest amount of partisanship for all years in the House and Senate appears in the redistributive category.

The one apparent fact about these findings is that there is no clear trend that has any direct bearing on the policy areas. It could be the case, however, that some salient trends are being masked by combining all recorded votes of a given bill to produce a single average. Other research offers one way around this problem by showing that patterns of partisanship vary consistently according to whether the vote deals with procedure (votes on rules, recommittal motions, and the like), substantive amendments, or passage-and-conference reports.[16] Rules and other procedural votes usually provide the clearest case of partisan challenge. For a variety of reasons, the minority party especially will employ rules votes, such as motions to recommit, to present a united front against the majority party or the administration.[17]

Consistent with these trends, the index-of-likeness scores were also tabulated according to the three types of recorded votes possible (substantive votes, votes on passage and conference, and procedural votes) within each of the policy areas. The results appear in Tables 22 and 23. The problem of small numbers of cases becomes a bit more severe, since many bills that had recorded votes did not have recorded votes for each of the three kinds. Again, the overall trends not related to the arenas observed in Tables 20 and 21 appear here as well (that is, variations in partisanship across administrations, similarity of House-Senate partisanship). In addition, clear distinctions exist for the three types of recorded votes regardless of arena. In only three of forty instances (including the overall averages) do passage-and-conference votes not exhibit the lowest degree of partisanship. Also, procedural votes generally exhibit greater partisanship than substantive and passage-and-conference votes. This appears most prominently in the cumulative averages.

In terms of variances in partisanship between arenas, the trends generally follow the mixed patterns already reported. Among the differences that do occur, constituent policies seem to reflect more party voting at times, as seen in the House during the 1969—74 period and in the overall averages. Relatively little partisanship is exhibited in the distributive category, especially in the House votes, and redistributive policy votes at times show low and high partisan voting. Interestingly, the pattern of conflictual politics observed in the regulatory arena does not manifest itself in any significant way in high partisanship.

Based on the above, it would seem reasonable to conclude that partisanship per se is of no particular import with respect to the arenas. This is not to say that party differences are unimportant in roll-call voting (though the absence of strong, consistent trends may be a function of the reputed decline of party). It might simply be the case that party exhibits itself in ways that are more subtle and generally less apparent than in simple aggregations of recorded votes. However, for the moment we must leave it at the absence of partisanship as a factor that bears directly on the distinction inherent in differing policy types.[18]

Substantive Analysis

Obviously, bills can be profoundly affected by the amendments proposed to them. And given the argument that the nature of policy engenders varying consequences, it is logical to extend the argument to parts of

Table 22: Index of Likeness for Recorded Votes in the House According to Substantive, Pass and Conference, and Procedural Votes

	Distributive			Regulatory			Redistributive			Constituent		
	Sub-stan-tive	Pass, Conf-erence	Pro-ced-ural	Sub-stan-tive	Pass, Conf-erence	Pro-ced-ural	Sub-stan-tive	Pass, Conf-erence	Pro-ced-ural	Sub-stan-tive	Pass, Conf-erence	Pro-ced-ural
1969–74	74.9% (6)	89.2% (9)	89.8% (3)	66.1% (3)	85.2% (10)	80.3% (1)	75.5% (3)	90.9% (8)	70.8% (2)	57.6% (4)	82.2% (9)	68.8% (1)
1964–68	48.5 (3)	78.2 (8)	49.0 (4)	62.8 (6)	80.9 (11)	49.3 (7)	50.7 (8)	72.5 (15)	49.9 (9)	52.9 (3)	76.6 (6)	29.0 (3)
1961–63	35.2 (2)	68.8 (6)	33.4 (3)	30.3 (1)	17.5 (1)	19.4 (1)	30.4 (2)	54.2 (8)	25.6 (6)	....	35.1 (3)	12.9 (2)
1954–60	.... (8)	82.4 (3)	54.0 (4)	43.0 (6)	75.2 (5)	52.1 (3)	80.3 (3)	82.1 (14)	42.7 (8)	17.6 (1)	79.0 (6)	72.0 (5)
Mean—all years	60.5 (11)	80.8 (31)	56.0 (13)	55.5 (14)	79.0 (28)	50.4 (14)	58.3 (16)	75.5 (45)	43.3 (25)	50.8 (8)	74.7 (27)	49.3 (11)

NOTE: Tabulation for the tables is the same as that for Tables 20 and 21. Obviously, not all bills have recorded votes in all categories.

Table 23: Index of Likeness for Recorded Votes in the Senate According to Substantive, Pass and Conference, and Procedural Votes

	Distributive			Regulatory			Redistributive			Constituent		
	Sub-stan-tive	Pass, Conf-erence	Pro-ced-ural	Sub-stan-tive	Pass, Conf-erence	Pro-ced-ural	Sub-stan-tive	Pass, Conf-erence	Pro-ced-ural	Sub-stan-tive	Pass, Conf-erence	Pro-ced-ural
1969–74	75.6% (7)	92.3% (6)	55.6% (2)	68.1% (7)	91.2% (8)	58.6% (4)	72.7% (6)	90.2% (8)	66.7% (4)	79.8% (6)	90.2% (8)	18.9% (1)
1964–68	49.2 (3)	76.9 (4)	……	71.4 (9)	80.4 (10)	62.9 (8)	62.3 (13)	68.2 (13)	55.8 (4)	77.8 (1)	80.9 (4)	……
1961–63	50.4 (4)	83.4 (6)	23.0 (1)	37.0 (1)	19.5 (1)	……	46.4 (10)	67.0 (9)	35.9 (3)	26.6 (3)	69.5 (2)	……
1954–60	73.1 (6)	92.7 (5)	10.6 (1)	66.9 (7)	76.9 (4)	51.0 (5)	55.9 (16)	86.1 (13)	32.3 (6)	83.6 (4)	87.3 (6)	78.4 (5)
Mean—all years	66.2 (20)	86.9 (21)	36.2 (4)	67.6 (24)	80.9 (23)	58.4 (17)	57.9 (45)	77.5 (43)	46.6 (17)	69.4 (14)	85.4 (20)	68.4 (6)

NOTE: Tabulation for the tables is the same as that for Tables 20 and 21. Obviously, not all bills have recorded votes in all categories.

policies as well (that is, amendments). Thus, all substantive amendments proposed to bills have been themselves categorized according to the four policy types, so that each substantive amendment may be compared with the bill as a whole and assessed in terms of its impact on the bill. Such a breakdown will also allow comparisons with other amendments and bills in the same and different categories. In addition, I will consider the other two categories of recorded votes (procedural, and passage and conference).

According to my thesis, constituent and distributive bills that contradict the usual pattern of few or no floor amendments do so on the basis of one of two factors: the introduction of redistributive or regulatory amendments (considered not germane to the policy), which bring with them by definition a greater level of political conflict; or, characteristics of the bill itself that involve other than purely distributive or constituent elements (see, for example, the case description of the Lockheed loan in Chapter 3). As another example, a redistributive bill may, by its characteristics as stated in the bill, have distributive elements that also affect its particular configuration (see the case of the Area Redevelopment Act in Chapter 4). It is also expected that the amendments to regulatory bills will themselves be regulatory, and that the amendments to redistributive bills will be redistributive but also distributive and regulatory as well. Finally, it is important to note that the unit of analysis here is the relevant clause, amendment, or portion of the bill.

Distributive Bills. As I argued in the previous section, distributive bills possess a low average rate of votes per bill. However, a quick scanning of Table 12 reveals a number of deviations from this expected pattern. The pertinent question is, Can we account for these deviations? And if so, is the reasoning consistent with the logic of the arenas of power? It should be stated again here that the characteristics of the policy areas do not and are not expected to yield perfectly consistent results all of the time. The observed results are not monocausal, and as the percentages discussed in Tables 18 and 19 indicate, other factors can and do intervene. The arguments presented here, however, will illuminate this discussion.

It is in fact the case that, almost without exception, those bills in the distributive category that do involve several votes per bill are mixed cases either because of amendments proposed or because of the nature of the bill itself. The forty distributive bills making up this category fall quite neatly into two categories: those with few recorded votes (generally none to three in the House, none to two in the Senate) and those with many recorded votes. This division, however, between pure distributive bills (usually with few amendments) and mixed cases (usually with more amendments) is not made on the basis of number of roll-call votes but rather according to the bill itself or the substance of the amendments to the bill. The deviant bills (those with large numbers of roll calls) illustrate the point. Fourteen bills exhibit high roll calls. Five of these deal with urban mass transit. Four of the five have high roll calls in comparison with the average distributive bill (they are numbers 6, 12, 27, and 80 in Table 12, with House and Senate roll calls of three and ten, two and five, two and six, and three and fifteen, respectively). The fifth (number 34, roll calls two and none) is a mass-transit bill for only the District of Columbia. The first two bills deal with general highway aid but include provisions for urban mass transit. In the case of the first bill, two of the three House votes and three of the ten Senate votes dealt with aid to urban areas for mass transit. Two of the other amendments in the Senate were regulatory provisions, dealing with the regulation of vehicles using the interstate road system. For the second bill, two of the five amendments in the Senate concerned urban mass transit, and one amendment was regulatory, related to the posting of signs on interstate highways. The other amendments offered to these bills are either distributive unrelated to mass transit or procedural. The amendments to bill number 27 deal exclusively with mass transit or procedural questions. The amendments to bill number 80 are made up of two regulatory provisions, two redistributive provisions, and the rest either mass-transit provisions or procedural matters.

Two reasons thus suggest themselves for this greater amending activity. The first is the presence of amendments not germane to the policy. Given the characteristics of regulatory and redistributive policies, the raising of regulatory and redistributive issues in the context of a distributive bill has the effect of engendering greater activity. The presence of these amendments, however, does not in and of itself explain this greater activity. The second reason for this greater activity can be found in the nature of the policy itself. Bills dealing with the construction and maintenance of roads and transportation generally are clearly distributive, because they involve disaggregable, tangible benefits to contractors, industries, and individuals. But urban mass transit, while still in the same category, presents a more ambiguous case. In being limited to urban (read "poor, minority, ethnic, blue-collar") areas and built to accommodate large numbers of passengers, this overtly distributive issue has touched on a class, if not redistributive, concern, because those most likely to use urban mass transit are those who might be characterized as lower-middle or even lower-class working members of ethnic and minority groups. Mass transit itself is primarily a function of densely populated areas. Thus, mass-transit policy, though still distributive by the nature of the categorization process (see Chapter 2), carries with it some redistributive implications. Those implications reflect themselves in the amending process.

This distinction stands out even more clearly when mass-transit bills are compared with the other bills in the distributive category that deal with other forms of transportation (highways, for example). Of the five bills that deal with the subject, four (numbers 13, 59, 111, and 152 in Table 12) have roll calls in the House and Senate of none and none, three and one, none and none, and two and two, respectively. All of those amendments are either procedural or germane to the substance of the bill (distributive). The fifth, highway beautification (number 70) has two House and five Senate recorded votes. Of those, two in the Senate are regulatory provisions related to billboard advertising, and the rest are either procedural or germane to the substance of the bill. This bill and the five mass-transit bills are all considered therefore to be mixed cases. The greater number of amendments bears out this assessment.

It should be pointed out here that the bills in the substantive categories discussed throughout do not automatically fall into any one category. Whether a bill is distributive, regulatory, redistributive, or constituent depends on the wording of the statute itself. For example, if a mass-transit bill were exclusively administrative in composition, it would likely be considered constituent. Several bills falling into the same substantive categories are in fact categorized in different arenas and are discussed later in this section.

Eight other bills also fall under the heading of mixed cases. Three of them are the three trade bills on the distributive list (numbers 96, 126, and 151). The numbers of recorded votes in the House and Senate are three and eleven, two and six, and two and four, respectively. Trade and tariff bills are also classically distributive,[19] although they can take on regulatory characteristics.[20] Regardless, they can and do result in the clash of groups, since (for example) trade policy that is protectionist for one group may in fact be harmful to the interests of another group that relies on the commodity in question. The aggregation of otherwise disaggregated interests in this way can be seen in farm policies, discussed in the section on regulatory policies.

Most of the other five distributive policies falling in the mixed category, because they deviate from pure distribution, possess a series of amendments not germane to the policy. The bill authorizing construction of the Alaskan pipeline (number 7) had six clearly regulatory amendments offered out of nine recorded votes in the House and twenty in the Senate. Another twelve amendments were constituent but directly related to questions of federal jurisdiction and rights to sue over questions pertaining to the pipeline. The rest of the votes were procedural. The bill itself thus had some regulatory elements. Similarly, the bill that authorized an emergency business loan to Lockheed suggested some redistributive questions (number 20; see Chapter 3). Because the bill involved the idea of granting a special privilege (that is, a loan) to a corporation, and by implication a broader class, it raised questions of "welfare for the rich." While other distributive bills might be viewed in the same light, this particular bill squarely confronted the redistributive implications because of what was implied in the policy itself.

An airport development bill (number 35) has, of two recorded votes in the House and eight in the Senate, three that are clearly redistributive (dealing with user taxes) and two that are regulatory (related to restrictions regulating the use of federal funds for certain kinds of construction). A bill dealing with education for the health professions (number 89) has three redistributive amendments (related to student loans) and one that is regulatory (barring discrimination), out of two House and four Senate recorded votes. Finally, a college academic-facilities bill has four redistributive amendments (related to taxation and special scholarships) out of two House and five Senate recorded votes. In all of the above cases, the remaining roll-call votes are procedural and administrative.

This dichotomy between pure and mixed cases can be neatly summarized by tabulating the mean number of recorded votes for each bill in the two divisions making up the forty distributive policies. The mean number of recorded votes per bill for the twenty-six pure cases is 1.2 in the House and 1.0 in the Senate. For the fourteen bills in the mixed category, the means are 2.8 in the House and 7.7 in the Senate. Among the recorded votes in the pure-cases category (there were thirty-two votes in the House and twenty-five in the Senate), all were procedural, constituent, or germane to the bill. A content examination of the twenty-six pure-case bills validated their clearly distributive characteristics.

Given this rather clear-cut distinction between pure and mixed cases, one can see how policy characteristics themselves bear directly on the process and outcome of legislation. It is possible for a pure distributive bill to be subject to several amendments beyond routine procedural votes (one such bill, number 87, has two House and six Senate votes), but the likelihood is clearly that the conflict will be resolved in committee, rather than on the floor. But when other policy provisions or characteristics intervene, because of either the nature of the bill itself or the types of amendments offered, the political characteristics are also affected.

Regulatory Bills. The regulatory bills under consideration present clear examples of bills that engender a high degree of floor activity based on the nature of the bill itself, rather than because of the proposal of amendments not germane to the policy. Of the thirty-one cases at hand, only one bill has recorded votes that are not either regulatory (that is, germane), procedural, or constituent. Bill number 14, the Equal Educational Opportunities Act, contained a single redistributive provision relating to children from low-income families. The high number of recorded votes for the regulatory bills indicates the disposition of regulatory policies to engender high floor

creativity.[21] It is evident that a regulatory bill need not automatically engender lots of floor activity, but it is abundantly clear that when disputes do
arise, they are likely to spill out of committee and onto the floors of
Congress.

As mentioned in Chapter 2, a regulatory policy need not involve a bald
assertion of police power by the state, incorporating fines and prison
sentences. That might be considered the pure case of regulation, but
certain conduct can also be induced by the use of incentives. The cases of
five farm bills provide good examples of the inducement of particular
behavior through the use of subsidies.

During the 1950s and 1960s, a series of farm-subsidy bills (numbers 69,
79, 95, 109, 143, and 159) was proposed by three presidents in order to
buoy up certain commodity markets. The bills closely resembled each
other in format and content. They were concerned with commodities such
as cotton, wheat, feed grains, dairy, poultry, rice, wool, soybeans, peanuts,
and livestock. Each crop represents a set of farmer interests, and all were
competing for favorable government actions in support of their commodity.
Without governmental intervention, commodity markets have a long history
of volatility that keeps most farmers on a rollercoaster of boom-and-bust
cycles. Farmers have a basic tendency to overproduce in an attempt to
increase profits. But the more production increases, the more available the
commodity becomes, and the more the price drops.[22] Thus, government
intervention involves the establishment of parity prices for farmers (prices
for goods established at a prior period of normalcy). Farmers' profits are
maintained by paying them subsidies, and in some cases by restricting the
flow of cheaper, imported items from abroad (import quotas). Farm benefits usually take the form of price-support loans, direct payments, acreage-
diversion payments, and the specification of acreage allotments. The
standard method of "enforcement" to be found in these farm bills is, on its
surface, purely voluntary. Farmers who comply with production and
acreage allotments and land-diversion programs (letting land lie fallow or
growing other crops on it) receive a combination of price supports, direct
payments, marketing certificates and land-diversion payments. Farmers
who do not comply must simply deal on the market and receive the current
market price for their commodities. While the government is not directly
dictating individual behavior, it is clear that farmers who do not comply
cannot successfully compete on the open market with those who have the
benefit of federal supports. Several legal experts have in fact noted that
"agricultural price-support laws are a form of economic regulation."[23]

It might seem that all interests could be easily placated, but the politics of
these bills indicate that this is not so, primarily because the interests are
closely related. In fact, the various commodity interests tend to fall into two
camps. One, including feed grains, wheat, cotton, rice, and soybeans,

favors high-subsidy programs as protection from market forces. But other commodity interests, such as livestock and dairy farmers, favor low price supports for certain commodities, especially feed grains, because they are themselves consumers of these products and therefore prefer to pay the lowest possible price for feed and other grains. Further, some of the largest producers of grains often oppose supports because in an open-market situation the large producers stand the best chance of surviving a plunge in prices and then monopolizing the market. Also, those livestock farmers who own operations large enough to raise their own feed grains would oppose high subsidies as well, since the subsidy restrictions would limit the production of feed grains for their livestock. In addition to commodities, then, farm size also bears on the position of farmers on subsidies. Farmers' organizations reflect these distinctions.

The American Farm Bureau Federation tends to represent more wealthy farmers in the Midwest and South, and as a consequence, it favors a free-market, low-subsidy situation. The National Farmers Union has traditionally represented the family farmer, especially in the Midwest and North Central states. Not surprisingly, it favors high supports. The National Grange, an organization slowly declining in influence, still shows strength in the Northeast and Northwest. It too tends to favor high supports. Consumer groups also play a role, generally favoring low price supports because they mean lower prices at the supermarket. Representatives of urban areas often sympathize with these groups because of their constituencies, though it is more difficult to identify the "consumer interest" than the farm interests.[24]

What is important to note about this multiplicity of interests is that they tend to aggregate around two poles, one favoring high supports, the other low supports. This broad bipolar tendency can disassemble, depending on the nature of the farm issue, but for the cases discussed here, the bipolar arrangement of groups has indeed tended to occur. What is interesting about these two coalitions is the class and regional overtones inherent in the debate between wealthy and smaller farmers over the question of government support of markets versus free enterprise.[25]

The case of these farm policies, then, illustrates several points. First, a policy can regulate without employing traditional negative sanctions. Second, regardless of that fact, pluralistic politics still emerge. But third, it may be the case that the more mixed pattern of politics (aside from the obvious distributive elements), in part resembling those of redistribution, is a response to the nature of the policy, insofar as it implies the awarding of benefits to large classes in the characteristic redistributive fashion rather than regulating individual conduct. While these farm policies are still considered regulatory, an element of redistribution is incorporated in the policy itself, and this then has probably yielded the somewhat redistributive nature of the politics as described above.

The regulatory pattern of politics seems quite clear. Patterns of floor activity are based on characteristics associated with the bill itself, rather than on amendments not germane to the policy. Floor activity, though not guaranteed, is very likely. Thus, presidents face a special challenge when involving themselves with regulatory policies. The absence of substantive amendments that are not regulatory is a clear indication that regulatory bills are poor choices for the attachment of concrete benefits or other nongermane amendments, given the highly visible and conflictual nature of regulatory policies. By way of analogy, a cowboy wanting to eat his lunch in the saddle would be foolish to pick a bucking bronco. An old nag would be much more suitable. It turns out in fact that bills in the next policy category are much more suited to this kind of amending activity.

Redistributive Bills. If there is a dominant political characteristic of redistributive policies, especially as it pertains to the president's program and Congress, it is the struggle over disaggregation. Given the broad, environmental effects of redistributive policies, the specific problem consists of combatting the tendency of congressmen to break down policies that are systemic in scope into specific, identifiable benefits that can then be dispensed in the manner of distributive policies. Others have noted that the breakdown of redistributive policies is often the price paid, especially by presidents, for passage of a bill.[26] That can be clearly seen in terms of substantive amendments proposed to redistributive bills considered here. Of the fifty-seven redistributive bills, twenty have recorded votes that are either distributive or regulatory in character (another seven redistributive bills have no more than one roll call in both houses). This pattern contrasts sharply with the pattern of amendments to regulatory bills, but it is similar to some of the mixed cases discussed in the distributive category. Bills with more recorded votes, however, do not necessarily have nongermane amendments. Some that do not are welfare reform, amendments to the Social Security Act, and the Economic Opportunity Act of 1964 (numbers 24, 74, and 82). From Table 12 it can be seen that the number of recorded votes runs the gamut from none to many, as was the case with regulatory policies. The overall averages, however, are lower than those of regulatory bills.

The fight over disaggregation, central as it is to redistributive policies and their politics, is especially important because it is so often waged between the president and Congress. Several examples illustrate this trend. The important breakthrough for the role of the federal government in education policy occurred in 1965 with the passage of the Elementary and Secondary Education Act (ESEA, number 73). For the first time, funds and aid were aimed specifically at school districts with high numbers of poor and unemployed. The cost of this new direction, however, was the inclusion of other, more distributive amendments. In addition to aiding poor school districts, for example, aid was also provided to colleges and universities and to state and local education agencies.[27] Also, the aid directives in the bill granted state and local agencies considerable discretion in designing plans of distribution and allotting federal funds. This in and of itself is an open invitation to disaggregate.[28] The 1974 revision of the ESEA (number 1) was even broader in its disaggregation. The formula that determined how aid was to be distributed resulted in allowing every school district in the country to receive ESEA funds![29]

The same pattern of disaggregation also appears in another area—housing. During the heyday of President Johnson's Great Society, considerable effort was made to improve urban life, especially for the poor and minorities. Two programs aimed at combatting urban decay were the Housing and Urban Development acts of 1965 and 1968 (numbers 75 and 46). The first, composed of a variety of provisions, included a rent-supplement program for those who were too well off to be eligible for public housing but were below the income level necessary to afford private housing. The question of the dispensation of this element of the program alone could provoke a distributive, and therefore disaggregative, response based on disputes over who should be included and excluded. Obviously, a program that targeted selected lower-income groups would be much more confined in its effects, which would be limited primarily to large cities. A program broadening the income range, however, would spread housing and rent supplements much more widely and therefore diffuse the benefits. In addition to this provision, however, the 1965 act also included provisions for special mortgages with no down payment for veterans; grants for sewer and water facilities, parks, beautification projects, and new college dormitories; and an increase of payments to businesses moved by urban renewal.[30] While some of these provisions might be considered themselves redistributive, it is evident that they are not central to the immediate objective of providing decent housing within the means of the poor (see detailed discussion, Chapter 4).

The 1968 act followed a similar pattern. In addition to a federal subsidy program for home ownership by lower-income families, provisions of that act included federal assistance to developers of new towns and communities, district planning aid for rural areas, reinsurance against riot losses for private insurance companies, flood insurance, federal assistance to nonprofit hospitals, federal mortgages on vacation homes, and assistance for college housing.[31] Again, much of the debate was over the question of where to set income limits for eligibility for homeowners' and rental-assistance programs. The passage of this bill was considered relatively easy. In fact, observers commented at the time that the ease of passage was largely attributed to the wide array of programs incorporated in the bill.[32] It need hardly be pointed out that this degree of disaggregation, inserted to facilitate the passage of both bills, occurred at a time when the president was not only of the same party as the congressional majority but an influential former denizen of its halls.

The discussion here has not made a clear distinction between bills that are more purely redistributive and those that present a significant degree of disaggregation (usually in a distributive direction). Some bills, such as an extension of unemployment benefits (number 3), amendments to the Older Americans Act of 1965 (number 17), and an authorization bill for the food stamp program (number 37) remained relatively pure in their scope. In part, this may be due to the fact that the elderly, the unemployed, and food-stamp recipients are found virtually everywhere in America. It may be the case that the more ambitious the redistributive program, or the less clearly defined the recipient group, the greater is the likelihood that compromises through disaggregation will be made.[33] One of the dilemmas presidents face is that it is the granting of just the sort of concessions outlined above that exposes a president to charges of giving in to special interests at the expense of the poor, the middle class, or the average working man. The president, of course, may not necessarily oppose such disaggregation. But whether he does or not, it is a characteristic of political life that stems from the nature of the policy.

Constituent Bills. It was previously observed that the final policy category, constituent policy, follows the pattern of distributive policies, at least in its low number of average recorded votes per bill. Like distributive bills, a few cases have numerous amendments, and also like distributive policies, the bills break up into two groups. Of the thirty-seven bills in this category, most are pure cases of constituent policy. That is, they deal fundamentally with in-house, administrative affairs that do not customarily draw much interest or attention from outside government circles. Bills dealing with the civil service (numbers 33, 39, and 165), government reorganization (numbers 40 and 132), extension of the national debt (numbers 19, 94, and 101), and federal salaries (numbers 32, 33, 86, 157, 158, and 165) are examples of classic overhead functions. Some of these measures, however, do attract attention from the outside, as can be seen by the larger number of amendments offered. For example, the matter of federal salaries for elected officials has always been an issue of at least symbolic importance to constituents and government watchers. Three of the bills dealing with federal salaries included provisions raising salaries for elected officials (numbers 32, 86 and 158). The number of House and Senate roll calls for each bill was two and four, one and eleven, and two and four, respectively. The other three bills dealing with federal salaries (numbers 33, 157 and 165) had four and ten, one and none, and none and none. The large number of roll calls for bill number 33, postal reorganization, was due to other issues raised in the bill having to do with labor regulations governing employees and procedural matters. Only one of the fourteen recorded votes dealt with pay raises.

Another pure constituent policy that has become prominent outside Washington circles is the matter of increasing the national debt. In very recent times, with the advent of Proposition Thirteen and the drive for a constitutional amendment to balance the budget, the size of the national debt has become an important campaign issue. Of the three bills under consideration here (numbers 19, 94, and 100), with roll calls in the House and Senate numbering three and nine, two and two, and two and two, respectively, only the latest (taken in 1972) indicates a rise in interest.

The second type of constituent bill is those that might be considered mixed cases, either because of the amendments offered to them or because of the nature of the policy itself. Of the thirty-seven constitutent bills, only four have amendments that are not germane to the policy. They are the Equal Rights Amendment (number 18), a bill increasing the debt limit (number 19), the postal reorganization bill (number 33) and the Amended Voting Rights Act of 1965 (number 38). The ERA had a series of regulatory provisions proposed related to the status of women in society. The bill on the debt had some redistributive provisions relating to tax matters, the postal reorganization bill had some measures related to labor regulations for postal employees, and the Voting Rights Act had some provisions having to do with enforcement. The number of House and Senate roll calls was two and ten, three and nine, four and ten, and two and twenty-two, respectively.

In addition to these mixed cases, a few bills were also more controversial because of the nature of the bill itself. Two of them, the ERA and the Amended Voting Rights Act of 1965, are mentioned above. Two others are the establishment of the Council on Wage and Price Stability (number 5) and the Civil Rights Act of 1957 (number 139). Roll calls for the latter two are two and four, and two and thirteen. All of these bills incorporate areas that, while still constituent in nature, also touch broad groups and interests in society. Other bills in the constituent list also directly affect groups in society (such as the statehood bills and immigration laws), but their scope and impact are not equivalent to these bills, as they are more strictly administrative acts of classification. Roll calls for the six mixed cases average 2.5 in the House and 11.3 in the Senate. The averages for the other thirty-one bills are 1.4 and 1.4. Again, the exercise has been to examine those cases that run counter to the dominant trend of relatively little floor activity in terms of the substance of bills.

Some questions might still remain about the classification of some bills, notably the civil-rights bills. As pointed out before, the classification by arenas is not conducted automatically according to the subject matter of the bills. An indication of this is the fact that two civil-rights bills have been classified as regulatory, while two others are considered constituent. The former two bills are clearly regulatory, because the provisions of the bill dictate individual conduct concerning discrimination in voting, housing, public accommodations, and the like. The latter two bills, however, are clearly constituent in makeup. To take the 1957 act as an example, creation of the federal Civil Rights Commission was the key provision. That act also allowed the president to appoint a new assistant attorney general, gave that attorney general the power to seek injunctions and levy fines, and extended the jurisdiction of federal district courts. While all these provisions had clear implications for the civil-rights movement, the statute itself is composed of administrative, overhead provisions.

Previously, I have argued that constituent policies are least conflictual and therefore are very amenable to presidential manipulations. A recent case serves to illustrate the ability of presidents to hold sway over at least one constituent policy area—budgeting. President Carter's troubles with the Congress were widely chronicled in the popular press. Thus it was all the more surprising (and pleasing, since it confirms the logic of my analysis) to read reports of a notable political success by Carter in holding the line set out in his budget resolution, approved by Congress in 1979. One reporter registered his own surprise, as well as that of a variety of Washington observers and participants, at the degree to which Carter's proposal was adhered to not only by the Congress, but by interest groups as well: "Even domestic interest groups, which have bitterly criticized the President's budget, operated on Capitol Hill this spring within the (budgetary) framework the Administration had developed."[34] Carter's "startling" success seems less of an anomaly in the light of policy analysis.

As indicated above, constituent policies seem to be gaining greater importance to interest groups and others in society. It is difficult to predict how far this trend will go and what effect it will have on presidential agendas, and for that matter on congressional ones. Carter, however, devoted a significant amount of his energy for domestic programs on constituent policies, including proposals to streamline the entire federal regulatory process, his reform of the civil service (see Chapter 3), revision of the CIA charter, federal election reform, creation of three new cabinet-level departments, including the Department of Natural Resources (later dropped) and separate Education and Energy departments, and a plan to overhaul the federal pay system.

Summary

The discussion in this chapter has focused heavily on bills and their characteristics (both policy and political). Of necessity, the emphasis has been more on congressional action, because all things that are legislative are also congressional. I have not lost sight of the fact, however, that the bills discussed herein are presidential proposals.

The political patterns we have observed match well with those projected. Where patterns have deviated, those deviations have been found to be consistent with variations traced back to the makeup of the bills themselves. The degree of floor activity, as measured by the number of roll-call votes, increased progressively from constituent, to distributive, to redistributive, to regulatory policies, with these patterns appearing more dramatically in the Senate than in the House. Partisanship was found to have no particular, consistent relationship to policy types. Substantive analysis of the bills revealed the existence in each policy area of two types of bills: those considered pure cases, which closely followed the ideal patterns associated with descriptions of the policy areas; and those considered mixed cases either because of the nature of the bill itself (such as a distributive bill with redistributive elements, like urban mass-transit measures), or as a result of amendments to those bills. The mixed cases were identified by the composition of the bill itself. The deviant political patterns were seen to flow from these characteristics.

7: The Four Presidencies and the Policy Environment

The presidency is an ongoing institution, yet it has changed in both form and style over the years. In part, this has been a response to the maturation of the legal and political system. But we usually assume that much of the changing nature of the presidency has sprung from the men we have elected to hold that office. In 1980 the nation elected a president acknowledged to embody a political philosophy rejected, if not discredited, some sixteen years earlier. The Reagan election represented a repudiation of the New Deal tradition (a tradition that Carter attempted to identify with in his unsuccessful bid for reelection) and, by extension, an affirmation of a new and more conservative policy agenda.

But what, if anything, does this mean for presidential-congressional relations? If my arguments throughout this work are correct, a Reagan mandate (and the leadership that implies), even as the forward line of "a new American conservatism," would not dramatically alter the fundamental policy patterns described to this point.

The conclusions of an exhaustive study of presidential-congressional relations reach a very similar conclusion. "Presidential legislative skills do not seem to affect support for presidential policies [in Congress] despite what conventional wisdom leads us to expect. Sources of information about presidential-congressional relations, particularly the press, seem to have focused upon the more unique examples of these relations, implying that what they were presenting was typical. When we rigorously and systematically evaluate the evidence, however, we reach different conclusions."[1]

To reach the conclusion that party ties, political skills, ability to propose innovative programs, ideological inclinations, and the like are all objectively unimportant for presidents in their dealings with Congress would still be too great a leap. These factors are, however, so much a part of the conventional wisdom (as discussed in the introduction and Chapter 1) that academics, journalists, and new presidents should all take notice. The whole point of my analysis has been to articulate an alternate explanation of interactions between the president and Congress. In keeping with this objective, analysis has spanned several stages, from a broad overview of a universe of bills to the examination of the details of several cases. In touching on several levels for the same set of data, I have tried to establish, as deliberately as possible, the validity of policy types in terms of their impacts on presidential programs.

At the outset, the case studies provided specific, descriptive accounts of eight successful presidential proposals (see Table 1 for a summary). The "special-interest president" operated in the distributive arena with limited efficacy. Presidential support had an impact, but only insofar as it coincided with the preferences of the congressional committees' leadership (as in the Wilderness Act). When some element of redistribution was present, the president's role was enhanced (Lockheed loan). The regulatory bills were political hot potatoes, both for the president and for Congress. As "presidential broker," the chief executive had the most vexatious time accommodating both his own interests and those of an array of interested congressmen and groups. Especially in the case of the crime control bill, Johnson was reduced to the role of an often-hapless referee.

The "public-interest president" associated with redistributive bills, on the other hand, exemplified the sort of presidential activism and leadership that Harold Laski, Clinton Rossiter, James MacGregor Burns, and others have extolled. The issues involved (housing, area redevelopment) sparked controversy, but the president was at the helm, steering and guiding the legislative ship through stormy seas. Constituent policies similarly afforded presidents political initiatives. The "administrative president" claim to sovereignty here, however, rested in the concern with overhead, administrative matters. Whether defense reorganization or civil-service reform, the president's longstanding status as head of the executive afforded him successes approached only in redistributive matters (but without the same degree of wrangling and bargaining).

In Chapter 5, we approached the four presidencies from a far more quantitative perspective, yet the numbers demonstrated general consistency and congruence with the cases. Overall, presidents proposed to and got from Congress more redistributive bills than any other type, followed by constituent and distributive, with regulatory bills trailing the list. Distributive proposals fluctuated with the president's electoral cycle (whereas redistributive bills did not), and the other policy types followed patterns suggested earlier in the chapter. The final analytical chapter dramatized political conflict over the president's bills by revealing that the greatest political storms centered over the president's regulatory bills, followed in order by redistributive, distributive, and constituent. Also, degree of party voting in Congress was found to have no relation to the four categories of bills. The descriptive portion of the chapter elucidated the difference in amendment patterns and clarified the difference between pure and mixed policy types (see Figure 3). The aim was to demonstrate not only that policy types make a difference for the president's program, but that the mixing of types also produces mixed results that vary with the components infused in a given bill.

Lest there by any confusion regarding the relation between the rank orderings of political conflict in Chapter 6 versus those of influence in Chapter 5, Table 24 illustrates their juxtaposition.

Table 24: Rank Orderings for Types of Bills According to Presidential Influence, Presidential Involvement, and Political Conflict

	Degree of Presidential Influence (Chaps. 3, 4)	Presidential Involvement and Success (Chap. 5)	Degree of Political Conflict (Chap. 6)
Constituent ("administrative")	1	2-3	4
Redistributive ("Public interest")	2	1	2
Distributive ("special interest")	3	2-3	3
Regulatory ("broker")	4	4	1

NOTE: 1 = highest; 4 = lowest

Thus, for example, while presidents push for and get redistributive bills in largest numbers, they have greater influence over constituent bills, in large part because of the lower level of political conflict associated with this policy type. The question was asked in the first chapter, Does the type of policy with which the president deals determine the shape of the political pattern? At least with respect to Congress and the president's annual legislative program; the answer is yes.

Presidential Interactions and Policy Types

Figure 7 summarizes in a more visual way the varying characteristics associated with presidential policy making as they have been set out up until now. The figure is an adaptation of the arenas-of-power scheme presented in Chapter 2 (Figure 2).

The headings in Figure 7 describe, in dichotomized fashion, two dimensions. The left-hand headings deal with the level of political conflict observed. As I noted at the start of Chapter 3, the four policy areas divide clearly into two groups: those engendering relatively little conflict in Congress (distributive and constituent) and those engendering relatively greater conflict (regulatory and redistributive). This was established by the amendment counts and the case studies. Note that the division of "low political conflict" and "high political conflict" coincides with the headings in the original arenas-of-power scheme in Figure 2 of "remote" and "immediate" likelihood of coercion. Thus, not surprisingly, relatively little political conflict occurs when the likelihood of coercion is minimal. It is the anticipation of governmental acts considered likely to directly affect behavior, whether of the individual or of the environment, that will generate the greatest debate and controversy.

A similar pattern can be observed for the other dimension. What is labeled "low presidential prerogative" and "high presidential prerogative" in Figure 7 coincides with the "applicability of coercion" dimension in the arenas scheme of "individual conduct" and "environment of conduct," respectively. This also follows a clear logic, because the nationally elected leader has greater influence over and concern with policies that are diffuse and widespread in their effect, and relatively less influence over and concern with policies that are very specific in their application. Considerations of the president as national leader are coincident with policies that are broader in scope. Policies that are more particularistic are, by their nature, more directly under the purview and prerogative of the particular congressmen and other political actors affected. Given this arrangement of marginal characteristics, the pattern of greatest to least presidential influence would seem to follow progressively from constituent, to redistributive, to distributive, to regulatory. My actual findings generally bear out this conclusion. While we saw in Chapter 5 that the president chooses to propose more redistributive bills than any other type, this does not contradict the conclusion that his greatest (easiest) successes occur for constituent policies, as noted. The cases indicate that the political costs paid by presidents for redistributive policies are greater for these than for constituent policies. In addition, the immediate political visibility and applicability of redistributive policies is likely to be far greater and therefore of more immediate political use to presidents than that of most constituent policies. It should, however, be noted that in recent years constituent policies have become more important as public issues. Interest in government reorganization, attempts to balance the federal budget, the recent countrywide movements to pass measures inspired by California's Proposition Thirteen, and a generalized renewal of the debate over the size and degree of influence government should have in affecting the lives of citizens—all these imply a shift in the agenda toward constituent issues. However, if the

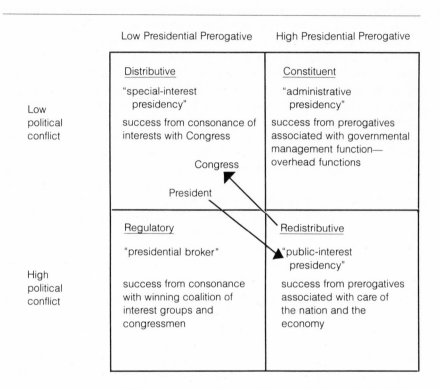

	Low Presidential Prerogative	High Presidential Prerogative
Low political conflict	**Distributive** "special-interest presidency" success from consonance of interests with Congress	**Constituent** "administrative presidency" success from prerogatives associated with governmental management function—overhead functions
High political conflict	**Regulatory** "presidential broker" success from consonance with winning coalition of interest groups and congressmen	**Redistributive** "public-interest presidency" success from prerogatives associated with care of the nation and the economy

Figure 7: The Arenas of Power Applied to Presidential Policy Making

case of Carter's civil-service reform is any indication, such a shift is much more superficial than might be otherwise supposed.

Within each box in Figure 7 is a description of how presidents are most likely to achieve their policy objectives through Congress. Success is possible for policies in each area, as is failure, but the likelihood of success, as noted, is greatest for constituent and redistributive policies. In the case of these two, the president benefits from the deference and responsibilities associated with management of government (and particularly the rest of the executive branch) and care of the nation. Distributive policies, particularistic in scope and concrete in the benefits they provide, are the jealous domain of individual congressmen and committees. When the president's distributive proposals coincide with the benefits sought by congressmen, success is likely. That success, however, derives less from presidential intervention (as in the case with constituent and redistributive policies) than from coincidence of interests. When the president violates the norms of congressional distribution, he is asking for a battle that will cost him dearly, whether he wins or loses.

If the normal political pattern for distributive policies can be described as calm, the pattern for regulatory policies is volatile. Here, the imposition of the president's own policy preferences is even more problematic. Not only is Congress likely to be splintered by such issues (and indeed is frequently reluctant to deal with them at all), but strong, if not pluralistic, pressure from interest groups is likely to be felt here more than elsewhere. The cases illustrated the more dramatic political conflicts and scope of policy changes associated with regulatory measures. The president is best off when he can mediate among groups and congressmen in the hopes of establishing a coalition that will see the bill through. The finding of least presidential influence over regulatory policies contradicts Lowi's earlier assessment that the president has greater influence here.[2]

The dotted arrows in Figure 7 indicate directions in which Congress and the president are likely to "pull" policies. The trend toward disaggregation of redistributive policies toward the distributive box has been amply demonstrated. On the other hand, the president will often be disposed to expand distributive issues toward the redistributive end. This movement can occur within as well as between boxes; that is, some distributive policies are likely to resemble redistributive policies more than others (for example, the Lockheed loan). Similarly, some redistributive policies will resemble distributive policies more than others.

It would complete the symmetry of this argument if it could be said that similar arrows could be drawn, and relationships established, between regulatory and constituent policies.[3] However, no clear evidence has appeared that would validate this proposed relationship. Despite the fact that the changes made in regulatory policies were more sweeping than for any other cases observed, those changes occurred within the context of regulation. The drive of interest groups, the Congress, and the president was not away from regulation toward some other policy type per se; rather, it involved disputes over the desirability and scope of regulation. In Johnson's crime bill, sentiment over gun regulation was divided between those who wanted it and those who did not. In the case of airline deregulation, most carriers opposed any major changes in the existing system, while a few carriers and the administration favored the relaxation of controls. The disputes centered on basic questions: Should we have regulation? If so, what should its scope and type be? While this implies "movement" within the regulatory box, there is no such observed constituent pattern. Congress tends to favor the trend toward disaggregation, but interest groups, the president, and Congress do not necessarily favor certain degrees of regulation. Interest groups, for example, who might be expected by the uninitiated to oppose regulation, frequently seek it. And when regulation is sought, it is not necessarily regulation by subsidy or some other, less coercive form. Constituent policies also do not exhibit any trends toward "movement" in the regulatory direction. As mentioned, constituent policies can possess mixed attributes in the way distributive policies do. There is, however, no clear movement discernible toward or away from mixed and pure cases or other policy areas, at least with respect to the president and Congress.[4]

In these distinctive ways, then, policy characteristics determine the shape of the president's political universe, at least as it relates to his dealings with Congress. It would be a mistake to oversimplify these processes and overgeneralize their applicability. Policy characteristics do not fall in the categories on a mutually exclusive basis; just as clearly, there is still a wide range of factors affecting what the president and Congress do that cannot be directly tied to policy characteristics. But the firmness of the findings validates the logic of the analysis in ways central to presidential behavior. And the clusters of characteristics associated with policy types can be clearly tied to the logic of the "four presidencies."

Applications to Existing Analysis of the Presidency

This research has shown how policy analysis applies to elements of presidential behavior primarily by examining new data and new cases. But this approach can offer much to existing studies of the presidency as well, and in doing so, it can increase our understanding and at the same time further validate the analysis. A few examples, arbitrarily selected, will serve to illustrate my point.

One study looked at President Carter's attempt to eliminate nineteen projects to develop water resources that had been approved by Congress. That attempt touched off a fierce political battle that left the President wounded. The author of the study attributes Carter's relative failure primarily to the usual set of factors associated with the Carter presidency—notably, his lack of political experience, his role as a Washington "outsider," his moralist background, his rationalist approach to policy making, and his personal disdain for compromise.[5] Although all of these elements operated at some level, the author himself notes that presidents in the past have usually deferred to Congress on such matters.[6] Clearly, both this tradition of presidential deference and Carter's own political drubbing over this issue are readily identifiable and understandable when we acknowledge that the issue was a classic distributive policy. A single case that seemed to arise from Carter's idiosyncracies becomes much more consistent with the experiences of previous presidents, as well as more predictable in terms of process and likely outcome when considered in the light of general policy characteristics (the "special-interest presidency").

The written accounts of Franklin Roosevelt's efforts to obtain passage of the Fair Labor Standards Act of 1938 hardly agree with the usual assessments of his presidency. Roosevelt labored for a year on the bill, "only to have it mutilated and emasculated by Congress at a time when both houses were 80 percent Democrat."[7] The labor bill involved redistributive elements (minimum wage standards), but its main purpose was "to eliminate as rapidly as possible labor conditions detrimental to the health, efficiency and general well-being of the workers."[8] In short, it was principally a regulatory bill. Roosevelt's inability to maintain the integrity of the bill is indicative, by this analysis, not so much of his own faults, but rather of characteristics associated with regulatory policies (yielding the "presidential broker").

We can observe a very similar pattern in an account of the Clean Air Act Amendments of 1977. This regulatory bill, pushed strongly by the Carter administration, nevertheless was resolved with little evident manipulation or influencing from the White House. Indeed, the floor manager of the bill commented that the politics surrounding the bill involved "the heaviest lobbying I've seen in 23 years in Congress."[9]

The president's involvement in redistributive policies, as identified in published accounts of presidential policy making, also conforms to the policy logic. One general assessment of economic policy making (usually redistributive) notes that, though the Constitution seems to assign such responsibilities to the Congress, the president has taken the initiative since the beginning of the republic in matters relating to developing fiscal policies, especially in the areas of taxation and expenditures.[10] The perspectives provided by an understanding of redistributive policies and their relation to the presidency (the "public-interest presidency") can be seen in a wide array of conventional case descriptions such as fiscal policy,[11] the Economic Opportunity Act of 1964,[12] and Medicare.[13]

These examples can be extended ad infinitum, but they need not be to make the fundamental point. The purpose of selecting the above examples from the literature is not to question the analyses of the authors, but rather to demonstrate how a diverse and seemingly contradictory series of policy cases related to the presidency can be employed beyond the intention of the authors (with the use of the policy framework) to provide a unified accounting of presidential policy making, thus enhancing the value of these cases. In doing so, our understanding of the presidency itself is increased.

Of Presidents and Policies

If presidential influence over legislative outcomes varies, as it does, what then does this say for prescriptions concerning present and future presidential behavior? If one were to assume the guise of Richard Neustadt, the prescriptive implications would be clear. The best way for presidents to maximize presidential influence and success (assuming, as Neustadt does, the desirability of these goals), at least with respect to Congress, would be to concentrate their legislative attentions on constituent and redistributive policy efforts, with perhaps a sprinkling of distributive bills aimed at pacifying particular congressmen and constituents. The high political costs and absence of immediate rewards connected with regulatory policies would discourage any major efforts in this area. Why, then, has the pattern for presidential behavior failed to follow such a prescription?

Aside from the fact that no president has ever heard of the arenas of power, presidents have not and are not likely to follow such a pattern, because presidential behavior is not purely instrumental. Patterns of policy making involve institutional and extrainstitutional demands, expectations, and needs, all of which focus upon the Oval Office (a fact Neustadt recognizes). Despite the high costs and low immediate political rewards associated with regulatory policies, there are times when policy needs can only be served through regulation, whether private interest seeks it or national interest impels it. Presidential action may be slow in coming, but a policy reaction, when it comes, is most likely to come from the president first. A good contemporary example is the nation's energy problem. Ever since the oil embargo of 1973, it has been clear to most that this and other Western societies were faced with an inexorable squeeze involving increasing demand, declining supplies, and a long-term price spiral. Presidents Nixon and Ford produced no concrete plan to counter these problems, and it was not until 1977 that Carter proposed his comprehensive energy package. What is most important about the four-year lag is not the absence of presidential action so much as the total lack of action by the Congress, the bureaucracies, and localities.[14] All of the other organs of government waited for the president to act. This example typifies the president's policy-making situation. Once Carter submitted his admittedly modest package, calling for a restructuring of crude-oil production, deregulation of natural gas, conversion to coal, increasing fuel economy in automobiles, and tax credits for home insulation and solar heating, the Congress and interest groups wasted little time in tearing into the proposal, particularly in the Senate. In this respect also the political shape of this primarily regulatory package fits the classic regulatory pattern. The political pattern was repeated early in 1979, when the House voted down a modest standby gas-rationing plan (though it was later passed). It was labeled a stunning defeat for Carter. As these cases illustrate, despite footdragging and reluctance in all quarters of government, it was and is the president who is expected to and usually does take the first step for important public issues, especially when other political actors are reluctant to do so.

The Carter administration provided an especially interesting case because the daily news reports offered contemporary confirmations of the logic of presidential continuities when considered in terms of policies and related political actions (in addition to the Carter cases discussed in previous chapters). For example, Carter sent a proposal to Congress in early 1979 to reduce costs for the ailing social-security program. It included such provisions as eliminating automatic death benefits paid in lump sums to all survivors of social-security recipients, so that only those in need would receive them; establishing a need requirement for children of social-security recipients attending college; and eliminating the minimum payment. These changes alone would save the social-security system over $400 million. Though the proposals were considered reasonable, Congress balked at the cuts. The reason, acknowledged in the press, was that Congress was treating these proposals not as manipulations to help rescue a floundering social program, but as reductions of concrete benefits that they did not want to be responsible for denying. Whether the cuts were necessary, just, or fiscally sound was not as important a concern as the fact that the denial or reduction of social-security benefits would offend groups and interests who were then recipients.[15] Such was the distributive congressional reaction to a redistributive proposal.

The centrality of distributive benefits to Congress was dramatized by two cases of policies important to Carter—the Panama Canal Treaty and the SALT II Treaty. Senator Herman Talmadge had been pushing for a direct-aid farm plan that officials of the Agriculture Department had opposed. But the week before the vote on the Panama Canal Treaty, the Agriculture Department withdrew its opposition to the Talmadge farm bill—by all accounts at Carter's behest—and the formerly wavering Talmadge announced his support for the treaty. Between the two Panama Canal Treaty votes, Talmadge was allowed to bring his farm bill to the floor on a special dispensation to obtain quick passage.[16]

More recently, Carter was faced with the problem of obtaining votes for the SALT II Treaty. One of the most important potential sources of support was Senate Majority Leader Robert Byrd. In May 1979 Byrd was reported to have talked with officials at the Environmental Protection Agency about the relaxation of pollution standards for the burning of coal. West Virginia, Byrd's home state, is a major coal producer, but burning the high-sulfur coal mined there causes more pollution than burning cleaner coal. Several government and congressional officials were quoted as saying that Byrd was trying to obtain the president's support for relaxed pollution restrictions in exchange for support of the treaty.[17]

These cases of vote buying and porkbarreling are certainly not unusual or startling to anyone familiar with the congressional process. They do illustrate, however, the importance senators attach to their own particular distributive interests (while the preceding example involves regulations, the effect of Byrd's proposal would have been to allow greater coal production and consumption in West Virginia and other coal states); the value placed on presidential approval, even for very particularistic policies; and the price a president often has to pay for a policy (in this case, two treaties) that does not have any readily disaggregable elements which might otherwise be used to buy support.

Extending the Analysis

The policy-politics logic of this project has incorporated a relatively narrow subsection of the political universe. The decision to limit this inquiry to the president's domestic legislative proposals for a twenty-year period proved to be sound because it facilitated a thorough analysis of an inadequately examined aspect of the presidency and policy making. It is evident, however, that the logic of this analysis might be extended beyond the present time frame. The other half of presidential policy making—nonlegislative policy making, incorporating executive orders, proclamations, decrees, and the like, all of which have the force of law without congressional approval—could be analyzed employing the same methods. While the emphasis here has been on factors affecting policy making, an analysis of executive orders could touch more directly on implementation. For example, is it true that the implementation of a presidential directive is more likely to occur if the directive deals with a redistributive policy, as compared to a regulatory policy? Does the general proportion of nonlegislative policy making for presidents follow the patterns of legislative policy making in terms of the distribution of policies across policy areas? And how does that affect the president's ability to deal with the bureaucracy?

My approach suggests a second avenue of analysis: a broadening of the historical perspective. An extension of the time dimension might reveal some fundamental trends in policy types and emphases that would inform an extended historical analysis about the activities not only of the president but also of the government itself. Indeed, it has already been suggested that much of what set off the New Deal era was Roosevelt's embracing of a whole series of redistributive policies that had formerly not been the concern of the federal government.[18] A detailed analysis of policies across historical eras might reveal trends about the relations of state to society that have not been evident from other analyses.

The arenas of power can also apply to comparative analysis. Several studies have attempted this cross-national approach in a general way,[19] indicating that it might provide a useful tool for comparison of executives across nations, at least for industrial democracies. Many have noted similarities in the fate of national executives, and policy comparisons might provide a convenient and commensurable method of analysis.

Finally, in making distinctions within the policy areas, our analysis opens the door to a further refinement. For example, in the distributive area we observed that bills fell into two categories, those that were pure or clear-cut cases, and those that were mixed. Such a division implies not only a dichotomy, but perhaps even a rank ordering of policies according to their degree of distributiveness. Such an alteration (which could, in theory, be applied to all the areas) would require a rethinking of the entire scheme. So ambitious an objective, however, awaits future labors.

Concluding Thoughts

Perhaps the final (not to say ultimate) question we are left with is that of governing itself. How can the system be effectively goaded to respond to the needs and problems of modern society?

One evident, recurrent nostrum fed the body politic has been the strong president (America's version of the man on the white horse). But how fruitful is this search for a strong activist when the analysis reveals that, in legislative mátters at least, recent presidents are pulled along by the same policy currents? If governing depends less on men than we thought, and more on policy constraints, then maybe we should alter the strong-president/weak-president vocabulary by talking instead about strong and weak policies, or more to the point, policies that are more and less susceptible to presidential influence. This is only a halfhearted suggestion, but it underlies the whole point of this book. Vietnam, Watergate, the decline of party, the rise of congressional incumbency, and increased mass disaffection with politics have all been credited with changing the face of the modern presidency. Yet the answers uncovered not only bear little relation to contemporary historical occurrences, they in fact challenge the usual assumptions about the ways in which the institution has been shaped. Our presidency is not simply an agglomeration of discrete administrations. It is a web composed of institutional and policy imperatives that shape, direct, and channel presidential activities into what we have come to label the "four presidencies." These "four presidencies" force us to give greater attention to the president's policy agenda, with the understanding that different segments of the agenda require different politics. The issues that a president pursues, in short, will have as much if not more to do with his success than his skills.

Appendix: Coding Procedures for the 5,463 Cases

The coding of bills into the four arenas-of-power categories has posed a major obstacle to the application of Lowi's theoretical scheme. One of the purposes of this book has been to rectify this problem by formulating a set of coding rules (in Chapter 2) and offering some illustrations. The detailed discussions in the case-study chapters and the chapter analyzing the set of 165 bills serve this latter purpose.

The coding procedures applied to the 5,463 cases in Chapter 5 are not illustrated in the same detail, however, and since this coding involves a large number of cases described in no more than a few sentences, some examples will be presented here to clarify these coding procedures. Coding guidelines are derived from the set of coding rules and the general characteristics of the policy arenas.

As mentioned in Chapter 5, the coding of this long list of cases was more problematic than that of the case studies and the 165 cases because of the sheer size of the list and the brevity of the bill descriptions. Nevertheless, most cases were not difficult to code because the descriptions provided concise summaries of the main points of these bills. (An intercoder-reliability score of .871 was obtained, based on the coding of 201 randomly selected cases drawn from the full list.) Also, many of the bills were repetitive, so that the same kinds of bills reappeared often throughout this period.

Presented below are some bills as they were summarized in the *Congressional Quarterly* Boxscore. The logic for many of these categorizations stems from the rules for classification and the description of the arenas categories in Chapter 2. The descriptions are presented in an order not related to the arenas categories, as this was the nature of the *CQ* presentation. These randomly selected summaries of bills are indicative of the coding that was involved across the twenty-year period.

"Regulate the sale of medical devices." When the description says the bill will regulate, we accept that this involves the manipulation of individual conduct through an implicit or explicit sanction. Regulatory.

"Exempt stationary sources from federal and state air and water quality laws and regulations." Though this bill involves the lifting of some controls, the fact of the removal of regulations is no less relevant than the imposition of regulations (see the case of airline deregulation). Regulatory.

"Replace enforcement conference and hearing mechanism [of the Environmental Protection Agency] with a provision for swifter public hearings as a prelude to issuance of abatement orders or requiring revision of standards." The EPA is principally concerned with regulation, but a bill that restructures its investigative mechanisms is administrative (concerned with overhead functions) and is therefore constituent.

"Appropriate $14 million in supplemental funds for the Department of Agriculture to liquidate contract authority required to build 500 miles of forest roads." The construction of forest roads is a particularistic project of the sort classically associated with porkbarreling. Distributive.

"Bring the Juvenile Court into the new District of Columbia Court of general jurisdiction." Questions of court (governmental) jurisdiction are procedural matters that determine where and when cases will be heard. Constituent.

"Extend the excise taxes on autos and telephone services at their present rate through December 31, 1971." Taxes are always considered redistributive, unless the bill outlines some other specific function, such as a regulatory tax (see Chapter 2). Redistributive.

"Establish the San Rafael Wilderness in Los Padres National Forest, California." The creation of national park lands is distributive (see Chapter 3).

"Provide $750 million for urban renewal programs." Urban renewal programs are targeted, in the legislation, to blighted, poor sections of cities, and are therefore aimed to help the disadvantaged. Redistributive.

"Increase Social Security payroll taxes (excluding hospital taxes) to 4.5% in 1969 and 5% in 1973." Again, tax-law changes. Redistributive.

"Enact legislation to create a federal electric bank and a federal telephone bank to provide additional sources of loans for rural electric and telephone co-operatives." A discrete benefit (loans) available to anyone within the category covered by "co-ops," subject to application guidelines, is distributive.

"Creation of a new cabinet-level Department of Labor and Business." Creation of an administrative department, involving changes in patterns of authority, is constituent.

"Extend the prohibition on purchase of firearms to alcoholics, in addition to minors, mentally ill, felons and drug addicts." Again, regulating additional conduct with the use of sanctions. Regulatory.

"Prescribe each step of the jury selection process for federal courts." Clarification of governmental procedures concerning jury selections. Again a matter of governmental authority. Constituent.

"Increase the federal minimum hourly wage standard to $1.40 in 1967 and $1.60 in 1968." The minimum wage is a salary floor for those at the bottom rung of the salary ladder, and it applies automatically to all at that level, across the board. Redistributive.

"Prescribe orders of procedure in the event of a President's incapacity by injury, illness, senility or other affliction." This is a matter of governmental (executive) authority and the conditions under which it may be exercised. Constituent.

"Authorize open space grants to cities for landscaping, installation of outdoor lights and benches, creating attractive cityscapes along roads and in business areas and for other beautification purposes." Beautification involves construction (public-works) projects available on a discrete basis to those cities that apply. Distributive.

"Repeal, on 1/1/66, the documentary stamp taxes on the issuance and transfer of stocks and bonds and on deeds of conveyance." A change in a tax is, again, redistributive.

"Delete from House tax bill the reduction in the rate of capital gains taxation." Once more, a change in a tax rate bill. Redistributive.

"Enact legislation to permit farmers to participate in a certificate program for wheat producers effective for the 1964 crop." A subsidy program available to wheat farmers on an application basis. Distributive.

"Increase funds in fiscal 1964 for aid to children through the public assistance and child welfare grant programs." Extension of a social-service program to a broad class of needy people, based on their condition. Redistributive.

"Direct the Federal Trade Commission to enforce regulations requiring lenders and vendors to disclose to borrowers in advance the amounts to be paid for credit." A directive, elaborating on disclosure laws, backed with enforcement. Regulatory.

"Extend the saline water conversion research program." Research programs involve the awarding of discrete benefits (research funds) to individuals and organizations, in the manner of a subsidy through an applications process. Distributive.

"Authorize an item veto of appropriation and authorization bills for the President." A bill authorizing an executive power over legislative activities. Constituent.

"Amend the Taft-Hartley Act to require employers to file non-communist affidavits." A requirement to submit statements to employers that prescribes a particular kind of individual conduct. Regulatory.

Notes

Preface

1. For a recent example of this, see James MacGregor Burns, *Leadership* (New York: Harper and Row, 1978).

2. Historians have a penchant for ranking presidents according to "greatness." See for example, Arthur Schlesinger, Sr., "Our Presidents: A Rating by Seventy-four Historians,"*New York Times Magazine,* 29 July 1962, pp. 12, 40–43.

3. In his exhaustive analysis of presidential character, James David Barber concludes that our salvation is precisely this—to elect good presidents (active-positives). Is this advice we can take to the polls? See *The Presidential Character* (Englewood Cliffs, N.J.: Prentice-Hall, 1977).

Chapter One

1. Aaron Wildavsky, ed., *The Presidency* (Boston: Little, Brown, 1969), p. ix.

2. Hugh Heclo, *Studying the Presidency* (New York: Ford Foundation, 1977), p. 5.

3. Norman C. Thomas, "Studying the Presidency: Where and How Do We Go from Here?" *Presidential Studies Quarterly* 7 (Fall 1977): 169.

4. Anthony King, "Executives," in *Handbook of Political Science,* ed. Fred Greenstein and Nelson Polsby (Reading, Mass.: Addison-Wesley, 1975), 5:173.

5. Ibid., p. 174.

6. See Francis Rourke, *Secrecy and Publicity* (Baltimore: Johns Hopkins Press, 1961).

7. Theodore Sorensen, *Decision-Making in the White House* (New York: Columbia University Press, 1963), p. 75. Ironically, the same accusation can be leveled against Sorensen.

8. King, "Executives," p. 174.

9. Emmet J. Hughes, *The Living Presidency* (Baltimore: Penguin Books, 1973), pp. 27–29.

10. D.W. Brogan, introduction to *The American Presidency,* by Clinton Rossiter, (New York: Time-Life Books, Time Reading Program Special Edition, 1960), pp. xv–xviii.

11. There have been a few attempts to systematize in a theoretically ambitious fashion factors related to character and personality. Most important are Barber, *Presidential Character;* and Erwin Hargrove, *Presidential Leadership* (New York: Macmillan, 1966). Barber's work has been seriously questioned on both theoretical and factual levels. See, for example, Alexander George,"Assessing Presidential Character," in *Perspectives on the Presidency,* ed. Aaron Wildavsky (Boston: Little, Brown, 1975), pp. 91–135; James Qualls, "Barber's Typological Analysis of Political Leaders,"*American Political Science Review* 71 (March 1977): 182–211. Barber's response is required reading. Despite these efforts, the dominant tendency has been to view each president as a unique actor.

12. See, for example, Leo Rosten, "The Washington Correspondents," in *The Presidency,* ed. Wildavsky, pp. 320–27; Timothy Crouse, *The Boys on the Bus* (New York: Random House, 1973), pp. 191–242; and Harry Kranz, "The Presidency v. the Press—Who Is Right?" in *Perspectives on the Presidency,* ed. Wildavsky, pp. 205–20.

13. Erwin Hargrove, *The Power of the Modern Presidency* (New York: Knopf, 1974), pp. viii, 7–12; also Thomas Cronin, *The State of the Presidency* (Boston: Little, Brown, 1975), pp. 24–39; Fred Greenstein, Larry Berman, and Alvin S. Felzenberg, *Evolution of the Modern Presidency* (Washington, D.C.: American Enterprise Institute, 1977), p. viii. For accounts by political scientists who worked for presidents, see, for example, James MacGregor Burns's account of a meeting with Kennedy, *Presidential Government* (Boston: Houghton Mifflin, 1973), pp. xv–xxi; Richard Neustadt's recounting of his happy days as an aide to Truman contrasted with working in the Nixon White House, "The Constraining of the President, *"New York Times Magazine,* 4 October 1973, p. 38; and Arthur Schlesinger, Jr.'s description of Kennedy in *A Thousand Days* (Boston: Houghton Mifflin, 1965), p. xi.

14. Several significant studies address these problems, but they will be discussed in appropriate sections.

15. Purposive behavior is defined as acting in a fashion designed to serve some end or goal. David Mayhew has utilized this approach with great success in his book *Congress: The Electoral Connection* (New Haven, Conn.: Yale University Press, 1974). Mayhew assumes that congressmen are single-minded seekers of reelection. In *An Economic Theory of Democracy* (New York: Harper and Row, 1957), Anthony Downs applies similar logic to the study of political parties by assuming that parties are units whose sole function is vote getting.

16. The formulation of the president's agenda is discussed in Paul C. Light, *The President's Agenda* (Baltimore: Johns Hopkins Press, 1981).

17. Robert Gilmour, "Central Legislative Clearance: A Revised Perspective," in *Perspectives on the Presidency,* ed. Stanley Bach and George Sulzner (Lexington, Mass.: Heath, 1974), p. 320. See also Aaron Wildavsky, *The Politics of the Budgetary Process* (Boston: Little, Brown, 1974), p. 35.

18. Gilmour, "Central Legislative Clearance," pp. 331–32.

19. Richard Neustadt, "Presidency and Legislation," in *The Presidency,* ed. Wildavsky, p. 559. See also Dale Vinyard, *The Presidency* (New York: Scribner's, 1971), p. 8; Rowland Egger and Joseph P. Harris, *The President and Congress* (New York: McGraw-Hill, 1963), p. 52; John F. Manley, "The Presidency, Congress, and National Policy-Making," *Political Science Annual* 5 (1974): 237; James Anderson, *Public Policy-Making* (New York: Praeger, 1975), p. 40; Burns, *Presidential Government,* pp. 198, 235–36, 351.

20. Neustadt, "Presidency and Legislation," p. 594.

21. William Goldsmith, *The Growth of Presidential Power* (New York: Chelsea House, 1974), 3:1397. See also my discussion in Chapter 4.

22. Ibid. Lawrence Chamberlain makes the same point; see "The President, Congress, and Legislation," in *The President: Roles and Powers,* ed. David Haight and Larry Johnson (Chicago: Rand McNally, 1965), pp. 303–4.

23. Mayhew emphasizes the importance of symbolic position taking and credit claiming, which aids congressmen by promoting reciprocity. See *Congress,* esp. pp. 52–61, 121–25. See also Richard F. Bensel, "Reciprocal Behavior and the Rules of the House of Representatives" (Ph.D. diss., Cornell University, 1978).

24. Senator Robert Byrd, quoted in "Senate Backs Canal Neutrality Treaty, 68–32," *Congressional Quarterly Weekly Report,* 18 March 1978, p. 675.

25. *Weekly Compilation of Presidential Documents,* 20 November 1978, p. 2025.

26. William F. Mullen, *Presidential Power and Politics* (New York: St. Martin's Press, 1976), chap. 2; Pendleton Herring, *Presidential Leadership* (New York: Farrar and Rinehart, 1940), p. 69; *Congressional Quarterly Almanac, 1972* (Washington, D.C.: Congressional Quarterly, 1972), p. 419.

27. Ronald Moe and Steven Teel, "Congress as Policy-Maker," *Political Science Quarterly* 85 (September 1970): 448.

28. Ernest Griffith, *The American Presidency* (New York: New York University Press, 1976), p. 100. Also Neustadt, "Presidency and Legislation," p. 594.

29. Richard Neustadt, *Presidential Power* (New York: Wiley, 1976), p. 152.

30. Each approach can be identified with one or a few important books. The institutional-legal perspective is found in Edward Corwin, *The President: Office and Powers* (New York: New York University Press, 1957). Personality and style are emphasized in Hargrove, *Presidential Leadership;* and Barber, *Presidential Character.* For the importance of the use of symbols, see Murray Edelman, *Politics as Symbolic Action* (Chicago: Markham, 1971). Socialization studies emphasize positive attachments to the president. See Fred Greenstein, *Children and Politics* (New Haven, Conn.: Yale University Press, 1969); David Easton and Jack Dennis, *Children in the Political System* (New York: McGraw-Hill, 1969). A cross-national confirmation of the importance of executives can be found in Fred Greenstein and Sidney Tarrow, *Political Orientation of Children* (Beverly Hills, Calif.: Sage Publications, 1970). Neustadt, *Presidential Power,* emphasizes power and influence. George F.

Milton, *The Use of Presidential Power: 1789*–1943 (Boston: Little, Brown, 1944); and Rossiter, *American Presidency,* are good sources for the role perspective.

31. Interestingly, the area of presidential elections is purposefully excluded from the otherwise inclusive bibliography on the presidency; see Greenstein, Berman, and Felzenberg, *Evolution of the Modern Presidency,* p. xii. A few key works on presidential elections are Nelson Polsby and Aaron Wildavsky, *Presidential Elections* (New York: Scribner's, 1976); Gerald M. Pomper, *Elections in America* (New York: Dodd, Mead, 1968); William Keech and Donald Matthews, *The Party's Choice* (Washington, D.C.: Brookings Institution, 1976).

32. A few of the important works on parties and party systems are: Austin Ranney and Willmoore Kendall, *Democracy and the American Party System* (New York: Harcourt, Brace, 1956); V. O. Key, *Politics, Parties, and Pressure Groups* (New York: Crowell, 1964); Hugh Bone, *American Politics and the Party System* (New York: McGraw-Hill, 1965); and Frank Sorauf, *Party Politics in America* (Boston: Little, Brown, 1976). Important works on voting and electoral behavior include Paul Lazarsfeld et al., *The People's Choice* (New York: Columbia University Press, 1944); Bernard Berelson, Paul Lazarsfeld, and William McPhee, *Voting* (Chicago: University of Chicago Press, 1954); Angus Campbell, Philip Converse, Warren Miller, and Donald Stokes, *The American Voter* (New York: Wiley, 1960), and *Elections and the Political Order* (New York: Wiley, 1966); and Norman Nie, Sidney Verba, and John Petrocik, *The Changing American Voter* (Cambridge, Mass.: Harvard University Press, 1976). Campaign finance is discussed in Alexander Heard, *The Costs of Democracy* (New York: Doubleday, 1962); Herbert Alexander's studies of presidential-year campaign financing from 1960 to 1976, and also his book *Financing Politics* (Washington, D.C.: Congressional Quarterly Press, 1976); and George Thayer, *Who Shakes the Money Tree?* (New York: Simon and Schuster, 1973). The relationship between journalism and political elections is discussed in Crouse, *Boys on the Bus;* Hunter Thompson, *Fear and Loathing: On the Campaign Trail, '72* (San Francisco: Straight Arrow Books, 1973); Joe McGinniss, *The Selling of the President 1968* (New York: Pocket Books, 1969); and Dan Nimmo, *The Political Persuaders* (Englewood Cliffs, N.J.: Prentice-Hall, 1970).

33. There is a clear disjunction in the literature between the study of presidential elections and the study of presidential behavior. The policy approach to be applied here may be useful in addressing this disjunction, but such an approach does not depend upon traditional studies of presidential elections. Any relevant sources will of course be cited.

34. Charles Roberts, ed., *Has the President Too Much Power?* (New York: Harper's Magazine Press, 1973); Charles Hardin, *Presidential Power and Accountability* (Chicago: University of Chicago Press, 1974); Hargrove, *Power of the Presidency;* Cronin, *State of the Presidency;* Charles Dunn, ed., *The Future of the American Presidency* (Morristown, N.J.: General Learning Press, 1975); Philip Dolce and George Skau, eds., *Power and the Presidency* (New York: Scribner's, 1976); Griffith, *American Presidency;* Mullen, *Presidential Power and Politics.*

35. This distinction is based in part on discussions with Michael E. Brown, to whom I am indebted. Peri Arnold and L. John Roos ("Toward a Theory of Congressional-Executive Relations," *Review of Politics* 36 [July 1974]: 417–19) make a

similar distinction between *is* and *ought,* constructing a two-by-two table based on the two dimensions. However, this compels the placing of all authors, in many cases artificially, along both dimensions. Clearly, some writers have an essentially normative intent, while others are interested principally in historical-factual chronicles. Writers who emphasize both are duly noted.

36. Cronin, *State of the Presidency,* p. 25.

37. Rossiter, *American Presidency.* Rossiter's book, once the most widely read book on the presidency, has been roundly criticized in recent years. Perhaps the most damning criticism is that the book employs circular logic. Rossiter believed that the president, through the exercise of his power, was the principal guardian and protector of liberty and democracy. This was so because the people supported the president in fulfilling this role. And the reason the people supported the president was that he used his power to support and defend liberty and democratic values. See, for example, Richard Loss, "Dissolving Concepts of the Presidency," *Political Science Reviewer* 4 (Fall 1974): 147–55.

38. Louis Koenig, *The Chief Executive* (New York: Harcourt, Brace, Jovanovich, 1975).

39. Harold Laski, *The American Presidency* (New York: Grosset and Dunlap, 1940).

40. Burns, *Presidential Government;* Rowland Egger, *The President of the United States* (New York: McGraw-Hill, 1972), p. vi. See also Walter Lippmann, *The Public Philosophy* (Boston: Little, Brown, 1955), chap. 5.

41. Richard Bolling, *House Out of Order* (New York: Dutton, 1965); Joseph Clark, *Congress: The Sapless Branch* (New York: Harper and Row, 1964).

42. Another early espousal of this view appears in Henry C. Lockwood, *The Abolition of the Presidency* (New York: Worthington, 1884).

43. William H. Taft, *The President and His Powers* (New York: Columbia University Press, 1967), originally published as *Our Chief Magistrate.* A good discussion of this perspective can be found in Roger Davidson, David M. Kovenock, and Michael K. O'Leary, *Congress in Crisis* (Belmont, Calif.: Wadsworth, 1966), pp. 17–25.

44. James Burnham, *Congress and the American Tradition* (Chicago: Regnery, 1959); Willmoore Kendall, *The Conservative Affirmation* (Chicago: Regnery, 1963); Alfred DeGrazia, *Republic in Crisis* (New York: Federal Legal Publications, 1965).

45. George Reedy, *The Twilight of the Presidency* (New York: New American Library, 1970).

46. Arthur Schlesinger, Jr., *The Age of Jackson* (Boston: Houghton Mifflin, 1946), *The Age of Roosevelt,* 3 vols. (Boston: Houghton Mifflin, 1957–60), and *A Thousand Days.* For his new view of presidential power, see *The Imperial Presidency* (New York: Popular Library, 1974). For other changes of opinion on the question of how much power the president should have, compare Henry Steele Commager, "Are We Creating a Dictator?" *New York Times Magazine,* 2 March 1941, p. 3, with *The Defeat of America* (New York: Simon and Schuster, 1974). Compare also the preface of Louis Koenig's second edition of *Chief Executive* (1968) with that of the third edition (1975).

47. Raoul Berger, *Executive Privilege* (Cambridge, Mass.: Harvard University Press, 1974). The Supreme Court recognized for the first time the doctrine of executive privilege in United States v. Nixon, 481 U.S. 683 (1974).

48. James Sundquist, "Needed: A Workable Check on the Presidency," *Brookings Bulletin* 10 (Fall 1973): 7–11.

49. Hargrove, *Power of the Modern Presidency;* Hardin, *Presidential Power and Accountability.*

50. The closest thing to a definitive work on this general subject is the massive Goldsmith, *Growth of Presidential Power.* See also Wilfred Binkley, *President and Congress* (New York: Random House, 1962).

51. See Louis Fisher's excellent *Presidential Spending Power* (Princeton, N.J.: Princeton University Press, 1975).

52. See, for example, Vinyard, *The Presidency,* pp. 25–29; Cronin, *State of the Presidency,* pp. 118, 326–27. Cronin, however, expresses the viewpoint that bigger has not necessarily meant better for the president.

53. Corwin, *The President.*

54. Schlesinger, *Imperial Presidency;* Berger, *Executive Privilege.*

55. Newton N. Minew, John B. Martin, and Lee M. Mitchell, *Presidential Television* (New York: Basic Books, 1973). There has been no satisfactory resolution of the dispute over whether presidents have, by and large, manipulated the press, or whether the press in fact cows the president. Daniel P. Moynihan, for example, feared that a balance weighing too heavily on the side of the press would be inimical to the interests of democratic government; see "The Presidency and the Press," *Commentary* 51 (March 1971): 41–52. See also Douglass Cater, "The President and the Press," *Annals of the American Academy of Political and Social Science* 307 (1956): 55–65; and Stanley Kelley, *Professional Public Relations and Political Power* (Baltimore, Md.: Johns Hopkins Press, 1956).

56. McGinniss, *Selling of the President;* Nimmo, *Political Persuaders;* Crouse, *Boys on the Bus.*

57. Neustadt, *Presidential Power,* pp. 77–100.

58. R. P. Nathan, *The Plot That Failed* (New York: Wiley, 1975). For more on the fate of the OEO, see Daniel P. Moynihan, *Maximum Feasible Misunderstanding* (New York: Free Press, 1970), pp. 153–60. Ford finally succeeded where Nixon failed, though Nixon laid the groundwork for Ford's coup de grace.

59. Rossiter, *American Presidency,* chap. 2; Koenig, *Chief Executive,* pp. 10–12.

60. Sorensen, *Decision-Making.*

61. Grant McConnell, *Steel and the Presidency* (New York: Norton, 1963), p. 114.

62. Robert Holt and John Turner, "Crises and Sequences in Collective Theory Development," *American Political Science Review* 69 (September 1975): 993. See also Herbert Simon, *The Science of the Artificial* (Cambridge, Mass.: MIT Press, 1969).

63. Alexander George also observes of Barber's books that "classification is often confused with diagnosis"; see "Assessing Presidential Character," p. 119.

64. Barber, *Presidential Character,* pp. 485–97.

65. David Easton, "An Approach to the Analysis of Political Systems," *World Politics* 9 (April 1957): 392.

66. Austin Ranney, "The Study of Policy Content," in *Political Science and Public Policy,* ed. Austin Ranney (Chicago: Markham, 1968), p. 7.

67. Ibid.

68. Henry Jones Ford, *The Rise and Growth of American Politics* (New York: DaCapo Press, 1967), p. 279.

69. Vinyard, *The Presidency,* pp. 6–13. A recent text on the presidency has attempted to focus on policy in describing the man and the office, though it does so in an unsystematic way. See William Lammers, *Presidential Politics* (New York: Harper and Row, 1976).

70. Stephen Hess, *Organizing the Presidency* (Washington, D.C.: Brookings Institution, 1976), pp. 151–52; Cronin, *State of the Presidency,* pp. 250–51.

71. Hargrove, *Power of the Modern Presidency,* pp. 123–24.

72. Arend Lijphart, "Comparative Politics and the Comparative Method,"*American Political Science Review* 65 (September 1971): 691. Harry Eckstein, "Case Study and Theory in Political Science," in *Handbook of Political Science,* ed. Greenstein and Polsby, pp. 96–97.

73. Adam Przeworski and Henry Teune, *The Logic of Comparative Social Inquiry* (New York: Wiley, 1970), chap. 1; Sidney Verba, "Some Dilemmas in Comparative Research," *World Politics* 19 (October 1967): 111–27.

74. Eckstein, "Case Study," pp. 92–94.

75. For a comprehensive listing of the significant case studies, see Fred Greenstein et al., *Evolution of the Modern Presidency,* pp. 303–1496.

76. Ruth Morgan, *The President and Civil Rights* (New York: St. Martin's Press, 1970); James Sundquist, *Politics and Policy* (Washington, D.C.: Brookings Institution, 1968); John Kessel, "The Parameters of Presidential Politics," *Social Science Quarterly* 55 (June 1974): 8–24.

77. Seyom Brown, *The Faces of Power* (New York: Columbia University Press, 1968); Keith Clark and Laurence Legere, eds., *The President and the Management of National Security* (New York: Praeger, 1969); Samuel Huntington, *The Common Defense* (New York: Columbia University Press, 1961); Thomas Halper, *Foreign Policy Crises* (Columbus, Ohio: Merrill, 1971); Roger Hilsman, *The Politics of Policy Making in Defense and Foreign Affairs* (New York: Harper and Row, 1971): and Richard Neustadt, *Alliance Politics* (New York: Columbia University Press, 1970).

78. Aaron Wildavsky, "The Two Presidencies," in *The Presidency,* ed. Wildavsky, pp. 230–43.

79. Aage Clausen, *How Congressmen Decide* (New York: St. Martin's Press,1973); Richard Fenno, *Congressmen in Committees* (Boston: Little, Brown, 1973), especially p. 45; Theodore J. Lowi, "Four Systems of Policy, Politics, and Choice," *Public Administration Review 32 (July–*August 1972): 298–310; Randall Ripley and Grace Franklin, *Congress, the Bureaucracy, and Public Policy* (Homewood, Ill.: Dorsey Press, 1976); and David Vogler, *The Politics of Congress* (Boston: Allyn and Bacon, 1974), chap. 6.

80. One possible exception is Kessel, "Parameters of Presidential Politics."

81. A good discussion of the problem of defining executives can be found in King, "Executives," pp. 175–83.

82. Theodore J. Lowi, *American Government: Incomplete Conquest* (Hinsdale, Ill.: Dryden Press, 1976), p. 451.

83. James Davis, Jr., *The National Executive Branch* (New York: Free Press, 1970), p. 22. See also Burns, *Presidential Government,* pp. 136–40.

84. Koenig, *Chief Executive,* p. 185. For a more general view of the historical evolution of the White House staff, see Cronin, *State of the Presidency,* pp. 117–51.

85. Lowi, *American Government,* p. 487. Independent agencies "are not intended to be directly responsive to presidential direction. Each operates under a broad delegation of power from Congress" (p. 488).

Chapter Two

1. See Daniel Lerner and Harold Lasswell, *The Policy Sciences* (Stanford, Calif.: Stanford University Press, 1951), chap. 9. For more on the purposes, uses, values, and limitations of classification schemes, see James Bill and Robert Hardgrave, *Comparative Politics: The Quest of Theory* (Columbus, Ohio: Merrill, 1973), p. 29; and Carl Hempel, *Aspects of Scientific Explanation* (New York: Free Press, 1965), chaps. 6 and 7. A good example of the use of classification schemes can be seen in Giovanni Sartori, *Parties and Party Systems* (Cambridge: Cambridge University Press, 1976).

2. See, for example, Thomas Dye, *Politics, Economics, and the Public* (Chicago: Rand McNally, 1966); Lewis Froman, "The Categorization of Policy Contents," and Robert Salisbury, "The Analysis of Public Policy," both in *Political Science and Public Policy,* ed. Austin Ranney (Chicago: Markham, 1968); Robert Salisbury and John Heinz, "A Theory of Policy Analysis and Some Preliminary Applications," in *Policy Analysis in Political Science,* ed. Ira Sharkansky (Chicago: Markham, 1970); and James Q. Wilson, *Political Organizations* (New York: Basic Books, 1973).

3. The development and application of this scheme can be seen in Theodore J. Lowi, "American Business, Public Policy, Case Studies, and Political Theory," *World Politics* 16 (July 1964): 677–715, "Making Democracy Safe for the World," in *Domestic Sources of Foreign Policy,* ed. James Rosenau (New York: Free Press, 1967), "Decision Making vs. Policy Making," *Public Administration Review* 30 (May–June 1970): 314–25, "Four Systems of Policy, Politics, and Choice," *Public Administration Review* 32 (July–August 1972): 298–310, "The Development of the Arenas of Power," in *Political Scientists at Work,* ed. Oliver Walter (Belmont, Calif.: Duxbury Press, 1971), and "Population Policies and the American Political System," in *Governance and Population,* Commission Research Reports, vol. 4 (Washington, D.C.: Government Printing Office, 1972), pp. 283–300.

4. The "immediate" and "remote" elements of the "likelihood-of-coercion" dimension correspond to H. L. A. Hart's distinction in law between primary and secondary rules; see *The Concept of Law* (New York: Oxford University Press, 1961).

5. Samuel Beer, "The Modernization of American Federalism," *Publius* 3 (Fall 1973): 49–96; James Grant, "The Administration of Politics," (Ph.D. diss., University of Chicago, 1972); George Greenberg, Jeffrey A. Miller, Lawrence B. Mohr, and Bruce C. Vladeck, "Developing Public Policy Theory," *American Political Science Review* 71 (December 1977): 1532–43; Judith Hartmann, "Bureaucracy, Democracy and the Administrative Official" (Ph.D. diss., University of Chicago, 1973); Michael T. Hayes, "The Semi-Sovereign Pressure Groups," *Journal of Politics* 40 (1978): 134–61; Francesco Kjellberg, "Do Policies (Really) Determine Politics? And Eventually

How?" *Policy Studies Journal,* Special Issue, 1977, pp. 554–70; Nancy Kornblith, "The Congressional Committee: Variance in Role and Functions" (M.A. thesis, University of Chicago, 1968); Joseph Penbera, Jr., "A Test of the Lowi Arenas of Power Policy Approach" (Ph.D. diss., American University, 1973); B. Guy Peters, John C. Doughtie, and M. Kathleen McCulloch, "Types of Democratic Systems and Types of Public Policies," *Comparative Politics* 9 (April 1977): 327–55; David Price, *Who Makes the Laws* (Cambridge, Mass.: Schenkman, 1972); Stuart Rakoff and Guenther Schaefer, "Politics, Policy, and Political Science: Theoretical Alternatives," *Politics and Society* 1 (November 1970): 51–77; Randall Ripley and Grace Franklin, *Congress, the Bureaucracy, and Public Policy* (Homewood, Ill.: Dorsey Press, 1976); L. John Roos, "Committee-Floor Relations in the U.S. Congress" (M.A. thesis, University of Chicago, 1969); Salisbury and Heinz, "Theory of Policy Analysis"; Jerrold Schneider, *Ideological Coalitions in Congress* (Westport, Conn.: Greenwood Press, 1979); T. Alexander Smith, "Toward a Comparative Theory of the Policy-Process," *Comparative Politics* 1 (July 1969): 498–515, and *The Comparative Policy Process* (Santa Barbara, Calif.: Clio Books, 1975); Robert J. Spitzer, "The Presidency and Public Policy: A Preliminary Inquiry," *Presidential Studies Quarterly* 9 (Fall 1979): 441–57; David Vogler, *The Politics of Congress* (Boston: Allyn and Bacon, 1974); Wilson, *Political Organizations;* William Zimmerman, "Issue Area and Foreign-Policy Process," *American Political Science Review* 67 (December 1973): 1204–12.

6. All information taken from Theodore J. Lowi, "American Business," "Decision Making," "Four Systems," and "The Arenas of Power" (manuscript), unless otherwise noted.

7. Raymond A. Bauer, Ithiel De Sola Pool, and Lewis A. Dexter, *American Business and Public Policy* (Chicago: Aldine-Atherton, 1972). Lowi's review of this book in fact provided him the first occasion to elaborate his approach.

8. Curiously, among the many works based on Lowi's arenas, virtually all simply ignore this fourth category, even though many of these studies have been completed since explication of the fourth area.

9. See, for example, Donald Wittman, "Parties as Utility Maximizers," *American Political Science Review* 67 (June 1973): 490–98; G. William Domhoff, *Fat Cats and Democrats* (Englewood Cliffs, N.J.: Prentice-Hall, 1972); and Walter Karp, *Indispensable Enemies* (Baltimore: Penguin Books, 1973).

10. For example, Wilson, *Political Organizations;* Kjellberg, "Do Policies Determine Politics?"; Richard Fenno, *Congressmen in Committees,* (Boston: Little, Brown, 1973) p. 45; Aage Clausen, *How Congressmen Decide* (New York: St. Martin's Press, 1973); Duncan MacRae, Jr., *Issues and Parties in Legislative Voting* (New York: Harper and Row, 1970), pp. 12–13.

11. Lowi, "American Business," p. 690.

12. Schneider, *Ideological Coalitions in Congress,* pp. 32–33.

13. See, for example, Kjellberg, "Do Policies Determine Politics?" pp. 558–68; Hayes, "Semi-Sovereign Pressure Groups"; Salisbury and Heinz, "Theory of Policy Analysis"; Rakoff and Schaefer, "Politics, Policy"; Lewis Froman, "An Analysis of Public Policies in Cities," *Journal of Politics* 29 (1967): 94–108.

14. See note 5. The extreme view on this kind of policy analysis is taken by Rakoff and Schaefer in "Politics, Policy": "Any effort to define policy once and for all...."

represents an exercise in futility" (p.69). Not surprisingly, they label Lowi's scheme "vague and empirically irrelevant" (p.77).

15. Wilson, *Political Organizations,* p. 329. See also Greenberg et al., "Developing Public Policy Theory," pp. 1534–36.

16. See Sartori's discussion of typologies in *Parties and Party Systems,* p. 290.

17. Wilson, *Political Organizations,* p. 328; George Greenberg et al., "Case Study Aggregation and Policy Theory" (Paper delivered at the Annual Meeting of the American Political Science Association, New Orleans, 4–8 September 1973), pp. 8–9.

18. I am especially indebted to John Green, with whom I spent many hours discussing these ideas.

19. Vogler, *Politics of Congress,* p. 303.

20. Ibid. See also Lowi, "Four Systems," p. 303.

21. Vogler, *Politics of Congress,* p. 311. The same evaluation is applied to foreign policy as well, though the president's dominance in foreign-policy matters, widely chronicled, is not included in this study.

22. Lowi, "Four Systems," pp. 302–3. On p. 304 Lowi presents a tabular summary of his evaluation of secondary-source case studies. Evidence assimilated from those cases confirms the arenas pattern and the progressive increase of presidential involvement in policies from distributive to redistributive.

23. Ripley and Franklin, *Congress,* p. 142.

24. Lowi, "Four Systems," p. 306.

25. Congressional activities of this sort are legendary. For example, David Mayhew identifies three activities considered essential for congressmen seeking re-election. One of these is credit claiming, which involves trafficking in what he calls "particularized benefits"; see *Congress: The Electoral Connection* (New Haven, Conn.: Yale University Press, 1974), pp. 51–52. Edward R. Tufte discusses "political gains accruing from giving population groupings benefits they want"; *Political Control of the Economy* (Princeton, N.J.: Princeton University Press, 1978), p. 26.

Chapter Three

1. William Tucker, "I Like Jimmy," *New York Times,* 9 September 1979, sec. 4, Op-Ed page.

2. Western development interests were certainly represented by the preponderance of congressmen from western states. In the House, nineteen of thirty-four Interior Committee members represented western states. In the Senate, the corresponding proportion was seventeen of eighteen.

3. See "Wilderness Bill Passed by House," *New York Times,* 31 July 1964, p. 1.

4. "Now the Wilderness Bill," *New York Times,* 29 July 1964, p. 32.

5. Paul E. Scheele, "President Carter and the Water Projects," *Presidential Studies Quarterly* 8 (Fall 1978): 348–64.

6. Berkeley Rice, *The C-5A Scandal* (Boston: Houghton Mifflin, 1971).

7. This was the unambiguous purpose of the expansion. Richard Witkin, "Lockheed's Rescue Plan May Aid Other Concerns," *New York Times,* 25 June 1971, p. 45.

8. "Burns Hedges on Lockheed Aid," *New York Times,* 17 June 1971, p. 59.

9. "Lockheed Loan Guarantee Bill Cleared on Close Votes," *Congressional Quarterly Almanac,* 1971 (Washington, D.C.: Congressional Quarterly, 1971), p. 157.

10. Ibid., pp. 155, 160.

11. Jacob K. Javits, "Needed: A New R.F.C.," *New York Times,* 11 July 1971, sec. 3, p. 12.

12. Adam Yarmolinsky, *The Military Establishment* (New York: Harper and Row, 1973), p. 18.

13. For a general overview of defense reorganization, see Department of Defense Reorganization Study Project, "Departmental Headquarters Study," 1 June 1978; Paul Hammond, *Organizing for Defense* (Princeton, N.J.: Princeton University Press, 1961); Henry Jackson, ed., *The National Security Council* (New York: Praeger, 1965); Blue Ribbon Defense Panel, *Report to the President and the Secretary of Defense* (Washington, D.C.: U.S. Government Printing Office, 1970).

14. "President's Stand," *New York Times,* 13 April 1958, sec. 4, pp. 1–2.

15. Martin Tolchin, "Grappling with the Monster Bureaucracy," *New York Times,* 23 July 1978, p.46.

16. Kathy Sawyer, "Carter's Civil Service Victory Confounds Capitol's Cynics," *Washington Post,* 14 October 1978, sec. A, p. 2. The legislation was considered unprecedented for its "sweeping scope" and "fleet rites of passage."

17. See Ann Cooper, "Civil Service Reforms Likely This Year," *Congressional Quarterly Weekly Report,* 16 September 1978, p. 2458.

18. Harlan Lebo, "The Administration's All-Out Effort on Civil Service Reform," *National Journal,* 27 May 1978, p. 838.

Chapter Four

1. Title 1 was an important component of the bill, but even the distribution of these benefits was founded in an attempt to promote law enforcement in localities, in order to facilitate what the rest of the bill mandated.

2. "House Rewrites and Passes Safe Streets Bill," *Congressional Quarterly Almanac,* 1967 (Washington, D.C.: Congressional Quarterly, 1967), p. 849.

3. The Constitution says: "The Supreme Court shall have appellate Jurisdictions, both as to law and fact, with such exceptions and under such regulations as the Congress shall make."

4. For example, John Herbers, "Democrats Work to Free Key Bills," *New York Times,* 1 January 1968, p.7.

5. Alexander Bickel, "The Senate Judiciary's Abominable Crime Bill," *New Republic,* 25 May 1968, p. 17.

6. Linda E. Demkovich, "The Pros and Kahns of Airline Deregulation," *National Journal,* 26 August 1978, p. 1359.

7. "Airline Deregulation," *Congressional Quarterly Almanac,* 1967, p. 554.

8. Area redevelopment is discussed in several books: John F. Bibby and Roger H. Davidson, *On Capitol Hill* (Hinsdale, Ill.: Dryden Press, 1972), chap. 6; David

Knapp, *Scouting the War on Poverty* (Lexington, Mass.: Lexington Books, 1971); Sar A. Levitan, *Federal Aid to Depressed Areas* (Baltimore: Johns Hopkins Press, 1964).

9. Ohio Congressman Clarence Brown feared that the program would be turned into a machine for the dispensing of political favors by the program administrator and that "every rural area in the U.S. can be declared a depressed area and come in and get funds." "Congress Enacts Area Redevelopment Bill," *Congressional Quarterly Almanac,* 1961 (Washington, D.C.: Congressional Quarterly, 1961), p. 254.

10. Tom Wicker, "Needy-Area Help Voted by House; Coalition Loses," *New York Times,* 30 March 1961, p. 1.

11. "Major Housing Legislation Enacted," *Congressional Quarterly Almanac,* 1965 (Washington, D.C.: Congressional Quarterly, 1965), p. 359.

12. Lawrence O'Kane, "President's Housing Message Scored by Many Here," *New York Times,* 4 March 1965, p. 19.

13. Again, supporting provisions of the bill buttress the central concern of the bill—federally supported housing.

14. A typical example of such an amendment was one proposed by a Pennsylvania congressman (and adopted by the House) that authorized grant-in-aid credit for expenses associated with an urban renewal project in Wilkes-Barre, Pennsylvania. The Senate version contained comparable additions; see "Major Housing Legislation Enacted," p. 373.

Chapter Five

1. A general outline of this and the other two approaches to presidential-congressional relations can be found in Roger Davidson, David M. Kovenock, and Michael K. O'Leary, *Congress in Crisis* (Belmont, Calif.: Wadsworth, 1966), pp. 15–37. See also John Saloma III, *Congress and the New Politics* (Boston: Little, Brown, 1969), chap. 2. James M. Burns presents a slight variation of the three approaches, which he ties to the early days of the Constitution, in *Presidential Government* (Boston: Houghton Mifflin, 1973), preface and chap. 1.

2. James Burnham, *Congress and the American Tradition* (Chicago: Regnery, 1959), p. 349.

3. The best outline of this approach is found in American Political Science Association Committee on Political Parties, *Toward a More Responsible Two-Party System* (New York: Rinehart, 1950).

4. For a summary of recent congressional reforms see *Origins and Development of Congress* (Washington, D.C.: Congressional Quarterly, 1976), chaps. 16, 25; Dom Bonafede, Daniel Rapoport, and Joel Havemann, "The President vs. Congress: The Score since Watergate," *National Journal,* 29 May 1976, pp. 730–48.

5. Chamberlain's findings are published in *The President, Congress, and Legislation* (New York: Columbia University Press, 1946), and in "The President, Congress, and Legislation," in *The President: Roles and Powers,* ed. David Haight and Larry Johnson (Chicago: Rand McNally, 1965), pp. 297–310.

6. Chamberlain, "The President," p. 304.

7. Ronald Moe and Steven Teel, "Congress as Policy-Maker," *Political Science Quarterly* 85 (September 1970): 467–68. Fisher and Ripley have also emphasized, though in a less systematic way, that the role of the Congress in policy making has been slighted: Louis Fisher, *President and Congress* (New York: Free Press, 1972); Randall Ripley, *Congress: Process and Policy* (New York: Norton, 1975), especially chap. 11.

8. Hugh Gallagher, "Presidents, Congress, and the Legislative Functions," in *The Presidency Reappraised,* ed. Rexford Tugwell and Thomas Cronin (New York: Praeger, 1974), especially pp. 232–33.

9. Goldsmith, *The Growth of Presidential Power* (New York: Chelsea House, 1974), 3: 1400.

10. Moe and Teel, "Congress as Policy-Maker," pp. 450–51.

11. Along conceptual lines, the empirical analyses as well as other evaluations actually touch on two dimensions of presidential-congressional relations. Relative influence can be examined on two bases: (a) in terms of introduction or initiation of legislation; and (b) in terms of formulation or the passage process of legislation. Moe and Teel find relatively high congressional influence because most legislative proposals follow the legislative circuit many times before being finally enacted; their study emphasizes the introduction-initiation aspect rather than influence over passage. In terms of antecedent initiation, a congressman is usually credited with the idea of the original proposal. Generally, the nature of legislative initiative is such that focusing on this aspect will invariably yield results indicating greater congressional influence.

The second aspect, legislative formulation or the passage process, is the dimension Chamberlain and Goldsmith touch on. While Chamberlain traced the antecedents of the legislation he evaluated, both he and Goldsmith were fundamentally concerned with the question of who was most responsible for passage. That dimension provided the basis for analysis.

For more on initiation, see Richard Pious, "Sources of Domestic Policy Initiative," in *Congress against the President,* ed. Harvey Mansfield (New York: Praeger, 1975), pp. 98–111; John R. Johannes, "Congress and the Initiation of Legislation," *Public Policy* 20 (Spring 1972): 281–309, "Where Does the Buck Stop?" *Western Political Quarterly* 25 (September 1972): 396–415, and "The President Proposes and the Congress Disposes—But Not Always," *Review of Politics* 36 (July 1974): 356–70.

12. Theodore J. Lowi, "Four Systems of Policy, Politics, and Choice," *Public Administration Review* 32 (July–August 1972): 301–9.

13. An additional fifty-one bills were eliminated due to an inability to classify them, because of either ambiguity or lack of information. The Boxscore was discontinued after 1974.

14. My thanks to John Green, Theodore J. Lowi, and Wendy Mink for their assistance in coding. An intercoder-reliability test was also conducted, using an outside coder. A random selection of 201 cases was drawn from the 4,563 domestic proposals. The result was an index of agreement between my coding and that of the outside coder, Gary Bryner (based on his coding of the 201 cases), of .871. (The formula was, number of agreed-upon cases divided by the total number of cases. Disputes were resolved between the author and the coder.)

15. For more on Boxscores and their limitations, see George C. Edwards III, *Presidential Influence in Congress* (San Francisco: Freeman, 1980), pp. 13–15. See also Stephen J. Wayne, *The Legislative Presidency* (New York: Harper and Row, 1978).

16. Since the percentages sum to 100 percent for each year in Table 3, variations in one area statistically affect variations in the other for each year. All correlations are negative because they sum to 100, and thus when one increases, the other three decrease, and vice versa; but there is no imperative that the correlations be necessarily high on this basis.

17. In paired comparisons, two columns of numbers are compared to each other at a time. Within these columns, the differences between each adjacent pair are compared with differences between pairs in the other column, to observe whether the difference in the adjacent set of numbers in the second column matches the direction of change. (If they do match, for example, if both go up, then the pair varies directly; if not, they vary inversely). The number of direct and inverse pairs are then totaled to indicate the degree of direct and inverse variation.

18. We may be undergoing a shift in the composition of the president's agenda with the current heightened awareness of and interest in problems of government organization and bureaucracy in the electorate. The implications of this will be discussed in the concluding chapter.

19. Richard Pious, *The American Presidency* (New York: Basic Books, 1979), p. 177.

20. A good general description of the president's historic claim to foreign policy preeminence can be found in Arthur Schlesinger, Jr., *The Imperial Presidency* (New York: Popular Library, 1974). The arenas have been applied to foreign policy in Theodore J. Lowi, "Making Democracy Safe for the World," in *Domestic Sources of Foreign Policy,* ed. James Rosenau (New York: Free Press, 1967); and William Zimmerman, "Issue Area and Foreign-Policy Processes," *American Political Science Review* 67 (December 1973): 1204–12. Presidential ascendancy over Congress in foreign policy is mapped by Aaron Wildavsky, "The Two Presidencies," in *Perspectives on the Presidency* (Boston: Little, Brown, 1975).

21. Edward R. Tufte, *Political Control of the Economy* (Princeton, N.J.: Princeton University Press, 1978). Several studies have examined differences in the content of an administration's policies, especially as they relate to the economy. Hibbs, for example, found that during Democratic administrations unemployment was driven downward, while it rose during the Republican administrations; the differences were apparently based in appeals to the differing constituencies of the two parties. Such a difference in the thrust of aggregate economic policies, while important, would not be reflected here, because both would be counted as redistributive. This reflects the differing aims and focuses of this study. Douglas A. Hibbs, "Political Parties and Macroeconomic Policy," *American Political Science Review* 71 (December 1977) 1467–87. For a more extensive bibliography, see Ripley, *Congress,* p. 112.

22. This information is also drawn from *Congressional Quarterly's* Presidential Boxscore.

Chapter Six

1. This was accounted for in the previous chapters, however, by looking at bill proposals (Chapter 5) and committee action (Chapters 3 and 4).

2. Descriptions and information from the annual volumes of the *Congressional Quarterly Almanac* were relied upon as the basis of information; in particular, the sections "Key Votes," "Presidential Boxscore," and on bill descriptions. In 1971 the House for the first time began recording "teller" votes in the Committee of the Whole. Including such votes in roll-call comparisons across chambers and across time (pre-and post-1971) would confound the analysis. However, none of the House roll calls utilized here were recorded teller votes. My thanks to Richard Bensel for pointing this out.

3. Thanks to John Green and Theodore J. Lowi for their assistance.

4. Committee action was covered, however, in the case-study chapters.

5. Woodrow Wilson, *Congressional Government* (New York: Meridian, 1956).

6. Barbara Hinckley, *Stability and Change in Congress* (New York: Harper and Row, 1971), pp. 82–83.

7. Stephen K. Bailey, *Congress in the Seventies* (New York: St. Martin's Press, 1970), p. 53.

8. Hinckley, *Stability and Change,* pp. 59–64.

9. See Theodore J. Lowi, "Four Systems of Policy, Politics, and Choice," *Public Administration Review* 32 (July–August 1972): 305–7. Lowi's data in table 2 indicate a generally inverse relation between the existence of floor creativity and committee creativity in terms of having the major influence over the final form of the bill. The only exception to this pattern seems to be regulatory policies, where both committee and the floor provide forums for significant changes in bills.

10. Randall Ripley, *Congress: Process and Policy* (New York: Norton, 1975), p. 75. See also Richard F. Bensel, "Reciprocal Behavior and the Rules of the House of Representatives" (Ph.D. diss., Cornell University, 1978).

11. See, for example, Lewis Froman, *The Congressional Process* (Boston: Little, Brown, 1967), p. 55; William Keefe and Morris Ogul, *The American Legislative Process* (Englewood Cliffs, N.J.: Prentice-Hall, 1968), p. 241. This is not to say that there is no difference but simply that, for my limited purposes, they will be treated the same. As John Manley wrote, "The mere adoption of closed rules indicates that the House is willing to rely on the Committee's judgment in countless decisions"; *The Politics of Finance* (Boston: Little, Brown, 1970), p. 222.

12. Froman, *Congressional Process,* especially pp. 5–15.

13. The standard percent figure is 10 percent. If the roll call vote was more than 10 percent for both yes and no on each vote, the vote was considered controversial.

14. The best statement on this is Julius Turner and Edward Schneier, *Party and Constituency* (Baltimore: Johns Hopkins Press, 1970). The authors show that partisanship varies according to issue area, which at best suggests that party differences may appear across the arenas categories as well. Important linkages between issue areas and party voting are discussed in Aage Clausen, *How Congressmen Decide* (New York: St. Martin's Press, 1973).

15. The index of likeness is set out in Turner and Schneier, *Party and Constituency,* pp. 41–42. It is discussed critically in W. Wayne Shannon, *Party, Constituency, and Congressional Voting* (Baton Rouge: Louisiana State University Press, 1968), p. 17.

16. Turner and Schneier, *Party and Constituency,* pp. 42–47.

17. See Lewis Froman and Randall Ripley, "Conditions for Party Leadership," *American Political Science Review* 59 (March 1965): 58.

18. As a final technical point, it has been noted that partisanship varies at times when congressmen are subdivided by region, especially Democractic congressmen from the South. This procedure, however, would not contribute to a resolution of the basic question of the relative degree of party voting according to party type. To break groups of congressmen within parties down into blocs is to break down the whole idea of party voting. Presidents are likely to have representatives from geographical regions that will be more inclined to support them, but that again does not address the question of the presence or absence of partisanship per se. To break down party in this way is, for present purposes, to break down the level of analysis.

19. See E. E. Schattschneider, *Politics, Pressures, and the Tariff* (Englewood Cliffs, N.J.: Prentice-Hall, 1935).

20. Raymond A. Bauer, Ithiel De Sola Pool, and Lewis A. Dexter chronicle this shift in a particular trade policy in *American Business and Public Policy* (Chicago: Aldine-Atherton,1972).

21. Not all bills, however, are controversial in terms of floor activity. There is no obvious dichotomy here for regulatory bills as there was for distributive bills, but some of the less controversial bills (in terms of floor activity) are clearly limited in scope and therefore in interest, such as the resolution of the West Coast dock strike (no. 15), the District of Columbia Court Reform and Criminal Procedure Act (no. 29), and the bill regulating bank mergers (no. 114). Marked changes can occur when opinions about a particular issue switch. A notable example is the military draft. Bills extending the draft in 1955 (no. 153) and in 1969 (no. 36) met with little evident resistance on the floor of either house. But in 1971 the bill to extend the draft met with a long series of roll calls—twelve in the House and fifty-six in the Senate. The intervening factor obviously was rising opposition to the Vietnam War.

22. A good general discussion of this can be found in "U.S. Farm Policy: A Free Market or Controls?" in *Issues of American Public Policy,* ed. John H. Bunzel (Englewood Cliffs, N.J.: Prentice-Hall, 1968), pp. 250–59.

23. Editors of the *Yale Law Journal,* "The Political Impasse in Farm Support," in *Public Policies and Their Politics,* ed. Randall Ripley (New York: Norton, 1966), p. 71.

24. "U.S. Farm Policy," pp. 256–59. See also Charles O. Jones, "The Agriculture Committee and the Problem of Representation," *American Political Science Review* 55 (June 1961): 358–67.

25. "It is difficult to ignore the loud sounds of an ideological battle [in agricultural assistance politics] waged on a familiar political-economic terrain. Old arguments over the government management of the economy versus unfettered free enterprise provided much of the firepower"; Clausen, *How Congressmen Decide,* p. 45.

26. Randall Ripley and Grace Franklin, *Congress, the Bureaucracy, and Public Policy* (Homewood, Ill.: Dorsey Press, 1976), p. 132.

27. Ibid., pp. 139–41.

28. James Sundquist, *Politics and Policy* (Washington, D.C.: Brookings Institution, 1968), p. 218.

29. Bensel, "Reciprocal Behavior," pp. 229–43.

30. "Major Housing Legislation Enacted," *Congressional Quarterly Almanac,*1965, p. 358.

31. "Housing Bill Provides Home-Buying, Riot, and Other Aid," *Congressional Quarterly Almanac,* 1968, pp. 314–20.

32. Ibid., pp. 321–23.

33. To state the matter another way, redistributive policies often beget distributive concessions. This is akin to what Lowi labels the "entropic" tendency of policies; that is, other policy types devolving toward distributive policy characteristics.

34. Roger Wilkins, "Amid Reports of Other Reverses, Carter Did Well in a Budget Test," *New York Times,* 28 May 1979, p. 27. An assistant director of the Congressional Budget Office was quoted as saying, "I was surprised . . . at the extent to which the interest groups entered the process this year with the assumption that they would have to tighten their belts and fight within the context of a smaller pie."

Chapter Seven

1. George C. Edwards III, *Presidential Influence in Congress* (San Francisco: Freeman, 1980), p. 202. Edwards also concludes that there are no major differences in congressional support for the legislative programs of Kennedy, Johnson, and Carter (pp.191–93) and that "Johnson's mastery of the legislative process seems to have had considerably less significance than conventional wisdom indicates" (p. 202). See my Chapter 5. Edwards's findings were the same for Republican presidents.

2. Theodore J. Lowi, "Four Systems of Policy, Politics, and Choice," *Public Administration Review* 32 (July–August 1972): 306.

3. Lowi talks about an "entropic tendency" of policies. He postulates that constituent, redistributive, and regulatory policies all exhibit a "winding down" or reduction toward the distributive policy type. No such specific, across-the-board tendency was observed here, but the notion is certainly not inconsistent with the relationships posited. See Theodore J. Lowi, "The Arenas of Power", (manuscript).

4. One might postulate, however, that movement between the constituent and regulatory areas similar to that observed between distributive and redistributive policies occurs and can be observed in the interactions of interest groups and the bureaucracy. This suggestion is purely speculative, though.

5. Paul E. Scheele, "President Carter and the Water Projects," *Presidential Studies Quarterly* 8 (Fall 1978): 359.

6. Ibid., p. 348.

7. Herman Finer, *The Presidency* (Chicago: University of Chicago Press, 1960), p. 79.

8. Louise Stitt, "State Fair Labor Standards Legislation," *Law and Contemporary Problems* 34 (Summer 1939): 456. See also John S. Forsythe, "Legislative History of the Fair Labor Standards Act," *Law and Contemporary Problems* 34 (Summer 1939): 464–90. Forsythe's assessments of the bill closely match the political characteristics associated with regulatory policies discussed herein; see especially pp. 489–90 of Forsythe's article.

9. Norman J. Ornstein and Shirley Elder, *Interest Groups, Lobbying, and Policymaking* (Washington, D.C.: Congressional Quarterly, 1978), p. 182.

10. Richard Pious, *The American Presidency* (New York: Basic Books, 1979), p. 293.

11. James Sundquist, *Politics and Policy* (Washington, D.C.: Brookings Institution, 1968) chap. 2.

12. Ibid., chap. 4.

13. Ibid., chap. 7.

14. Bureaucrats were aware of the energy problem but were obliged to wait for a political initiative.

15. Joseph Nocera, "Insecurity," *New Republic,* 7 April 1979, p. 10. Nocera also discusses the disaggregation of Carter's 1977 comprehensive tax reform plan by the Ways and Means Committee.

16. "The High Cost of Herman Talmadge," *New Republic,* 1 April 1978, p. 5.

17. Drummond Ayres, Jr., "Byrd Denies Tying Arms Treaty Vote to Coal Rule," *New York Times,* 6 May 1979, p. 27.

18. Lowi, "Four Systems," pp. 298–310.

19. T. Alexander Smith, *The Comparative Policy Process* (Santa Barbara, Calif.: Clio Books, 1975); Theodore J. Lowi, "Public Policy and Bureaucracy in the United States and France," in *Comparing Public Policies,* ed. Douglas Ashford (Beverly Hills, Calif.: Sage Publications, 1978), pp. 177–96.

Bibliography

"Airline Deregulation." In *Congressional Quarterly Almanac*. Washington, D.C.: Congressional Quarterly, 1977.

Annual Chief Justice Earl Warren Conference on Advocacy in the U.S.A. *The Powers of the Presidency*. Cambridge, Mass.: Roscoe Pound–American Trial Lawyers Foundation, 1975.

Arnold, Peri, and L. John Roos. "Toward a Theory of Congressional-Executive Relations." *Review of Politics* 36 (July 1974): 410—29.

Ayres, B. Drummond, Jr. "Byrd Denies Tying Arms Treaty Vote to Coal Rule." *New York Times,* 6 May 1979, p. 27.

Bailey, Stephen K. *Congress in the Seventies*. New York: St. Martin's Press, 1970.

Barber, James David. *The Presidential Character*. Englewood Cliffs, N.J.: Prentice-Hall, 1977.

Bauer, Raymond A., Ithiel De Sola Pool, and Lewis A. Dexter. *American Business and Public Policy*. Chicago: Aldine-Atherton,1972.

Bensel, Richard F. "Reciprocal Behavior and the Rules of the House of Representatives." Ph.D. dissertation, Cornell University, 1978.

Berger, Raoul. *Executive Privilege*. Cambridge, Mass.: Harvard University Press, 1974.

Bickel, Alexander. "The Senate Judiciary's Abominable Crime Bill." *New Republic,* 25 May 1968, p. 17.

Bill, James, and Robert Hardgrave. *Comparative Politics: The Quest for Theory*. Columbus, Ohio: Merrill, 1973.

Black, Henry C. *The Relation of the Executive Power to Legislation*. Princeton, N.J.: Princeton University Press, 1919.

Bryce, James. *The American Commonwealth*. New York: MacMillan, 1981.

Burnham, James. *Congress and the American Tradition*. Chicago: Henry Regnery, 1959.

"Burns Hedges on Lockheed Aid." *New York Times,* 17 June 1971, p. 59.

Burns, James MacGregor. *Leadership*. New York: Harper and Row, 1978.

———.*Presidential Government*. Boston: Houghton Mifflin, 1973.

Chamberlain, Lawrence H. "The President as Legislator." In *President and Congress,* edited by Joan MacLean. New York: Wilson, 1955.

———. *The President, Congress, and Legislation.* New York: Columbia University Press, 1946.

———. "The President, Congress, and Legislation." In *The President: Roles and Powers,* edited by David Haight and Larry Johnson. Chicago: Rand McNally, 1946.

Clausen, Aage, *How Congressmen Decide.* New York: St. Martin's Press, 1973.

"Congress Enacts Area Redevelopment Bill." In *Congressional Quarterly Almanac.* Washington, D.C.: Congressional Quarterly, 1961.

Cronin, Thomas. *The State of the Presidency.* Boston: Little, Brown, 1975.

Davidson, Roger, David M. Kovenock, and Michael K. O'Leary. *Congress in Crisis.* Belmont, Calif.: Wadsworth, 1966.

Davis, James, Jr. *The National Executive Branch.* New York: Free Press, 1970.

DeGrazia, Alfred. *Republic in Crisis.* New York: Federal Legal Publications, 1965.

Easton, David. "An Approach to the Analysis of Political Systems." *World Politics* 9 (April 1957): 383–400.

Editors of the *Yale Law Journal.* "The Political Impasse in Farm Support." In *Public Policies and Their Politics,* edited by Randall Ripley. New York: Norton, 1966.

Edwards, George C. *Presidential Influence in Congress.* San Francisco: Freeman, 1980.

Egger, Rowland, and Joseph P. Harris. *The President and Congress.* New York: McGraw-Hill, 1963.

Finer, Herman. *The Presidency.* Chicago: University of Chicago Press, 1960.

Ford, Henry Jones. *The Rise and Growth of American Politics.* New York: DaCapo Press, 1967.

Froman, Lewis, *The Congressional Process.* Boston: Little, Brown, 1967.

Gallagher, Hugh G. "Presidents, Congress, and the Legislative Functions." In *The Presidency Reappraised,* edited by Rexford Tugwell and Thomas Cronin. New York: Praeger, 1974.

George, Alexander. "Assessing Presidential Character." In *Perspectives on the Presidency,* edited by Aaron Wildavsky. Boston: Little, Brown, 1975.

Gilmour, Robert. "Central Legislative Clearance: A Revised Perspective." In *Perspectives on the Presidency,* edited by Stanley Bach and George Sulzner. Lexington, Mass.: Heath, 1974.

Goldsmith, William. *The Growth of Presidential Power.* New York: Chelsea House, 1974.

Greenstein, Fred, Larry Berman, and Alvin S. Felzenberg, *Evolution of the Modern Presidency.* Washington, D.C.: American Enterprise Institute, 1977.

Griffith, Ernest S. *The American Presidency.* New York: New York University Press, 1976.

Hargrove, Erwin. *The Power of the Modern Presidency.* New York: Knopf, 1974.

Heclo, Hugh. *Studying the Presidency.* New York: Ford Foundation, 1977.

Herring, Pendleton. *Presidential Leadership.* New York: Farrar and Rinehart, 1940.

Hess, Stephen. *Organizing the Presidency.* Washington, D.C.: Brookings Institution, 1976.

"The High Cost of Herman Talmadge." *New Republic,* 1 April 1978, p. 5.

Hilsman, Roger. *The Politics of Policy Making in Defense and Foreign Affairs.* New York: Harper and Row, 1971.

Hinckley, Barbara. *Stability and Change in Congress.* New York: Harper and Row, 1971.

Holt, Robert, and John Turner. "Crises and Sequences in Collective Theory Development." *American Political Science Review* 69 (September 1975): 979–94.

"House Rewrites and Passes Safe Streets Bill." In *Congressional Quarterly Almanac.* Washington, D.C.: Congressional Quarterly, 1967.

"Housing Bill Provides Home-Buying, Riot, and Other Aid." In *Congressional Quarterly Almanac.* Washington, D.C.: Congressional Quarterly, 1968.

Hughes, Emmet J. *The Living Presidency.* Baltimore: Penguin Books, 1973.

Huntington, Samuel. "Congressional Responses to the Twentieth Century." In *The Congress and America's Future,* edited by David Truman. Englewood Cliffs, N.J.: Prentice-Hall, 1973.

Javits, Jacob K. "Needed: A New R.F.C." *New York Times,* 11 July 1971, sec. 3, p. 12.

Johannes, John R. "The President Proposes and Congress Disposes—But Not Always." *Review of Politics* 36 (July 1974): 356–70.

———. "Where Does the Buck Stop?—Congress, President, and the Responsibility for Legislative Initiation." *Western Political Quarterly* 25 (September 1972): 396–415.

Kaplan, Abraham. *The Conduct of Inquiry.* New York: Chandler, 1964.

Kendall, Willmoore. *The Conservative Affirmation.* Chicago: Henry Regnery, 1963.

Kessel, John. "The Parameters of Presidential Politics." *Social Science Quarterly* 55 (June 1974): 8–24.

King, Anthony. "Executives." In *Handbook of Political Science,* edited by Fred Greenstein and Nelson Polsby. Reading, Mass.: Addison-Wesley, 1975.

Koenig, Louis. *The Chief Executive.* New York: Harcourt, Brace,Jovanovich, 1975.

Laski, Harold. *The American Presidency.* New York: Grosset and Dunlap, 1940.

Lebo, Harlan. "The Administration's All-Out Effort on Civil Service Reform." *National Journal,* 27 May 1978, p. 838.

Light, Paul C. *The President's Agenda.* Baltimore: Johns Hopkins University Press, 1981.

Lijphart, Arend. "Comparative Politics and the Comparative Method." *American Political Science Review* 65 (September 1977): 682–93.

"Lockheed Loan Guarantee Bill Cleared on Close Vote." In *Congressional Quarterly Almanac.* Washington, D.C.: Congressional Quarterly, 1971.

Lockwood, Henry C. *The Abolition of the Presidency.* New York: Worthington, 1884.

Loss, Richard. "Dissolving Concepts of the Presidency." *Political Science Reviewer* 4 (Fall 1974): 133–68.

Lowi, Theodore J. "American Business, Public Policy, Case Studies, and Political Theory." *World Politics* 16 (July 1964): 677–715.

———. *American Government: Incomplete Conquest.* Hinsdale, Ill.: Dryden Press, 1976.

———. "The Arenas of Power." Typewritten manuscript.

———. "Decision Making vs. Policy Making." *Public Administration Review* 32

(May-June 1972): 314–25.

———. "Four Systems of Policy, Politics, and Choice." *Public Administration Review* 32 (July-August 1972): 298–310.

"Major Housing Legislation Enacted." In *Congressional Quarterly Almanac*. Washington, D.C.: Congressional Quarterly, 1965.

Manley, John F. "The Presidency, Congress, and National Policy-Making." *Political Science Annual* 5 (1974): 227–73.

McConnell, Grant. *Steel and the Presidency*. New York: Norton, 1963.

Moe, Ronald, and Steven Teel. "Congress as Policy-Maker." *Political Science Quarterly* 85 (September 1970): 443–70.

Mullen, William F. *Presidential Power and Politics*. New York: St. Martin's Press, 1976.

Nagel, Ernest. *The Structure of Science*. New York: Harcourt, Brace and World, 1961.

Nathan, R. P. *The Plot That Failed*. New York: Wiley, 1975.

Neustadt, Richard E. "Presidency and Legislation." In *The Presidency,* edited by Aaron Wildavsky. Boston: Little, Brown, 1969.

———. *Presidential Power*. New York: Wiley, 1976.

Nocera, Joseph. "Insecurity." *New Republic,* 7 April 1979, p. 10.

"Now the Wilderness Bill." *New York Times,* 29 July 1964. p. 32.

O'Kane, Lawrence. "President's Housing Message Scored by Many Here." *New York Times,* 4 March 1965, p. 19.

Ornstein, Norman J., and Shirley Elder. *Interest Groups, Lobbying, and Policymaking*. Washington, D.C.: Congressional Quarterly, 1978.

Pious, Richard M. *The American Presidency*. New York: Basic Books, 1979.

———. "Sources of Domestic Policy Initiatives." In *Congress against the President,* edited by Harvey C. Mansfield. New York: Praeger, 1975.

"President's Stand." *New York Times,* 13 April 1958, sec. 4, pp. 1–2.

Przeworski, Adam, and Henry Teune. *The Logic of Comparative Social Inquiry*. New York: Wiley, 1970.

Ranney, Austin. "The Study of Policy Content." In *Political Science and Public Policy,* edited by Austin Ranney. Chicago: Markham, 1968.

Reedy, George. *The Twilight of the Presidency*. New York: New American Library, 1970.

Ripley, Randall. *Congress: Process and Policy*. New York: Norton, 1975.

———, and Grace Franklin. *Congress, the Bureaucracy, and Public Policy*. Homewood, Ill.: Dorsey Press, 1976.

Rossiter, Clinton. *The American Presidency*. New York: Time-Life Books, Time Reading Program Special Edition, 1960.

Rourke, Francis. *Secrecy and Publicity*. Baltimore: Johns Hopkins University Press, 1961.

Sawyer, Kathy. "Carter's Civil Service Victory Confounds Capitol's Cynics." *Washington Post,* 14 October 1978, sec. A, p. 2.

Scheele, Paul E. "President Carter and the Water Projects." *Presidential Studies Quarterly* 8 (Fall 1978): 348–64.

Schlesinger, Arthur, Jr. *The Imperial Presidency*. New York: Popular Library, 1974.

"Senate Backs Canal Neutrality Treaty, 68-32." *Congressional Quarterly Weekly Report,* 18 March 1978, p. 675.

Shannon, W. Wayne. *Party, Constituency, and Congressional Voting.* Baton Rouge: Louisiana State University Press, 1968.

Shull, Steven A. *Presidential Policy Making.* Brunswick, Ohio: King's Court Communications, 1979.

Sorensen, Theodore, *Decision-Making in the White House.* New York: Columbia University Press, 1963.

Spitzer, Robert J. "The Presidency and Public Policy: A Preliminary Inquiry." *Presidential Studies Quarterly* 9 (Fall 1979): 441–57.

Stitt, Louise. "State Fair Labor Standards Legislation." *Law and Contemporary Problems* 34 (Summer 1939): 456.

Sundquist, James. "Needed: A Workable Check on the Presidency." *Brookings Bulletin* 10 (Fall 1973): 7–11.

———. *Politics and Policy.* Washington, D.C.: Brookings Institution, 1968.

Taft, William H. *The President and His Powers.* Originally published as *Our Chief Magistrate.* New York: Columbia University Press, 1967.

Tolchin, Martin. "Grappling with the Monster of Bureaucracy." *New York Times,* 23 July 1978, p. 46.

Tufte, Edward R. *Political Control of the Economy.* Princeton, N.J.: Princeton University Press, 1978.

Turner, Julius, and Edward Schneier. *Party and Constituency.* Baltimore: Johns Hopkins University Press, 1970.

U.S., Congress, House. *House Reports.* 87th Cong., 2d sess., 1962. H. Rept. 1406.

"U.S. Farm Policy: A Free Market or Controls?" In *Issues of American Public Policy,* edited by John H. Bunzel. Englewood Cliffs, N.J.: Prentice-Hall, 1968.

Vinyard, Dale. *The Presidency.* New York: Scribner's, 1971.

Vogler, David. *The Politics of Congress.* Boston: Allyn and Bacon, 1977.

Wayne, Stephen J. *The Legislative Presidency.* New York: Harper and Row, 1978.

Wicker, Tom. "Needy-Area Help Voted by House; Coalition Loses." *New York Times,* 30 March 1961, p. 1.

Wildavsky, Aaron, ed. *The Presidency.* Boston: Little, Brown, 1969.

———. "The Two Presidencies." In *The Presidency,* edited by Aaron Wildavsky. Boston: Little, Brown, 1969.

"Wilderness Bill Passed by House." *New York Times,* 31 July 1964, p. 1.

Wilkins, Roger. "Amid Reports of Other Reverses, Carter Did Well in a Budget Test." *New York Times,* 28 May 1979, p. 27.

Wilson, James Q. *Political Organizations.* New York: Basic Books, 1973.

Witkin, Richard. "Lockheed's Rescue Plan May Aid Other Concerns." *New York Times,* 25 June 1971, p. 45.

Yarmolinsky, Adam. *The Military Establishment.* New York: Harper and Row, 1973.

Index